KV-012-615

Religions, Rights and Laws

FOR FIONA

Religions, Rights and Laws

A. Bradney

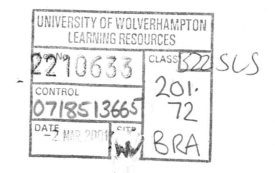

UNIVERSITY OF WOLVERHAMPTON
LEARNING RESOURCES

Acc No. 2210633   CLASS 322 SUS

CONTROL 0718513665   201. 72

DATE -2 MAR 2001   SITE W   BRA

Leicester University Press
Leicester, London and New York
Distributed in the United States and
Canada by St. Martin's Press

Leicester University Press
(a division of Pinter Publishers Ltd.)

First published in 1993

© A. Bradney, 1993

Apart from any fair dealing for the purposes or research of private study, or criticism or review, as permitted under the Copyright, Designs and Patents Act, 1988, this publication may not be reproduced, stored or transmitted, in any form or by any means, or process without the prior permission in writing of the copyright holders or their agents. Except for reproduction in accordance with the terms of licences issued by the Copyright Licensing Agency, photocopying of whole or part of this publication without the prior written permission of the copyright holders or their agents in single or multiple copies whether for gain or not is illegal and expressly forbidden. Please direct all enquiries concerning copyright to the Publishers at the address below.

Editorial offices
Fielding Johnson Building, University of Leicester,
Leicester, LE1 7RH, England

Trade and other enquiries
25 Floral Street, London, WC2E 9DS *and*
Room 400, 175 Fifth Avenue, New York, NY 10010, USA

A. Bradney is hereby identified as the author of this work as provided under Section 77 of the Copyright, Designs and Patents Act, 1988.

British Library Cataloguing in Publication Data
A CIP catalogue record for this book is available from the British Library

ISBN 0 7185 1366 5

Library of Congress Cataloging-in-Publication Data
A CIP catalog record for this book is available from the Library of Congress

Typeset by Saxon Graphics Ltd, Derby
Printed and bound in Great Britain by Biddles Ltd., Guildford and King's Lynn

Contents

Preface

This book is concerned with legal systems in Great Britain. Although British citizens can benefit from the European Convention on Human Rights and the work of the European Court of Human Rights, the Convention constitutes a foreign jurisprudence with traditions that are very different from those of the legal systems of Great Britain. I have therefore, with some regret, excluded discussion of this system from my book. For the reasons that I have tried to set out in chapters 1 and 2, the primary purpose of this book is not to provide an exposition of legal rules. However, in so far as I have discussed the current state of the legal systems in Great Britain, I have intended to do so as of 31 July 1992.

I presented earlier versions of some of the ideas to be found in this volume in a paper given at the 'Law and Politics' conference at the Queens University of Belfast and to staff seminars at the Law departments of the City University, the University of Keele and the University of Leicester. I am grateful to the participants at those various events for their comments. Parts of chapter 8 previously appeared as articles in the *Juridical Review* and the *Oxford Journal of Legal Studies*. I am grateful for the publisher's permission to reprint these sections. Mahendra Solanki read a draft of chapter 5 and made a number of helpful comments on my reading of Salman Rushdie's work. Finally, Fiona Cownie discussed almost the entire volume with me. I benefitted from her ideas. She will be glad that I have, at last, finished.

Part 1:

The Problem

1 Introduction

Very little has been written about the relationship between religion, rights and legal rules within Great Britain. St John Robilliard's book, *Religion and Law*, is the only monograph that is directly concerned with this general topic.[1] Some other books, for example Sebastian Poulter's, *English Law and Ethnic Minority Customs*, cover topics which overlap with consideration of religion and law.[2] There are also a limited number of monographs which take as their subject particular issues which relate to religion and law.[3] Finally, there is a small amount of periodical literature. Nevertheless, notwithstanding these works, the total quantity of material, whether of an academic or a professional nature, is limited . An incautious observer might deduce from this the proposition that, within Great Britain, there is very little to say about the relationship between rights, religions and laws. Yet this would seem unlikely. Other jurisdictions, notably the United States, have generated a vast literature commenting on the relationship between religion and law.[4] True, such jurisdictions generally have written constitutions protecting religious liberty and, sometimes, providing for the separation of church and state. There is thus a particular focus for commentary. The unwritten nature of the United Kingdom constitution, and the lack of positive legal protection for individual rights, means there is a less obvious centre for enquiry. But an unwritten constitution is still a constitution. Great Britain still has religions and laws and there is, indeed, a legally established church in part of the country.[5] *Prima facie*, the relationship between religions, rights and laws within Great Britain seems to be a suitable subject for analysis.

No religion is proscribed within Great Britain.[6] A multiplicity of faiths exist alongside each other. Although variants of the Christian faith remain the dominant form of religion within Great Britain, the number and size of other faiths is rapidly increasing. In 1970 the community membership of non-Trinitarian and other religions was 1.7 million people. By 1987 it had risen to 4.3 million people and it has been estimated that, by the year 2000, membership will be 5.7 million people. At the same time the community membership of Trinitarian[7] churches has fallen from 40.4 million people in 1970 to 37.5 million people in 1987 with an estimated membership of 36.1 million people in 2000.[8] In terms of numbers, the most significant new non-Christian faith is Islam with community membership growing from 0.3 million people in 1970 to 1.5 million people in 1987 with an estimated membership of 2.2 million people by

2000. However, there are also substantial numbers of Sikhs and Hindus as well as lesser numbers of other faiths.[9] At the same time, as the number of non-Christian religions represented in Great Britain grows, the balance of forms of Christianity also changes. Thus, for example, whilst Anglican and Roman Catholic church membership has declined between 1970 and 1990,[10] the membership of 'black' churches[11] has generally grown.[12] Citizens and aliens are, in law, free to choose which, if any religion they wish to follow. According to *The Times*, the journal of record, it is 'self-evident...that there should be no coercion in matters of religion'.[13]

Freedom of religion accords with the United Kingdom's obligations under international law. The United Kingdom is a signatory to the European Convention on Human Rights under which, '[e]veryone has the right to freedom of expression, conscience and religion'.[14] The United Kingdom is also a member of the United Nations, whose Declaration on Human Rights holds that, '[e]veryone has the right to freedom of thought, conscience and religion'.[15] However, whilst a willingness to shoulder such obligations might betoken something about the political or philosophical climate within the United Kingdom, international law has only limited legal importance in municipal law, being no more than an aid to statutory interpretation.[16] Nevertheless, though obligations under international law do not, of themselves, signify anything about the state of municipal law, there is ample evidence to suggest that judges within the legal systems of Great Britain adhere to the notion of freedom of religion. Scrutton LJ's dictum in *Re Carroll*, '[i]t is, I hope, unnecessary to say that the Court is perfectly impartial in matters of religion',[17] and Cross J's comment in *Neville Estates Ltd* v. *Madden*, '[a]s between different religions the law stands neutral',[18] are but two examples of a common feature of judgements where religion becomes a matter of apparent consequence. Judges have consistently denied that there is any legal import in the religion of litigants before them. Freedom of religion is, apparently, a defining characteristic of legal rules within Great Britain.

Were the concern of this book Northern Ireland, rather than Great Britain, the starting point would be somewhat different. In Northern Ireland a social divide between two religious communities, the Catholic and the Protestant, is reflected in a legal system which attempts to remedy the resulting conflict; most notably in the existence of the Fair Employment (Northern Ireland) Act 1989 and the Fair Employment Commission set up to administer that Act. A recognition of the importance of religion within Northern Ireland society plays a part in the Northern Ireland legal system. It could be argued, it is this very fact, religious conflict in Northern Ireland and religious freedom within Great Britain, that describes and explains the gap between the social mores of the two societies. Moreover, it could be said, the features of the Northern Ireland legal system which show a special regard for religion reflect a reformist attempt to reach the stage found within the legal systems of Great Britain where religion is of no account.

If freedom of religion is the norm within the legal systems of Great Britain, and if judges are neutral about the religious beliefs of those before them, there is little purpose to this volume. To say that there is freedom of religion, to say that there is no compulsion in matters of religion, is (if true) to foreclose all questions except, is this a desirable situation? There might, at most, be a place for a book which describes those laws which provide for this happy state of affairs. However, there remains the question, is it correct to say, in any simple but meaningful sense, that there is freedom of religion within Great Britain?

Religion is both belief and practice. The two are inseparable. To say 'I adhere to a particular faith' is also to say 'I believe I should follow the precepts of that faith'. Believers may fail in their practice. However, they will account that failure blameworthy. What they cannot do is deny the necessity of such practice.[19]

In the United States the First Amendment to the American Constitution permits not free belief in religion but 'free exercise' of religion.[20] As Pfeffer observes, '[t]here is no need for a constitutional guaranty protesting freedom to believe, for, as the common-law adage has it the devil himself knows not the thoughts of man'.[21] Freedom to believe can hardly be denied. It is freedom to express one's beliefs and freedom to practise one's beliefs that are at issue. Within Great Britain, in the absence of any law positively asserting a general right to the free practice of religion, this idea finds expression in the fact that the exigencies of particular religious practices will, on occasion, exempt a believer from the normal requirements of law. Thus, for example, under the Road Traffic Act 1972 it was a criminal offence to ride a motor-cycle without a crash-helmet.[22] A male Sikh must wear a turban.[23] Thus it was impossible for an observant male Sikh to ride a motor-cycle and comply with the 1972 Act. To meet this difficulty the Motor-Cycle Crash-Helmets (Religious Exemption) Act 1976 was passed, giving Sikhs an exemption from this particular requirement of the 1972 Act.[24] Outlining the need for such legislation, the proposer of the Bill, Sidney Bidwell MP, asked '[c]an we seriously say that we are carrying on our tradition of religious tolerance if...society imposes its will in such a way that a Sikh begins to turn away from his family religion...?'[25] In this instance a desire for tolerance led to the conclusion that both belief in a religion and practice of the tenets of that religion must be permitted.

There is no complete list of British legal rules granting exemptions or providing for novel procedures because of practices occasioned by religious observance. Some examples are relatively well known. One instance is the marriage ceremonies of both The Religious Society of Friends ('Quakers') and Jews which are given special recognition under the Marriage Act 1949.[26] Another is the fact that Jews are exempt from some of the normal restrictions on Sunday trading if they have a conscientious objection to working on the Jewish sabbath.[27] Other examples are more obscure. For example, the Secretary of State has power to exempt Christian Scientists from certain regulations governing nursing homes and mental nursing homes.[28] All such rules, whether well known or not, can be seen as examples of a practice which owes its historical antecedents to the Toleration Act of 1689.

The unofficial title of the 1689 Act gives a misleading impression of the contents of the statute.[29] Whilst it excused certain Christians from penalties for their practices which had arisen because of a number of previous statutes and allowed them to worship providing that that worship was not conducted behind locked doors, it applied only to Protestant nonconformists who believed in the Trinity.[30] As a measure of toleration one of the main defects of the 1689 Act was that it did not apply to Roman Catholics.[31] Indeed, as late as 1829, the Roman Catholic Relief Act included, alongside various measures for increased tolerance towards Roman Catholics, other provisions designed to provide for the 'gradual suppression and final prohibition of "Jesuits and members of other religious orders, communities and societies of the Church of Rome"'.[32] However, despite this and other defects, the 1689 Act did introduce into law the principle that a person might be excused, because of the dictates of their religion, from a legal penalty which would otherwise apply.[33]

Once it is accepted that legislation, of the type exemplified by the Toleration Act 1689, should play a part in the legal system then it is no longer possible accurately to contend that the law takes no account of religion. Legal rules which reflect a policy of tolerance are precisely concerned with a person's religion. Courts concerned with construing these rules apply themselves to the question of the religious beliefs of litigants before them. Moreover, in applying these rules, the court's concern is not with mere matters of mechanical interpretation, but with issues which touch upon the very nature of religion.[34] For example, in a series of cases concerning interpretation of paragraph 6(5) of Schedule 1 of the Trade Union and Labour Relations Act 1974, a provision permitting conscientious objection to trade union membership, the matter at issue was whether the 'religious beliefs' of the litigants meant that they could not belong to a trade union. In the end it was decided that application of this rule turned on an assessment of the subjective religious belief of the litigant in question.[35] In such areas of the law, pace Scrutton LJ and Cross J, it is clear that the courts are neither neutral to, nor unconcerned with, the religion of the persons before them. This is not to say that such concern of itself necessarily undermines the principle of religious freedom.

The idea that a person should be excused penalty under law because of their religious beliefs springs naturally from a belief in freedom of religion under law.[36] However, a conceptual problem arises once this idea is implemented through legislation. Any such piece of legislation is, necessarily, in one sense, an act of discrimination. One group is given different treatment. The treatment which is different is intended to be more favourable. If one group, why not another? Under the 1989 Employment Act Sikhs are exempted from any regulation requiring the wearing of safety helmets on construction sites.[37] If Sikhs are to be exempt should not Rastafarians be given the same exemption? On the basis of various Biblical injunctions such as Leviticus 21:5[38] Rastafarians believe that hair should not be cut.[39] The consequent dreadlocks are likely to prevent a Rastafarian wearing a safety helmet. Why are Rastafarians not exempted? Equally, if a group is granted an exemption in one situation should it not be granted a similar exemption in other areas? If Sikhs are exempted from wearing safety helmets on construction sites does it not then follow that they should be similarly exempted in, for example, power stations?

In debate on s 11 of the Employment Act 1989, in answer to arguments about possible extensions of the exemption, Lord Strathclyde, on behalf of the Government, observed that Sikhs in the construction industry were a special case because there was, 'no similar concentration of Sikhs in any other industry'[40] and, implicitly, because there was no similar concentration of any other relevant religion in the construction industry. However, if it is true, 'that there should be no compulsion in matters of religion', and if, as Sidney Bidwell argued with regard to motor-cycle crash-helmets, such laws are necessary as an expression of religious tolerance, Lord Strathclyde's position is not necessarily appropriate. To demand that a Rastafarian choose between employment in the construction industry and the dictates of his faith is, *prima facie*, a form of compulsion in religion. Such laws create a penalty for religious observance leading the adherent to ask how much their religion means to them; a penalty and a question which does not arise in the case of exempted religions. The laws operate in the same way as laws relating to theft. A person may steal but if they do so they will be fined or imprisoned. A person may be a Rastafarian but, if they are, they may not be a construction worker. In both cases there is a sanction for performance. This penalty, this compulsion, arises if any Rastafarian considers employment in the construction industry. From the perspective of consideration of compulsion in religion the situation is not altered whether there be one or 20,000 Rastafarians involved.

Lord Strathclyde's approach to religious freedom involves taking account of other factors in addition to the exigencies of religious practice and the desirability of avoiding compulsion in matters of religion. Religious freedom is to be measured against other matters. It is not difficult to think of examples of the kind of factors that pragmatically might be taken into account in determining the extent to which someone might be permitted to practice their religion without penalty arising because of the operation of law. The exemption for Sikhs in the construction industry appears to have owed much to political pressure from the Sikh community.[41] The weight of political pressure is one factor. Administrative convenience, the needs of others and the integrity of the law are three other examples of factors that might, in other instances, be taken into consideration.

For many there might be no surprise in finding that freedom of religion is a relative rather than an absolute matter. It might be argued that, as has been observed in relation to other supposed freedoms, no freedom is total. Thus, for example, Shabbir Akhtar, in one of his contributions to the debate on the publication of *The Satanic Verses* has written that, '[t]he freedom to express opinions on political and religious matters has to be restrained in the interests of social harmony'.[42] Each freedom needs to be put in the balance and a freedom may weigh differently in that balance from case to case.

The United States Supreme Court's approach to the First Amendment illustrates a view of freedom of religion which involves weighing the importance of this freedom against other freedoms. Reviewing the First Amendment's apparent absolute prohibition on measures to prevent the free exercise of religion, Chief Justice Waite observed that, '[l]aws are made for the government of actions, and while they cannot interfere with mere religious beliefs, they may with practices'.[43] This approach was later confirmed by Justice Robert's pronouncement that, 'the [First] Amendment embraces two concepts – freedom to believe and freedom to act. The first is absolute but, in the nature of things, the second cannot be. Conduct remains subject to regulation for the protection of society.'[44] The free practice of religion remains important. '[O]nly those interests of the highest order and those not otherwise served can overbalance legitimate claims to the free exercise of religion.'[45] However, freedom of religion is only part of the argument.

The proposition that freedom of religion is or should be relative is, itself, a matter for argument, but, if it is true that this is the approach which is adopted in Great Britain, two observations follow. First, the original statement in this chapter, taken from *The Times*, could no longer be seen as being accurate. It would not be possible to accept that, within Great Britain, there is no compulsion in matters of religion. The difference between saying that there is freedom of religion in Great Britain and freedom of religion is something to be taken into account is not a merely a matter of a slight rewording. To say that freedom of religion is relative is to say that there may be compulsion in matters of religion in at least some cases. To say that freedom of religion is something to be taken into account is necessarily to raise, as a pressing and immediate concern, questions like what other things should be taken into account and when? Secondly, to say that freedom of religion should be weighed in the balance to assess its relative importance is to use a common, powerful and wholly misleading metaphor. To weigh something in the balance it is necessary to know the measure of the balance. To say a pencil weighs less than an elephant involves an explicit or implicit use of a measure of weight. In relation to freedoms what is that measure? It is not enough to consider first one thing and then another to say that one has balanced one thing against another. If the metaphor of balance is to have real meaning, rather than to conceal an arbitrary process by which one appears to provide a rational justification for a conclusion that has in fact already been arrived at, both things considered must be analysed in the light of some previously delineated criteria. What is the measure used when assessing freedom of religion? What takes the place of weight?

Answering the questions in the last paragraph, as well as determining the exact nature of the treatment of religions within the legal systems of Great Britain, provides the subject matter for this book. The aim is not to produce a lengthy catalogue of legal rules, but rather to analyse how notions of legal rules, religions and rights interrelate within Great Britain. This aim determines the structure of the book.

In order to see how legal rules, religions and rights affect each other within the legal systems of Great Britain it is first necessary to make a preliminary survey looking at how some basic concepts can be used. Only after this has been done, is it possible to move on to apply them to particular areas of the legal systems within Great Britain with a view to seeing whether a general account is possible. It might seem frivolous to begin a book with a chapter devoted not to the ostensible subject matter of the book but to more basic philosophical concerns. The next chapter deals with matters which have highly developed literatures, spanning several academic disciplines, attached to them. To presume to condense this scholarship into a chapter might appear to be an act of impertinence normally only to be found in student crammers. However, no matter how jejune the account which follow will be, the chapter is necessary. Any analysis, whatever its subject, which lacks an account of its method and terminology is thereby impoverished. Where writers have a clear grasp of method and terminology, yet omit this material from their text, the reader is deprived of the defence of the choice of method and terminology that the writers would offer. If discussion of the method and terminology is omitted because the writer has not yet fully articulated it to herself or himself and is thus unable to rehearse it for the reader, the analysis itself is that much more likely to be incoherent or contradictory. How can one use that which one does not fully understand?

General observations such as the above take on particular force in areas such as the one which is the subject of this book. Where a topic has been a constant focus for academic enquiry within a particular discipline concepts and methods will become familiar simply by their continual usage. These do not need to be explicitly discussed for there to be some level of mutual understanding between writer and reader since the meaning of the concepts and methods has been taken on by both through a form of osmosis. This process has deficiencies. It carries with it the probability that contradictions or lacunae in terminology or method will occur but will never be fully revealed because the manner of analysis, as opposed to its object, has never been made a central object of concern. However, this process does allow some degree of communication on the basis of at least a minima of shared understanding of meaning or use. By contrast, in Great Britain, in relation to religions, rights and laws, all the central concepts are problematic and may be understood by writer and reader in different ways. No process of the professionalisation of knowledge has yet created a core of accepted usage.

Moreover, in this area, the frequency of usage that there is does not always clarify meaning. An illustration of this phenomenon can be seen in the use of the idea of 'religious tolerance'. This idea has already been deployed twice in this chapter. It was first encountered in discussion of the Tolerance Act of 1689 and then later seen used to justify special legislative treatment of Sikhs. However, the fact that notions of tolerance in matters of religion have formed part of the conceptual apparatus for arguments about freedom of religion in Great Britain for the last 400 years does not mean that this idea has acquired any greater clarity. Nor does it mean that whatever content it has achieved has remained the same from century to century or thinker to thinker. Jordan, at the beginning of his treatment of the development of religious toleration in England in the sixteenth century, observed that, '[t]here can be little doubt that the modern tolerance towards religious diversity has a large content of indifference' but went on to observe that, in its beginnings, religious tolerance implied very different things about the polity.[46] Then, religious tolerance implied neither indifference towards religion nor the positive assertion of liberty of religion but, rather, the negative idea of the withdrawal of state interference over a strictly limited range of individual activity.[47] The varied and sometimes fluid meaning given to the idea of religious tolerance is a common feature of terminology in this area. In the context of such dangerously uncertain ideas there must be some attempt to give solidity to concepts being used. This is true both in the cases of base concepts like notions of rights as well as in the case of more specific ideas like 'neutrality' and 'tolerance'. At the very least it is necessary to offer stipulative definitions enabling the reader to see where and why they depart from the arguments put forward.

Notes

1. St John Robilliard, *Religion and the Law: Religious Liberty in Modern English Law* Manchester University Press, 1984.
2. S. Poulter, *English Law and Ethnic Minority Customs* Butterworths, 1986. See also S. Poulter, *Asian Traditions and English Law: A Handbook* Runnymede Trust with Trentham, 1990.
3. See, for example, C. Crowther, *Religious Trusts* George Ronald, 1954.
4. For the period between September 1988 and August 1989 the 1989 volume of the American '*Index to Legal Periodicals*' lists 46 articles under the heading 'Freedom of Religion'. There are also 6 other headings in the same volume, listing other articles, which deal with religion.
5. The Welsh Church Act 1914 s 1 disestablished the Church of England in Wales.
6. 'Great Britain' is used in its strict sense to include England, Scotland and Wales but exclude Northern Ireland.
7. Trinitarian churches are those Christian churches which believe in the unison of the Holy Trinity in one godhead. Broadly speaking, they are the main-stream Christian denominations. Non-Trinitarian churches include groups such as Mormons and Spiritualists that some may not regard as Christian.
8. P. Brierley (ed.), *UK Christian Handbook 1989/90* MARC Europe, 1988, p.151. These are figures for the United Kingdom rather than Great Britain; separate figures for Great Britain not being available. Community membership is not the same as active membership. Numbers of active members are smaller than those who nominally hold themselves out as belonging to a particular faith. Moreover the ratio of nominal to active members varies from faith to faith. Thus, whilst there were 6.9 million active members of the Trinitarian churches in 1987 there were 0.9 million active Muslims; the latter representing a much higher proportion of the community membership. (These figures are once again taken from the *UK Christian Handbook* but are conveniently abstracted in *Social Trends 20* Central Statistical Office, 1990, p. 166.)
9. Brierley, *op. cit.*, p. 151.
10. Brierley, *op. cit.*, p. 149.
11. That is Pentecostalist churches with a congregation drawn predominantly from those with a West Indian or African ethnic background.
12. Brierley, *op. cit.*, p. 153. The most complete survey of the current composition of the Christian churches in England is to be found in P. Brierley, '*Christian' England* MARC Europe, 1991.
13. *The Times*, August 14th, 1984.
14. Article 9(1).
15. Article 18.
16. *per* Diplock LJ in *Salomon* v. *Commissioners of Customs and Excise* [1967] 2 QB 116, C.A., at pp. 143–144.
17. [1931] 1 KB 317, C.A., at p. 336.
18. [1961] 3 All ER 769, Ch.D., at p. 781.
19. A belief in a god does not necessarily lead to the view that that god's commands should be obeyed. For example, dualistic religions may distinguish between an evil and a good god where only the latter's commands should be obeyed. Thus Zoroastrians' belief in the existence of both Ahura Mazda, the creator of all that is good, and Angra Mainyu, the source of evil. (See M. Boyce, *Zoroastrians* Routledge and Kegan Paul, 1979, particularly at pp. 19–21.) Equally some Christian Gnostic traditions appear to countenance either a belief in a duality of gods or a god whose commands should not be wholly obeyed. (See E. Pagels, *The Gnostic Gospels* Penguin Books, 1982, pp. 55–57.) A concern with the dictates of religions and a concern with the dictates of gods are different things.

20. Though see below at p. 7 for the difficulties in interpreting this provision.
21. L. Pfeffer, *Religious Freedom* National Textbook Company, 1977, p. 33.
22. Road Traffic Act 1972 s 32(3).
23. Ratan Singh Bhanga 'Prachin Panth Prakas 16: 1-36' in W.H. McLeod (ed.), *Textual Sources for the Study of Sikhism* Manchester University Press, 1984, p.73. See also W. Cole and P. Sambhi, *The Sikhs* Routledge and Kegan Paul, 1978, pp. 110-112.
24. This provision is now found in the Road Traffic Act 1988 s 16(2).
25. Standing Committee F, 23 June 1976, col 6. In a similar fashion Sikhs have also been exempted from any regulations requiring the wearing of safety helmets on construction sites. (Employment Act 1989 s 11).
26. Marriage Act 1949 ss 47 and 26(1)(d).
27. Shops Act 1950 s 53.
28. Registered Homes Act 1984 s 37.
29. The practice of giving statutes official short titles is a relatively modern one. The Short Titles Act 1896, which retrospectively gave many statutes official short titles, lists an 1888 Act as the latest statute which, prior to the 1896 Act, lacked an official short title.
30. The Act is discussed in E.N. Williams, *A Documentary History of England: Vol 2* (1559–1931) Penguin Books, 1965, chp 7. This chapter also contains a somewhat shortened form of the Act itself. For further discussion of the Act see W.S. Holdsworth, *History of English Law: Vol VI* Methuen and Co, 1924, pp. 200-202.
31. Toleration Act, 1689 s 17.
32. Roman Catholic Relief Act 1829 ss 28–38.
33. For a list of the principle moves towards religious toleration in the nineteenth century, the period of greatest legislative change, see Robilliard, *op. cit.*, Appendix. For discussion of the change in the relationship between church, state and legal systems which began with the Reformation see W. S. Holdsworth, 'The State and Religious Nonconformity: An Historical Retrospect' (1920) *Law Quarterly Review*, 339.
34. The courts are very rarely concerned with matters of mechanical interpretation. (See, for example, P. Goodrich 'Reading the Law' Basil Blackwell, 1986 particularly at pp. 105–121) However, there are some instances when judges consciously apply themselves to a problematic concept and others when, at least explicitly, they treat a concept as both given and obvious and its application as mechanical. The religious belief of a litigant more usually falls into the former category.
35. *Cave and Cave* v. *BRB* [1976] IRLR 400, I.T., *Goodbody* v. *BRB* [1977] IRLR 84, I.T., *Saggers* v. *BRB (No 2)* [1978] IRLR 435, E.A.T.
36. Which is not to say that it follows inevitably from such a belief.
37. Employment Act 1989 s 11.
38. 'They shall not make baldness upon their head, neither shall they shave the corner of their beard, nor make any cuttings in the flesh.'
39. The Biblical authority for not cutting hair and the importance of dreadlocks for Rastafarians are discussed by Cashmore in E. Cashmore, *Rastaman* Allen and Unwin, 1979, pp. 156–161.
40. *Hansard*, HL, Vol 511, col 744, October 16, 1989
41. See the remarks made by Lord Trefgarne announcing the Government's intention to introduce the exemptions contained in s 11. *Hansard*, HL, Vol 510, col 524, July 14, 1989.
42. S. Akhtar, 'Is Freedom Holy to Liberals?' in *Free Speech* Commission for Racial Equality, 1990, p. 18.
43. *Reynolds* v. *United States* (1878) 98 US 145 at p. 166. The Supreme Court distinguished positive actions, in the instant case an attempt to contract a

polygamous marriage, which could be made the subject of legislation and negative actions, such as not getting medical attention for a child, which, in *R.* v. *Wagstaffe* (10 Cox Cr Cas 531) had been held not to amount to manslaughter.

44. *Cantwell* v. *Connecticut* (1940) 310 US 296 at pp. 303-304.
45. *per* Chief Justice Burger in *Wisconsin* v. *Yoder* (1972) 406 US 205 at p. 215.
46. W. Jordan, *The Development of Religious Toleration in England* George Allen and Unwin, 1932, p. 15.
47. Jordan, *op. cit.*, p. 19.

2 A statement of method

Introduction

In a review of Rheinsteins's book, *Marriage Stability, Divorce and Law,* Abel drew a distinction between, 'a law book and a book about law'.[1]

> A law book...is a work of legal doctrine. It is a study of the rules which legal institutions apply, or which regulate the behavior of those institutions. The study identifies, defines, organizes, and criticizes the rules by means of criteria proper to the legal system – it rationalizes them in Weber's sense...By contrast, a book about law is a mode of reflection upon the legal system.[2]

This distinction, although particular in its specifics, is not unique in its general form. Thus, for example, Campbell and Wiles draw a similar distinction between socio-legal studies and the sociology of law in their 1976 article, 'The Study of Law in Society in Great Britain'.[3] For them, in socio-legal studies, 'the hegemony of law is accepted and furthered...the nature of the legal order is treated as unproblematic...[and] the general functions of law in society tends to be taken for granted...'.[4] However, in the sociology of law, '[t]he focus is no longer on the legal system, known and accepted, but on understanding the nature of social order through the study of law...The goal is not primarily to improve the legal system, but rather to construct a theoretical understanding of the legal system in terms of the wider social structure.'[5]

Making distinctions, such as those above, draws attention to the problematic nature of thinking, and thus writing, about law. Law, it appears, may be understood in many different ways. In thinking one seeks understanding; but an understanding of what? What is the precise nature of the question about law being asked and by what criteria is the answer to be judged? The distinctions drawn by Abel or Campbell and Wiles would suggest that to say that one seeks an understanding of law is not enough. Nor is it sufficient to indicate a general area of enquiry – to say, for example, that this book is about the relationship between religions and legal rules in Great Britain. To do this suggests the direction of one's gaze but it is necessary to go beyond this to know what one is looking for in choosing to enquire into the relationship between religions and laws. Asking questions about the type of thinking done is not a prolegomenon distinctive to studies of law. On the contrary, it is a necessary feature of enquiry in any area. At one level, the point is a simple one; that answers can be no more precise than the questions that they are linked with.[6]

A bald statement of the subject matter of a book communicates to the reader not just by virtue of what it says in lexical form but because of the implications and suppositions aroused in the reader's mind. To say, 'I am writing a book about conveyancing', even if the word conveyancing itself is understood, in itself means almost nothing to the reader.[7] The meaning that the statement takes on comes in the light of known professional tendencies of books about conveyancing; the particular associations with specific forms of argument, accepted questions, 'known' answers, forgivable lacunae in logic and so on. 'A book about conveyancing' implies something about the audience for the book, that it will be practitioners, and thus something about its form, that it will contain doctrinal law with a bent to issues prevalent (in the author's mind) in practice. It is not, of course, that it could not be otherwise. Books about conveyancing might normally be meditations on the politics of land use. However, they are not and this form of meaning is constructed in the light of what has been the case not what might have been.[8]

To say that one is, 'writing a book about conveyancing' is not a value-free act. Subjects, disciplines and movements are not neutral enclosures within which individuals work; mere generic descriptions freely chosen by particular individuals. 'The intellectual writes both for and against his peers.'[9] An important part of intellectual life is the search for recognition. To say that you work within a particular area is designed, in part, to aid this search for recognition. There are rewards for writing within a group; difficulties for those writing outside. Groups will affect what is published and what, of that which is published, is studied.[10] To work within such groups is, in Kuhn's terminology, to work within a 'normal science'.[11] The acceptable problems, methods and modes of answer are dictated by what has gone before. Questions, methods and modes of answer may be found unacceptable not only because they lack intellectual coherence but also because they lack any fit within the canon of the discipline. Thus, typically, those working within the discipline of law deny not the existence of questions other than those that they ask about law but, rather, the legitimacy of treating of such other questions within a law school. For example, Carrington has argued that those who are nihilists (and therefore question whether legal principle is anything more than a cosmetic phenomenon) should leave law schools, 'perhaps to seek a place elsewhere in the academy'.[12]

The acceptance of the terminology, problems and discourse of an area which is, at least in part, involved in avowing an intention to write within any particular area is an intellectual strength. It allows work to proceed from positions that have already been established on the basis of arguments already settled. For this reason, it is possible to argue that, '[w]e are dwarfs...but dwarfs who stand on the shoulders of giants, and small though we are, we sometimes manage to see farther on the horizon than they'.[13] Intellectual work can be seen to have the possibility of advancing over generations. However, a difficulty also emerges.

> A description which contains no critical reflection on the position from which it is articulated can have no other principle than the interests associated with the unanalysed relation that the researcher has with his object.[14]

A 'law book', using Abel's terminology, is susceptible to such criticism because, *inter alia*, the criteria, which it uses, 'those proper to the legal system,' are themselves unexamined. It is, by definition, only a contingent answer to whatever question it started by asking. It docs not ask itself, for example, why it is asking the questions, whether those questions are valid (or even internally coherent) or whether the criteria by which answers are judged are anything more than plausible language accepted within a particular group. Writing 'a book about conveyancing' involves accepting limitations on the legitimate extension of questions; involves taking that which is problematic as axiomatic. On one level such a book, whatever the skill and effort shown in writing, will thus be nothing more than a formal exercise in dogmatics.[15] A 'book about law', again using Abel's terminology, goes further than a law book in its enquiry, and in that way is better, because the internal criteria of the legal system are themselves the object of examination. But a book about law written as, 'a mode of reflection upon the legal system,' is susceptible to precisely the same criticism as a law book, for exactly the same reasons, if its own terms of discourse are not themselves subject to examination. It is always necessary to look at the forms within which we claim to be working, to place ourselves,

> ...inside these dubious unities in order to study their internal configurations...to ask...what unities they form...by what right they can claim a field that specifies them in space and a continuity that individualizes them in time; according to what laws they are formed; against the background of which discursive events they stand out; and whether they are not, in their accepted and quasi-institutional individuality, ultimately the surface effect of more firmly grounded unities.[16]

Understanding involves an understanding of the process by which we achieve understanding. If this is so then a book about law involves beginning with consideration of matters which lie wholly outside law (however law is conceived) so that the foundation of the work can be established.[17] There is no advance in interrogating the criteria of a legal system if the criteria by which we do that, those common to the discipline within which we work, are not themselves interrogated. To fail to do this is merely to exchange one set of suppositions for another. There is no improvement if 'books about law' turn out to be, for example, economics books, philosophy books or sociology books that take as their subject law. Because of this, whilst there are successful law books, books which may succeed in their own terms by using criteria internal to the legal system, there can be, in their own terms, no successful books about law (although there may be, in their own terms, successful economics books, sociology books, etc., which take as their subject law). To succeed in its own terms a book about law must be more than a book about law. *Pace* Abel, there are no books about law. There are law books and then there are books.

Writing a book

What, then, is necessary in writing a book?
   Husserl argued that,

> Philosophy – wisdom (*sagesse*) – is the philosopher's quite personal affair. It must arise as *his* wisdom, as his self-acquired knowledge tending towards universality, a

knowledge for which he can answer from the beginning, and at each step, by virtue of his own absolute insights.[18]

We seek to know things, not to believe them. As 'radically beginning philosophers',[19] each must begin again, putting in doubt all convictions previously accepted.[20] The philosopher does not differ in this from the rest of humanity. '[C]uriosity, the desire to know things as they are, is a craving no less native to the being of man, no less universal through mankind, than the craving for food and drink.'[21] The search for knowledge is a part of being human. Seen in one way, because of the ontological priority of self over all other forms, the search for knowledge is all there is to being human. The philosopher is distinguished from others only by the rigor brought to the search.[22]

Anything accepted, without personal challenge, is belief rather than knowledge. Moreover, being accepted unchallenged, the belief is vague and vapid. The person holding the belief does so loosely; unaware of the parameters of the belief, unsure of even the nature of the limitations and unresolved doubts that make that particular thing belief rather than knowledge, still less aware of the precise dimensions of those limitations and doubts.[23] We cannot rely on the arguments of others in any instance because to accept, without personal test, the arguments of others, knowing that we have, at some point, found arguments of others wanting, would be an act of faith. In this context faith generates belief but forbids knowledge.

Anything which is merely accepted is a loss; a genufluction to the ignorance, lethargy or mortality of the philosopher. Anything which is merely accepted is also a flaw, a weakness in the theorising of the philosopher which, no matter how seemingly trivial, because it might tear apart the fabric of that philosophy, does tear apart the fabric of that philosophy. One cannot *know* that a belief is of trivial import; one can only *believe* in it unimportance. The goal in philosophy is wisdom – knowledge – and thus anything which exists merely at the level of belief is for the philosopher, a fundamental flaw. It is the nature of something as a belief which makes it a flaw, not the content of the specific belief. Its potential, the unknown capacity of what it might do, means that because it is a belief it is a fundamental flaw in the philosophy.

Belief can creep into, and unsettle, the most subtle philosophy. Kropotkin criticises Hobbes's contention that the life of primitive man was brutish, nasty and short. He argues that, on the contrary, early societies were characterised by their communitarian spirit.[24] For the argument in this chapter it is not the truth of Kropotkin's alternative proposition that matters but the nature of his argument. Hobbes's views on the life of early man are mere conjecture (as, perhaps, are those of Kropotkin). No answer to Kropotkin's charges are to be found in the texts of Hobbes other than counter-assertion. But if Hobbes' view on this matter is fundamentally flawed so, as Kropotkin argues, is his political philosophy. It is not enough to take his assertion as an axiom for the philosophy which follows. If the assertion is an axiom that which follows is merely a web of words. Those words may have a beautiful and skilful structure but they have no philosophical connection with their apparent referent, human nature. Without that connection what is the philosophy a philosophy of?

In the context of this argument it is not the reified structure of any philosophy which is at issue but, rather, the person's ability to personally account for it. Thus, that which may be knowledge for one person, can become mere belief for another. Akhtar has described the way in which, in the context of the debate on the publication of Salman Rushdie's *The Satanic Verses*, freedom of speech has become a holy value, something beyond rational debate, for some of those commenting on the Muslim reaction to the affair.[25] Even if foundational claims can be justified in the case of some arguments for freedom of speech, knowledge of those claims will only exist for those who have personally thought through the appropriate arguments. Those who take on trust writings which are thought to justify an absolute assertion of freedom speech, and which may in fact justify such an assertion if the arguments contained in the writings are properly thought through, merely believe in freedom of speech.[26] Their beliefs, as beliefs, have no higher intellectual status than any other beliefs. As in this case, so in other examples.

The above might be thought to put an unreasonably high demand on any philosophising. I, at any rate, am ignorant, lazy and mortal; so are we all. Perhaps we all feel that, at most, like Newton, we are merely playing with brightly coloured pebbles on the shores of the ocean of truth.[27] We accept our intellectual efforts are desultory. For this reason it may be thought that to eschew all beliefs in favour of knowledge, to recognise what is contingent, what is provisional, and to search for something deeper and surer, is a course we are only capable of, if at all, in a small discrete area. Thus we limit the scope of our attempt. We become just psychologists or just philosophers, just sociologists or just historians. And then only in an accepted sub-set of our chosen discipline. We work upon accepted questions within an accepted structure seeking answers to be measured against accepted criteria. To follow Husserl is to set standards according to which we can be almost certain our work will fail. Better to choose the more limited possibility where there is some hope of success.

Fear of failure is not an argument. It is an emotion. Even a virtual guarantee of failure is not an argument. If the enterprise itself is valid, if radical philosophising is possible only in the form Husserl describes, and if radical philosophising is at some point necessary, then the fact that we may fail is irrelevant. If we search for wisdom (the deepest form of understanding), and that presumably is the end goal of any intellectual pursuit, not just philosophy understood in a narrow professional sense, then that is the path which we must take. Other approaches available do not even offer the possibility of the apodictic certainty that is sought. They can only generate ever more sophisticated beliefs. With other approaches we can be sure that, whatever our abilities, the search is endless, not just now but for all time, because in these cases the search is conceptually without end. More sophisticated beliefs, accepted as beliefs, can lead only to ever more sophisticated beliefs which always are, and always will be, lost in a maze of unresolved questions, unable to identify even the entrance to the maze. What we get from our attempt at radical philosophy may turn out to be a lesser form of philosophy, thus may not be wisdom, but that does not disturb the nature of what we have to try to do: and, by the very attempt at radical philosophy, we become more able to say of our philosophy at this point we miss, or there exceed the mark. Thus our philosophy becomes stronger. That we are likely to fail in our eventual goal is a matter of personal, not intellectual, concern. And, perhaps, not even of personal concern: 'For us, there is only the trying. The rest is not our business'.[28]

There have been, and are, many who deny the ontological or epistemological possibility of apodictic certainty. Post-modernism and pragmatism are but two of the more notable contemporary intellectual fashions that stand in opposition to the possibility of making foundational claims.[29] However, even for those who argue that absolute knowledge is conceptually unattainable, the necessity of the search for such knowledge may remain. In this spirit Kolakowski has argued that,

> [W]e can speak of the relativity of knowledge in the sense that the same collection of facts admit of different theoretical explanations becoming narrower as science progresses, though it never disappears altogether...Truly absolute knowledge, either in the sense of mentally reproducing the whole universe or of formulating a law of unalterable and final validity, is an unattainable goal to which we can only approximate indefinitely. In so doing, however, we can come to possess an increasingly full and accurate picture of reality as a whole.[30]

However, not all those rejecting the possibility of absolute knowledge would accept any value in pursuing it as a goal. Lyotard has argued that, '[i]n contemporary society and culture – postindustrial society, post-modern culture – ...[t]he grand narrative has lost its credibility...regardless of whether it is a speculative narrative or a narrative of emancipation'.[31] In his view, in order to understand social relations, we need, 'a theory of games which accepts agonistics as a founding principle'.[32] Any approach, such as this, provides a strict limitation to the possibility of doubt.

In *On Certainty* Wittgenstein wrote that, '[i]f you tried to doubt everything you would not get as far as doubting anything. The game of doubting itself presupposes certainty.'[33] To go through the process of explaining doubt, to go through the questioning process, involves a use of language which must not itself be doubted. 'It may be...that *all enquiry on our part* is set so as to exempt certain propositions from doubt, if they are ever formulated. They lie apart from the route travelled by the enquiry.'[34] The act of doubting itself implies a certainty.

> All testing, all confirmation and disconfirmation of a hypothesis takes place already within a system. And this system is not a more or less arbitrary and doubtful point of departure for all our arguments: no, it belongs to the essence of what we call the argument.[35]

If that which was taken as certain for the purpose of the doubting is itself then made the subject of doubt, this can only be possible on the basis of some new assumed certainty. And so on, *ad infinitum*. It is not just that we lack a language to express radical doubt. Rather, it is that there can be no such radical doubt. The technique of doubting must necessarily destroy the possibility of perfect doubting. It is possible to doubt only within a frame of reference. 'What counts as an adequate test of a statement belongs to logic. It belongs to the description of the language-game.'[36] It is never possible to doubt the frame of reference. To have a context within which it makes sense to doubt a frame of reference is to create a new frame of reference within which the old frame is simply part of the grammar of the new; to create a new frame of reference within which the old frame of reference is no longer a frame of reference.

> I did not get my picture of the world by satisfying myself of its correctness; nor do I have it because I am satisfied of its correctness. No: it is the inherited background against which I distinguish between true and false.[37]

Following this argument, within the frame of reference things may be doubted; a reconsideration of a frame of reference which involves changing that frame involves a process which is akin to that of a religious conversion.[38] Although Wittgenstein's arguments lead to a philosophical rejection of the possibility of notions such as apodictic certainty, incontrovertible foundations or any unity of knowledge it does not therefore follow that the language games which are revealed are to be found within a vacuum. Arguments such as those used by Wittgenstein, and adopted and expanded by Lyotard, may provide a limitation to the philosophical process of doubt but they do not foreclose the possibility of further moves, of a qualitatively different kind, beyond the mere description of the grammar of different examples of language games. If, as Lyotard notes, the games 'do not carry within themselves their own legitimation, but are the object of a contract, explicit or not, between the players',[39] there must be some sense in which that contract is a 'contract'.[40] Wittgenstein's argument is not that there are only language games but that within a strictly defined notion of philosophy there is only the study of language games. 'If the true is what is grounded, then the ground is not *true* nor yet false.'[41] But, for Wittgenstein, there still *is* the ground. 'If someone asked us "but is that *true?*" we might say "yes" to him; and if he demanded grounds we might say "I can't give you any grounds, but if you learn more you will think the same."'[42] Even if the arguments of Wittgenstein are accepted there is still some purpose in searching for the ground. However, even within the range of arguments that Wittgenstein addressed himself to, there are difficulties inherent in the notion of 'language games' and the consequent opposition to radical philosophising.

Kripke, in his commentary on the rule and private language arguments in Wittgenstein's *Philosophical Investigations*, has argued that the sceptical nature of Wittgenstein's arguments appears to lead to the conclusion that, for Wittgenstein, '[t]here can be no such thing as meaning anything by any particular word.'[43] The essence of Kripke's arguments can be seen in an example taken from mathematics (though, as Kripke observes, exactly the same problems occur in, 'all meaningful uses of language').[44] Kripke argues that, following Wittgenstein's observations, it is never possible for one person alone to say that they are obeying a rule when they work in a new situation. Kripke's example is of the sum $68+57=125$. This sum conforms to the rule of addition normally symbolised by '$+$' or 'plus'. Kripke postulates the rule of addition known as '$\oplus$' or 'quus'. Quus is the rule of addition where $x \oplus y = x + y$ provided that both x and y are less than 57 but otherwise $x+y$ equals 5.

> Ordinarily, I suppose that, in computing '$68+57$' as I do, I do not simply make an unjustified leap in the dark. I follow directions I previously gave myself that uniquely

determine that in this new instance I should say '125'. What are these directions? By
hypothesis, I never explicitly told myself that I should say '125' in this very
instance.[45]

If someone has never before had an occasion to calculate the sum of 57 and 68
nothing in their past behaviour or mental history will determine whether they
have followed the plus rule or the quus rule in their past additions and thus
nothing determines which they should follow in this new calculation.[46] Given
these observations the problem of how language (which constantly deals with
new situations), conceived of as rule directed behaviour, is ever possible is
generated. 'Wittgenstein's main problem is that it appears that he has shown *all*
language, *all* concept formation, to be impossible, indeed unintelligible.'[47]

For Kripke the conditions for the assertibility of the plus rule (and thus the
possibility of language) can only be given once 'we widen our gaze from
consideration of the rule follower alone and allow ourselves to consider him as
interacting with a wider community'.[48] A single person can never say that they
should use either the plus or quus rule. The justificatory arguments for saying
that one means plus and not quus in the presence of a new calculation lie in one
person's provisional assertion that plus is what others would say.[49] However,
this suggestion, that assertibility is to be found in claiming to follow the usages
of a community, is itself open to objection.

> [W]hat is the community except a collection of persons? And if each of those persons
> is supposed to take his orders about meaning solely from the others, it follows that
> none of them takes orders. The whole semantic house of cards is based upon our
> taking in each other's washing, or would if there were any laundry to wash.[50]

The metaphor adopted by writers such as Wittgenstein and Lyotard, 'language
game', itself suggests the problematic assumption inherent in their arguments;
that there is at least one group of people playing the same game, where playing a
game involves one person replicating the essential behaviour of another. People
play by the same rules and, in playing by the same rules, they play the game.
However, playing a game may be a more individualistic process than either
Wittgenstein or Lyotard allow for.

Umpires and referees are present in games not just to adjudicate on
infractions of rules by players but to supplement the player's knowledge of the
rules. Individual players, having only a limited knowledge of the rules,[51]
literally play by a different set of rules one from another. Equally, players play
not just according to such knowledge of the rules as they have. They also play,
and count themselves as winning or losing, by reference to a set of purely
personal drives. Thus, for example, people who play 'social squash' do not see
themselves as being continually beaten (if that happens) but rather as 'playing
social squash' in which there is no winning or losing or where winning or losing
is not the driving feature of the game. For sports psychologists playing a game
involves more than the rules of the game. For example, they write of players
who fear success and therefore do not give of their full effort[52] and of the
psychology of winners (and losers).[53] There seems little to suggest that the
practice of game playing[54] has the form which is implicit within the work of
Wittgenstein.

It is, of course, imaginable that two people belonging to a tribe unacquainted with games should sit at a chess-board and go through the moves of a game of chess; and even with all the appropriate mental accompaniments. And if *we* were to see it we should say they were playing chess.[55]

But we would only mean by that attribution that the making of various moves which accorded with known rules by seemingly sentient creatures led us provisionally to conclude that a game was being played. Inferred by that game description would be the presence of a one or more of a range of psychological phenomena of the type described above. Their absence would deprive the activity of its game character. The computer that plays chess is not performing the same kind of activity as the Grand Master that it beats.[56]

Games players play private games.[57] There are only private games.[58]

Unpacking the metaphor of language games in the manner above suggests a very different notion of what is involved in doubting to that suggested by Lyotard or Wittgenstein. If doubting is done in the context of a language game then doubting is, in the final analysis, a private activity by the doubter. Doubting is not done in the context of a fixed frame of reference. Nor is it something which involves the presence of a community. Rather, it is a process more akin to the improvement of a breed of dogs.

> The breeders who devised the standard and created the breed...started with neither a perfect standard nor perfect specimens; they started with a general idea of what they wanted and a multiplicity of variously crude specimens with which to begin their breeding. One improves one's understanding of the general by the particular; one improves the particular by referring it to the general.[59]

Each person improves their own breed. They may compare their work with their (imperfect) knowledge of the work of others but their work never becomes a public matter. They work, as they must, for themselves and by themselves.

To say that radical doubt is possible is not to say that it is easy. What is being sought through the process of radical doubt may be seen as being nothing more than a clarification of terms. But this process of clarification must be understood as being something larger than a search for consistent usage, coherent expression and stipulative definition (important though these matters are and despite the fact that, here, the work will attempt to provide precisely these things.) If the analysis is to be anything more than a series of conditional statements, a form of higher journalism constituting only ephemeral comment on ephemeral conditions, it is here that the work must be grounded. However, added to the intellectual difficulties of this process are the psychological problems. Rousseau may have been expressing a common fear when he wrote that he believed in God, 'because doubt is too violent a state for me to endure'.[60] Nevertheless, if radical doubt is a possible it is also necessary.

Languages of rights

Languages of rights are shot through the relationship between religions and legal rules in Great Britain. Competing tongues allege different, contradictory

rights on the basis of diverse, incompatible premises. Whether any of these
languages are in any sense accurate or helpful (or even whether or not they are
internally coherent) is not, at this juncture, to the point. Such languages are part
of the very phenomenon under consideration. Any attempt at a comparative
description of these languages, and after that an analysis of them, presuppposes
some criterion against which to measure them. Such a criterion cannot be found
in a formal analysis of the meaning of 'right' within a particular language
game.[61] Rather, it is necessary to provide a criterion against which to measure
why something is a right; to provide a criterion which will establish moral right.
It is at this point that the nature of the human being becomes a vital issue.

> What men ought to do depends on what they are. My ethics will be determined by my
> view of human existence.[62]

For each person their own individual existence precedes everything else.

> Should I die in misery and squalor, heeded by no-one, of no material consequence in
> the world, I should be no less human...My radical autonomy on the other hand (my
> being an end in myself) is necessary (necessary in the strict sense) to my conception of
> myself as human.[63]

Whereas, for each of us, the world is contingent on our effort in knowing it
(and is thus created by us) our individual existence merely is. The world may be
more than our contingent experience but, nevertheless, we can never know it as
more than our contingent experience. Our own existence is by contrast, for us,
direct experience. Our perception of the world is based upon apparatus, touch,
sight, hearing and so forth, that we know to be flawed.[64] Although, this does
not justify discounting entirely the phenomena of apparent appearance[65] our
knowledge of the relationship of that perceived phenomena to other things is
of a different, lower order to our knowledge of self. Thus, for each of us, our
individual existence has priority over the world. Individual existence is
therefore free. We are not, in ourselves, bound.[66] Limitations to ourselves, to
our action, to our manner of being, are ones that we make, that we accept.
When we claim that, 'I do something because of x', the 'I' precedes the 'x'. Thus
the claim, if advanced as the ultimate justification for an action suggesting we
could not have chosen otherwise, is illegitimate. 'X', being dependant on 'I',
cannot bind, therefore cannot justify 'I'. Such a claim is a form of lie to self.[67]
In accepting 'x' as a limitation we make 'x' a limitation and it is a limitation only
because of that acceptance.

Many writers have denied, or been taken to deny, the possibility, or at least
the priority, of direct knowledge of self.[68] Hume, for example, in his *Treatise
on Human Nature*, argues that, '...when I enter most intimately into what I call
myself, I always stumble on some particular perception or other...'.[69] Hume
argues that all we know are perceptions. Individual perceptions are not, in
themselves, self. Therefore, we cannot know of self. Perceptionless, we do
not exist, according to Hume. 'When my perceptions are removed for any time,
as by sound sleep, so long am I insensible of myself, and may truly be said not to
exist.'[70] However, if perceptionless we do not exist, in what sense are *my*
perceptions mine? Without a concept of self, perceptions are simply free-

floating entities which are only conventionally attached to a concept of personhood.[71] What, then, would such perceptions be?[72] It seems better to argue that because of our perceptions (not because of the content of those perceptions) we know of self.[73] Similarly we can deal with Freud's argument that we have direct experience of the ego but not the id.[74] Following this argument our awareness of the id comes, if at all, through introspective speculation rather than through direct intuition. We have no priority over another (for example our analyst) in making claims of knowledge of our id. However, as Sartre has written, though this distinction may be fruitful in furthering psychoanalytic treatment, it is ontologically unsound.[75] To cast the id as a censor determining, or partially causing, our actions (of us both not us) is, implicitly, to claim the id as a limitation over which we have no control. However, the id is of us as much as is the ego. Our intuitive awareness of self may be masked. We may hide our selves from self. Nevertheless we remain, at all times, aware of self. The notions of ego and id themselves demand the notion of underlying self.[76] To write of the intuitive awareness of self is not the same thing as writing of the easy apprehension of self. As Husserl argues, '...when descriptive theory of consciousness begins radically...[i]ts beginning is the pure – and, so to speak, still dumb – psychological experience'.[77] Intuitive awareness of self, direct knowledge of self, is not the same thing as attention to the superficial phenomenona of everyday life.

Sperry's brain-bisected patients pose another order of problem for the idea of the *cogito* to that exemplified, in different ways, by Hume and Freud. Sperry reported two patients who had, for medical reasons, had the hemispheres of their brain surgically separated. In both patients he observed elements of separate consciousness in the two divided hemispheres of the brain.[78] If Sperry's observations are accurate the brain does not necessarily, in the Cartesian sense, think.[79] Parfit has then gone on to ask, on the basis of this phenomenon, how our notions of personal identity would be effected if we were able to imagine a person who was able, at will, to split and rejoin the two hemispheres of their brain.[80] Plainly both Sperry's brain-bisected patients and Parfit's thought-experiment provide considerable challenges to notions regarding the relationship between body, mind and self. However, of themselves, they seem to do nothing to challenge the basic idea of the Cartesian ego. The chronology of the *cogito* is precise. I think therefore I am. '[A]t any particular time this experience [of apodictic certainty] offers only a core that is experienced "with strict adequacy", namely the ego's living present...'.[81] The concept of the *cogito* can equally well accommodate the concepts of one mind, one mind becoming two, two becoming one or one mind continuing alongside a rudimentary consciousness, depending on which interpretation of the brain-bisected phenomenon is preferred. '[T]here is no sense in which a split-brain patient could *feel* double – even if we assume that there are two quasi-independent spheres of consciousness inside his skull.'[82] But it is this feeling of double which is required for an effective challenge to the notion of the *cogito*.

Another objection to the form of argument in the *cogito* is that it refers only to one way of thinking; only to one way of conceiving self. It has been said that some people's view of self is inherently relational; that they can only see themselves in the context of their contact with others.[83] If this is so then an image of self as the one thing of which one can have absolute certainty is true only of some people; for those people who think in a non-relational way. If, however, it is true only for some people, even for those people for whom it is true, that truth takes on a different ontological form. It would, then, no longer be an apodictic certainty for all of those whom we would normally see as being fellow humans.

The *cogito* is in part an empirical proposition. It says that each person, if put to the question, can doubt everything except his or her own existence.[84] To dispute this it is necessary to argue of an individual not just that that person normally sees himself or herself in relation to other people but that that person cannot but see themselves in relation to other people. Moreover, what is required from that individual is not a simple rejection of the idea of himself or herself as separate from others but a rejection, in good faith, of the notion that the idea could be true.

Many writers have made 'the selflessness and self-abnegation' they see as being common amongst women a central tenet in their work.[85] Clearly, at least in the United Kingdom and perhaps in the world as a whole, women carry out the majority of tasks associated with caring for others.[86] This bifurcation in workload might well be seen as being associated with different modes of thinking. Those who see themselves, can only see themselves, in association with others are those who are more likely to have the empathy necessary to care for others. Gilligan's book, *In a Different Voice*, is replete with examples of the different attitudinal responses of women and men to questions about self and the way in which these differences alter what Gilligan refers to as moral reasoning.[87]

Some writers have been quite clear that, upon the basis of Gilligan's work, attitudes to self common to, or common amongst, women lead to radical consequences in moral theorising and hence to radical differences in addressing the language of rights. They have argued that any language of rights is, in itself, inappropriate for those who see themselves, not as individuals, but as persons eternally situated within a network of relationships.[88] A difference in conception of self, as suggested earlier, leads to a different view of ethics.

However, whatever the validity of Gilligan's arguments, they address a different order of moral theorising to that discussed in this section. Her arguments present no challenge to the *cogito* because they simply do not consider how people might see themselves. The questions asked by Gilligan, the surveys she quotes and those she carried out herself, relate not to how people *can* see themselves but how people *do* see themselves. Gilligan's work offers no evidence that anybody, let alone any group of people, cannot but see themselves in relation to others. Gilligan's interest in perception of self is at the level of societal reality; how people see themselves in the particular social context in which they find themselves. Her analysis is of the the various characters of those whom she surveys but,

> ...what is called character is purely a structural distinction and presents itself as a slight gap between the person's modes of behaviour and the objective behaviour prescribed for him by his milieu. This gap in turn does not express nature but history, in particular the complexity of origins and the actual degree of social integration.[89]

That women, but not men, in a particular society do not commonly perceive themselves as individuals is instructive in terms of questions relating to social construction but not germane to questions regarding the nature of self.[90]

Even within that feminist writing, in the United Kingdom or elsewhere, that might be characterised, very loosely, as separatist, positing men as the enemy with whom there is neither the possibility of compromise or amity, the essential difference between women and men seems to be perceived of at the level of social construct; albeit a determinant construct.[91] As Duchen has observed,

> In Great Britain, the question of whether or not women are inately different from men, and what the significance of that difference might be, has been generally dismissed by feminists as essentialism and does not find much currency except with feminists involved in psychology or psychoanalysis.[92]

In general feminist writing has not set out to challenge the philosophical basis of the *cogito*.[93]

If the individual is existentially free, the individual is action.

> ...for human reality, to be is to choose oneself; nothing comes to it from outside or from within which it can receive or accept. Without any help whatsoever, it is entirely abandoned to the intolerable necessity of making itself be – down to the slightest detail.[94]

Action is that choosing which involves the formulation, sometimes we would say (incorrectly) the re-formulation, of the world. Each individual must, at all times, design the world; it is not created for them. Ignorance, the unconscious formulation of the world, might seem an easier, therefore preferable, course. However, a person in a state of ignorance is like an old roof in a rain storm; knowledge, like rain, might always leak in. Ignorance is unstable.

> *Why* truth, and not rather untruth or indifference to truth? Because each particular life and being needs a fortress within which to preserve and protect itself and from which to reach out in search of aggrandizement and more power, and truth is this fortress.[95]

My action can only be morally justified by my conscious desire to do it. In acting I am responsible only to myself. I cannot truthfully say, 'I do this because society demands it of me,' or 'I do this because it is my duty,' or, 'I do it because of this moral value'. All these formulations imply that I am bound to the actions by some outside cause. However, my experience of the outside is always contingent on my existence. Morally, I may do 'that which society demands of me' but only if I act in full consciousness of my freedom; not because of 'society's demands'. It is necessary to explain or justify my action, not to attempt to deny the conundrum by suggesting that the action was unwilled. If a person is, the only moral value can be to act in full consciousness of this knowledge.

To act morally is to act authentically. Authenticity connotes full awareness of self. If I act without authenticity, I lie. If I act on the basis of bad faith, reckless inattention or wanton ignorance I act without authenticity.[96] It is the authenticity of the action that makes it moral not its 'goodness', 'benefit to the greatest numbers' or 'compliance with duty'. One looks to the actor to judge the morality of the action not to the action or the result of the action.

We may presume, although not know, the existence of others. Another person's apparent existence may be no more than my contingent experience. However, I can only reject my neighbour's existence at the expense of accepting 'a kind of Brahamic annihilation of consciousness'.[97] My experience of my neighbour is of the same form as my experience of all points of the external world. I cannot unilaterally reject my neighbour without rejecting the world as a whole. But if I reject the world then I reject consciousness. However, my neighbour's nature is as hidden from me as that of anything else in the external world. My acceptance of my neighbour as a replica of me, as another (thus specifying my neighbour's nature) is an act of will.

Although my neighbour may be a simulacrum, she or he appears to replicate me. If I accept my neighbour as being like myself, as another human, then my neighbour must also have existence preceding anything else. My neighbour is also free. Although my experience of my neighbour is contingent, I must treat my neighbour as myself. If, having accepted my neighbour's existence as being like myself, I do not treat my neighbour as being free, knowing that I am free, but, rather, treat my neighbour as any other object, then I lie. To act morally, I must be as aware of my neighbour's freedom as I am aware of my own.

Out of the phenomenology above arises an ethic. If it is morally right for me to treat myself as being free in essence then, since others are like me, I must treat them as free in essence. Equally, as against them, I must also have a moral right to be treated by those others as free in essence. In this case something being (morally) right also means each individual has a (moral) right.[98] The right only arises once I have gambled on the existence of others. As a Cartesian ego I am, in Wittgenstein's much-quoted phrase, 'a limit of the world'.[99] As such there is no person and no thing for me to have a right against.[100] However, once I have acknowledged the existence of others, both I and the others have a moral right to be treated as human (that is, as a person existentially free); each person has a moral duty to treat others in the same way. 'The right of radical autonomy is obviously not a positive right (not something to be granted or taken away by some positive institution).'[101] Rather it is a corollary of humanness.

Only an individual can possess a moral right. In analysing history, interpreting social geography, or similar exercises, terms like class, race and community may be used. In such exercises they have a methodological significance, providing a short-hand description of the interrelationship between great numbers of individuals. However, none of these terms have any deeper meaning than this. Although we may sensibly discuss the role of class, refer to a sense of community or describe the different effects of race, no class, community or race actually exists in the same way that an individual exists. An individual can proceed by way of analogy from knowledge of self to presumption of other selves. No such analogy is possible in seeking to derive the notion of a group from knowledge of the individual.[102] A group exists only so long, and in so far, as it is ordered as such by an individual.

It may be argued that treating the individual, rather than a group, as the fundamental entity is inaccurate since it ignores the fact that individuals live in relation to each other. Kamenka argues that such ideas of,

...the *droits de l'homme*, as opposed to the *droits du citoyen*, are nothing but rights of the member of civil society, ie of egoistic man, of man separated from man and from common life and being.[103]

He goes on to write that the,

the human right to freedom is not based on the connexion of man with man but rather on the separation of man from man. It is the right of separation, the right of the limited individual, limited unto himself...[104]

Following this view, the approach described in previous passages is vitiated by the fact that individuals have no place, no sense of identity, except by measuring themselves against others or by tracing their bonds with others. Thus, in the early Christian Church, the members of the Church were seen only as part of an organic whole.

For as the body is one, and hath many members, and all the members of the body, being many, are one body; so also is Christ.
For in one Spirit were we all baptized into one body, whether Jews or Greeks, whether bond or free; and were all made to drink one Spirit.[105]

On this basis the individual is no more an entity independent of the group than the foot is an entity independent of the group. Strike the foot from the body and it dies; separate the individual from the group and it has no life. If it has no separate existence it can neither be morally right nor have moral right. As a social being the individual cannot be separated out from the society in which she or he lives.

The individual is a set of statuses, rules, and other intrinisically social positions and relationships that devolve upon a mere biological entity in the course of the more or less patterned interactions that make up social life. The individual's rights (if any) and duties, indeed his interests and desires, objectives and purposes, are incomprehensible apart from the language, the norms and beliefs, the institutions and arrangements that make up a social order.[106]

That individuals are normally seen as part and parcel of the society in which they live is, at least within Great Britain, patently the case. It may also be true that, more widely,

[i]n the vast majority of human societies, in time and space, until very recently...a view of human society [as an association of individuals, founded logically on or historically on contract] would have been hotly contested; indeed, most cultures and languages would not have had the words to express it plausibly.[107]

Finally, it may be a general psychological truth that people, in their everyday perceptions, feel that their identity is dependant on others; that they cannot but see themselves as a member of a society. None of this, however, disturbs the centrality of the status of the individual in ethical argument since this is based not upon our conventional feelings and actions but upon the question of what we are.

Lyotard suggests that, 'each of us knows that our *self* does not amount to much'.[108] Those who believe this might then seek strength through their relationships with others. But each such relationship, if founded on a belief in our connection with others, is false. These relationships rehearse intimacies that never existed. Rather, we each have the experience that the closer we get to another person the more we realise how little we know about them. Thus, Gabriel García Márquez has remarked of his wife, 'I now know her so well that I haven't the slightest idea what she is really like'.[109] We each have the feeling that in public places we live our private lives. Even in our most intimate moments we must fail to connect with others. By virtue of our humanity we lack the necessary knowledge. Because we each amount to everything, we cannot know others. As the Chinese novelist, Zhang Xianling, has written

> I don't speak English, nor do I understand French, so in conversations with foreigners I have lost my own tongue. In conversing with the Chinese, however, I have begun to sense that we Chinese do not understand each other's words. In the end, I can only tell myself what I say.[110]

So it is for all of us. In such a context love is the only stable relationship because love is the only relationship that does not presume effect or reciprocity.[111] But love does not negate solitude. Love is a relationship only with self.

If the individual is free then it must follow that no legal rule can negate the radical autonomy of self. This is to say not that no legal rule ought to negate the radical autonomy of self but that, no matter what form or content the rule, a legal rule cannot negate the radical autonomy of self. Sanctions imposed by legal rules, whatever the nature of those sanctions, must be powerless when faced with the intransigence of absolute subjectivity.[112] However draconian the sanction, it would be a lie for an individual to say that he or she obeyed the rule because of the sanction. Obedience to a rule will always occur because of an individual's choice. Since a legal rule cannot make anyone do anything, it is not possible to criticise a legal rule because of the damage it does. The damage is done by the individual(s) who choose to obey the rule. When the criticism of the legal rule relates to damage that the rule does to those other than the person obeying the rule this point, though still accurate, is of little consequence. The injustice of a rule in relation to, for example, the poor remains an injustice even if the poor are damaged not by the rule but by those obeying the rule. However, the distinction between damage being done by a rule and damage being done by those who obey the rule becomes vital if the criticism is that the rule, in some sense, damages those who obey it. The rule cannot damage them; only their obedience is damaging. But what sense is there in criticising the rule if the root error is in the psychology of those who obey the rule? Removing the rule alters nothing; it is the disposition to obedience that is in question.

Despite this, the concept of the radical autonomy of the individual does give a purchase for a critique of legal rules. Using the notion of radical autonomy legal rules can be criticised, not because of their effects, but because of their lack of legitimacy. All legal rules affect the autonomy of individuals. Rules, and their sanctions, put constraints on the behaviour of individuals. In itself this is not a matter for criticism. At this level rules may be measured as good or bad using criteria such as economic efficiency, social worth, 'formal justice'[113] or the like. However, if a legal rule purports to usurp the radical autonomy of the individual, treating the individual not as an end but as a means, then the rule is susceptible to a much deeper criticism. The claims that such rules make are simply lies and it is this failure in honesty which is a more compelling criticism than the comparatively trivial complaint that the rules engender social injustice or are economically inefficient. Such rules are illegitimate in the sense that no autonomous individual can take heed of them and in the sense that they present a false picture of the world. That which the rule commands may be taken up by the individual as the content of their behaviour but, in making the content of the rule their project, the individual is not obeying the rule. Rather the individual is, as he or she must, continuing to freely choose his or her own course of action. Such rules can only be obeyed, in the full sense of the word, by individuals who act in bad faith.

Detmold has asked,

> How could it be the case that I (any of us) accept against reason the imposed will of another and still retain my human status?; I become the other's tool or slave...This conception of human nature – what it is, fundamentally, to be a human person – is sufficient ontological justification for the conception of a primary human right.[114]

These 'strong rights'[115] that each individual has – the rights inherent in their own existential freedom – measure the legitimacy of legal rules in any social system. Since they relate to humanness they are not culturally based but are, rather, criteria against which to judge each culture.[116]

Powerful though it is, the notion of the radical autonomy of the individual does not provide a criterion for assessing every legal rule. A rule which creates a speed limit of 30 miles per hour does not challenge the radical autonomy of an individual. Their autonomy is effected but the rule contains no implicit reflections on the humanness of those to whom the rule applies. The merit of such a rule must be assessed solely by criteria other than radical autonomy. However, a rule which makes an arbitrary distinction between people (for example, saying that left-handed people can drive at 40 miles per hour but right-handed people can only drive at 30 miles per hour) does challenge individuals radical autonomy, not because of the command inherent in the rule (the speed limits) but because making an arbitrary distinction between human beings is to treat one or both groups as not being fully human.[117] As has been seen above, I cannot justify treating myself in an arbitrary fashion. I am responsible for each of my actions and must act conscious of that responsibility. Once I have gambled on their existence I must treat others as myself. Therefore I cannot make arbitrary distinctions between others. Again, this does not mean that the notion of radical autonomy will provide the only criterion for judging legal rules that make distinctions between human beings. Someone may wish to argue that a rule is bad without wishing to argue that it is illegitimate. A speed limit of 150 miles per hour in built up areas would be a bad idea even though nobody's radical autonomy would be challenged.

Notes

1.   R. Abel, 'Law Books and Books about Law' (1973) 23 *Stanford Law Review*, 175 at p. 175.

2. Abel, *op. cit.*, pp. 175–176.
3. C. Campbell and P. Wiles, 'The Study of Law in Society in Great Britain' (1976) 10 *Law and Society Review* 548.
4. Campbell and Wiles, *op. cit.*, p. 553.
5. *loc. cit.*
6. Some of the arguments below have been rehearsed, in a somewhat different context, in A. Bradney, 'And that man dying' in F. Patfield and R. White (eds), *The Changing Law* Leicester University Press, 1990.
7. The subject 'conveyancing' is, of course, an example taken more or less at random. The strength of the remarks that follow in the main text at this point vary proportionate to the degree to which the area of a book could be said to be a 'subject'.
8. Such associations are not immutable. For example, in Great Britain, in the 1920s, the term 'family law' would have meant little if anything, in the 1960s it would have meant a largely doctrinal subject associated with a particular social form and in the 1980s a rather eclectic area with vestiges of doctrinal study increasingly dominated by socio-legal studies and some theoretical work.
9. R. Debray, *Teachers, Writers, Celebrities* New Left Books, 1981, p. 238.
10. See, for example, M. Booth, *British Poetry: 1964 to 1984* Routledge and Kegan Paul, 1985, Part 1.
11. T. Kuhn, *The Structure of Scientific Revolutions* University of Chicago Press, (2nd ed., 1970) Chp III.
12. P. Carrington, 'Of Law and the River' (1984) 34 *Journal of Legal Education* 222 at p. 227.
13. U. Eco, *The Name of the Rose* Secker and Warburg, 1980, p. 86. There are a number of different versions of the original source for this quotation. Sir Robert Burton attributes a similar remark to the Latin poet, Didacus Stella (R. Burton, *The Anatomy of Melancholy: Vol 1* Clarendon Press, 1989, p. 12). (Merton discusses Burton's suggestion in R. Merton, *On the Shoulders of Giants* Free Press, 1965, pp. 3–8.) However, given the setting of his novel, Eco is probably thinking of the later version of the quotation that John of Salisbury attributes to Bernard of Chartres (John of Salisbury, *The Metalogicon* University of California Press, 1962, p. 167).
14. P. Bourdieau, *Homo Acedemicus* Polity Press, 1980, p. 16.
15. Law books are not unique in being open to this kind of criticism. In the same way there are also philosophy books, sociology books, economics books, and so forth.
16. M. Foucault, *The Archaeology of Knowledge* Tavistock Publications, 1972, p. 26.
17. In this context, the metaphor 'foundation' should be understood as indicating a beginning, further back than which the thinker purports to establish it is impossible to go. Thus a thinker who decries foundational thinking, a search for the Ideal or any similar pursuit may still have a foundation though he or she will see it merely as a beginning. See further p.19.
18. E. Husserl, *Cartesian Meditations* Martinus Nijhoff, 1960, p. 2. It is possible to see a validity in this statement even if one rejects all of the philosophy that Husserl then develops from it; the personal necessity for an attempt at 'radical philosophy' is distinct from an acceptance of Husserl's phenomenology.
19. Husserl, *op. cit.*, p. 6.
20. To enter into this question is not a new thing. 'If we imagine the philosophical discussion of the modern period reconstructed as a judicial hearing, it would be deciding a single question; how is reliable knowledge (*Erkenntis*) possible.' (J. Habermas, *Knowledge and Human Interests* Polity Press, 1987, p. 3.)
21. A.E. Housman, *Selected Prose* Cambridge University Press, 1961, p. 16. Curiosity is neither a choice nor a product of socialisation. Everybody must strive to understand the world because they, and only they, create the world. Housman's

'Introductory Lecture', from which this quotation is taken, is an extended meditation on the nature of this search for knowledge.

22. 'Philosophy as synoptic vision is obviously not the province of a single academic discipline.' R. Rorty, *Consequences of Pragmatism* The Harvester Press, 1982, p. 30. We are philosophers by virtue of the form of our thinking, not the source of our income or the place of our publications. We are philosophers by virtue of the fact that we start a journey without maps.

23. Even for those who dispute the possibility of anything other than belief, their beliefs must be as precise as is possible within their schemata.

24. P. Kropotkin, *Ethics* Prism Press (no date) pp. 148–155.

25. S. Akhtar, *Be Careful with Muhammed!* Bellew Publishing, 1989, pp. 58–61.

26. A flavour of the necessary process and difficulties involved in making another's writings knowledge for oneself is caught in Jorge Luis Borge's story 'Pierre Menard – Author of Don Quixote'. Menard sets himself the task of writing chapters from *Don Quixote*; not of putting himself exactly in the position of Cervantes, and thus rewriting *Don Quixote* but, 'to continue being Pierre Menard and to arrive at *Don Quixote* through the experiences of Pierre Menard'. (Jorge Luis Borges, 'Pierre Menard – Author of Don Quixote' in Jorge Luis Borges, *Fictions* Calder and Boyars, 1965, p. 46). Even when Menard succeeds, the exactly rewritten chapters of *Don Quixote* take on a different meaning; the respective contents of Cervantes' and Menard's versions being read in the different contexts of the lives and beliefs of their two authors. (See further J. Sturrock, *Paper Tigers* Clarendon Press, 1977, pp. 163–165 and M. Stabb, *Jorge Luis Borges* St. Martin's Press, 1970, pp. 95–97.) In fact, in tracing through the arguments which lead to and are involved in another's work, the reader will usually feel compelled to depart from that work because they will have a differing view to the writer on the relative merits of competing arguments. Unless one can follow Menard's path fully one can never take on board another's arguments completely.

27. Sir David Brewster, *Memoirs of the Life, Writings and Discoveries of Sir Isaac Newton Volume 2* Johnson Reprint Corporation, 1965, p. 409.

28. T.S. Eliot 'East Coker' in *Four Quartets* Faber and Faber, 1959, p. 31.

29. See J. Lyotard, *The Postmodern Condition: A Report on Knowledge* Manchester University Press, 1984, and R. Rorty, 1982, *op. cit.*, and *Contingency, irony and solidarity* Cambridge University Press, 1989.

30. L. Kolakowski, *Main Currents in Marxism Vol 1* Oxford University Press, 1981, p. 396. Kolakowski himself has written that, 'the phenomenology [of Husserl] was the greatest and most serious attempt in our century to reach the ultimate sources of knowledge'. L. Kolakowski, *Husserl and the Search for Certitude* Yale University Press, 1975, p. 4.

31. Lyotard, *op. cit.*, p. 37.

32. Lyotard, *op. cit* ., p. 16.

33. L. Wittgenstein, *On Certainty* Basil Blackwell, 1974, para. 115.

34. Wittgenstein, *op. cit.*, para. 88.

35. Wittgenstein, *op. cit.*, para. 105.

36. Wittgenstein, *op. cit.*, para. 82.

37. Wittgenstein, *op. cit.*, para. 94.

38. Wittgenstein, *op. cit.*, para. 92.

39. Lyotard, *op. cit.*, p. 10.

40. Accepting, of course, that the use of the term 'contract' is metaphorical.

41. Wittgenstein, *op. cit.*, para. 205.

42. Wittgenstein, *op. cit.*, para. 206.

43. S. Kripke, *Wittgenstein on Rules and Private Language* Basil Blackwell, 1982, p. 55.

44. Kripke, *op. cit.*, p. 7.

45.   Kripke, *op. cit.*, p. 10.
46.   Kripke, *op. cit.*, chp 2.
47.   Kripke, *op. cit.*, p. 62.
48.   Kripke, *op. cit.*, p. 89.
49.   Kripke, *op. cit.*, p. 90.
50.   A.J. Ayer, *Wittgenstein* Weidenfeld and Nicholson, 1985, p. 74.
51.   For example, see the comment by the then General Secretary of the Association of Cricket Umpires, that, '[i]t is a sad fact that many Players, at all levels of the game, have only a superficial knowledge of the Laws…' (T. Smith, *Cricket Umpiring and Scoring* Dent, 1980, p. 6). Equally, there is no compelling reason to suppose umpires have a complete knowledge of rules.
52.   B. Cratty, *Psychology in Contemporary Sport* Prentice-Hall, 1983, p. 126.
53.   See, for example, A. Beisser, *The Madness of Sports* Charles Press Publishers, 1977, chp 14.
54.   Or learning game playing.
55.   L. Wittgenstein, *Philosophical Investigations* Basil Blackwell, (2nd ed., 1958) para. 200.
56.   Wittgenstein seems to have rarely attempted game playing. Monk's description of Wittgenstein's taking up and abandoning tennis in a matter of seven days is a rare instance of Wittgenstein showing any personal interest in game playing. (R. Monk, *Ludwig Wittgenstein* Jonathan Cape, 1990, p. 76.) In the absence of any academic study this comparative poverty of personal experience may have given Wittgenstein a very poor picture of the nature of game playing.
57.   It is possible to conceive of a formal nature of games which is different to the actual practice of playing games and to argue that it is this formal nature which Wittgenstein is concerned with in his arguments. (See, for example, H. Finch, *Wittgenstein – The Later Philosophy* Humanities Press, 1977, p. 78.) However, for Wittgenstein '"obeying a rule" is a practice' (Wittgenstein, 1958, *op. cit.*, para. 202). If obeying a rule is a practice surely so must playing a game be a practice and that practice must be the actual practice and not just the formal practices described by the rules of the rule-book. (Even if Wittgenstein did see games playing in terms of formal practices alone this would only lead to the conclusion that his use of the metaphor is invalid as an empirical referent.)
58.   Precisely the same arguments can be adduced if the metaphor of a contract replaces that of the game. (See, for example, n. 40 *supra*.) Contracts are personal matters differing in their content for each of the parties. (See H. Beale and T. Dugdale, 'Contracts Between Businessmen: Planning and the Use of Contractual Remedies' (1975) 2 *British Journal of Law and Society* 45 and S. Macaulay, 'Non-Contractual relations in Business' (1963) 28 *American Sociological Review* 55.
59.   Yvor Winters quoted by Dick Davis in D. Davis, *Wisdom and Wilderness* The University of Georgia Press, 1983, p. 156. My use of this extended metaphor may be different to that intended by Winters. It certainly differs from Davis's exegesis of the passage. (Davis, *op. cit.*, p. 157.)
60.   Jean-Jacques Rousseau, *Lettre a M. de Voltaire sur la Providence*.
61.   As, for example, may be found in the work of Hohfeld. See W. Hohfeld, *Fundamental Conceptions as Applied in Judicial Reasoning* Yale University Press, 1923.
62.   J. Wild, 'Existentialism as a Philosophy' in E. Kern (ed.), *Sartre* Prentice-Hall, 1962, p. 146.
63.   M. Detmold, *Courts and Administrators* Weidenfeld and Nicholson, 1989, p. 116.
64.   R. Descartes, *Discourse on Method* Penguin Books, 1968, p. 53.
65.   Husserl, *op. cit.*, pp. 19–20.
66.   '…by the sole fact that I am conscious of the causes which inspire my action, these causes are already transcendent objects for my consciousness; they are outside. In

vain shall I seek to catch hold of them; I escape them by my very existence. I am condemned to exist forever beyond my essence, beyond the causes and motives of my act. I am condemned to be free.' J.P. Sartre, *Being and Nothingness* Philosophical Library (no date), p. 439.

67. A lie or other form of deception involving deceit of self is to be avoided because it involves one in contradiction. Such a lie is to say 'p' and 'not p' at the same time. Thus Ackroyd has Oscar Wilde say, 'I have lied to so many people – but I have committed the unforgivable sin, I have lied to myself.' (P. Ackroyd, *The Last Testament of Oscar Wilde* Abacus, 1984 p. 2. See also J. P. Sartre, *op. cit.*, pp. 48–49.) A lie to another person does not have the same form. Therefore it is not to be avoided for the same reason. A tells B 'not p' knowing 'p' to be the case. For A no contradiction is involved.

68. Some of these objections are discussed in Detmold, *op. cit.*, at pp. 136–141.

69. D. Hume, *Treatise of Human Nature: Book 1* Penguin Books, 1969 p. 300. See generally Book 1, Part IV, Section VI, 'Of Personal Identity'.

70. Hume, *op. cit.*, p. 300.

71. Detmold, *op. cit.*, p. 139.

72. Not what are perceptions perceptions of since we know that they may be of nothing; as, for example, in dreams.

73. Thus, also, Lichtenberg's argument that all we should say is 'here is thinking'. Thinking does not infer a thinker only if we accept free-standing thought (which is not to say that the concept of thinking infers a corporeal thinker).

74. See particularly S. Freud, *The Ego and the Id* 1923.

75. Sartre, *op. cit.*, pp. 50–54.

76. 'The very essence of the reflexive idea of hiding something from oneself implies the unity of one...' Sartre, *op. cit.*, p. 53.

77. Husserl, *op. cit.*, p. 38.

78. R. Sperry, 'Brain Bisection and Mechanisms of Consciousness' in J. Eccles (ed.), *Brain and Conscious* Experience Springer, 1965.

79. Sperry's original observations lay themselves open to a number of different interpretations. In discussion after the presentation of Sperry's paper one participant asked 'whether this evidence really justifies us in saying that there are really two minds here ...shouldn't we say rather that they are capable in a way that we are not, because of the corpus callosum, they are capable of attending to part of their hemispheric activity at a time?' (Sperry, *op. cit.*, p. 312.) Since Sperry's original papers the surgical process of brain bisection has been described and a number of different experiments done on brain-bisected humans, monkeys and cats. (See, for example, M. Gazzaniga, *The Bisected Brain* Appelton-Century Crofts, 1970.)

80. D. Parfit, *Reasons and Persons* Clarendon Press, 1984, chp 12.

81. Husserl, *op. cit.*, p. 22.

82. V. Ramachandran, 'Twins, Split Brains and Personal Identity' in C. Josephson and V. Ramachandran, *Consciousness and the Physical World* Pergamon Press, 1980, p. 140.

83. See, for example, C. Gilligan, *In a Different Voice* Harvard University Press, 1982.

84. '[T]he capacity to judge correctly and to distinguish the true from the false...is naturally equally in all men...I have never supposed that my mind was out of the ordinary...'. Descartes, *op. cit.*, p. 27.

85. The phrase is taken from K. O'Donovan, *Sexual Divisions in Law* Weidenfeld and Nicholson, 1985, p. 207, but the idea is one in general use.

86. Apart from women's domestic role within the family much of women's waged work is associated with caring or nurturing forms of employment such as nursing, teaching, secretarial assistance, etc. See, for example, A. Coote and B. Campbell, *Sweet Freedom* Basil Blackwell, (2nd ed., 1982) chp 2.

87. Gilligan, *op. cit.*
88. See, for example, A. Bottomley, S. Gibson and B. Meteyard, 'Dworkin, Which Dworkin? Taking Feminism Seriously' (1987) 14 *Journal of Law and Society* 47 at pp. 54–55.
89. J.P. Sartre, *The Family Idiot: Vol 1*, The University of Chicago Press, 1981, p. 62.
90. The same points can be made with respect to the later collection of essays edited by Gilligan, and to which she makes several contributions *Mapping the Moral Domain*. The 'mapping' is of the domain as it exists within one culture rather than of existential moral structure. (See C. Gilligan, J. Ward and J. McLean Taylor with B. Badige (eds) *Mapping the Moral Domain*, Harvard University Press, 1988.)
91. See, for example, 'Extract from a radical lesbian tract' in C. Duchen, *French Connections* Hutchinson, 1987, pp. 91–93.
92. Duchen (ed.), *op. cit.*, p. 55.
93. It is easy to find examples of feminist writing which appear to accept the ontological priority of individual existence. Thus, for example,

   'I Begin by presuming that I am free.
   I begin with nothing, no form, no content...'
   (A. Dworkin, *Women Hating* E.P. Dutton, 1974, p. 198.)

   'I presume that I am free.
   I act.'
   (Dworkin, *op. cit.*, p. 199.)

   '[M]y energy belongs to me, not to women any more than men, not to the movement, to which I never swore an oath of allegiance.'
   (M. Dhavernay, 'Hating Masculinity Not Men' in Duchen, *op. cit.*, at p. 103.)
94. Sartre, *Being and Nothingness*, *op. cit.*, pp. 440–441.
95. R. Hollingdale, 'Introduction' to F. Nietzsche, *Thus Spake Zarathustra* Penguin Books, 1961, p. 26.
96. There are other considerations, other forms of reason, which will justify action. I might wish to justify my actions socially, politically, patriotically, etc. Some of these other ways of reasoning will be invalid because they are immoral; because they contradict my knowledge of my freedom. Many will begin where my knowledge of my freedom leaves me a number of different potential courses. For example, to say I must do this because I am British is immoral because it implies that my Britishness precedes and takes priority over 'I'. This, of itself, is immoral. To say that, taking into account the geographical area in which I was born, I choose to do this, may or may not be immoral, depending on the other reasons for my action and the nature of the action.
97. R. Kirkpatrick and F. Williams, 'Translator's Introduction' in J. P. Sartre, *The Transcendence of the Ego* Octagon Books, 1972, p. 25.
98. White has argued that a distinction should be drawn between being right and having a right. See A. White, *Rights* Clarendon Press, 1984, pp. 95–100. Even if one accepts the validity of his method of argument (which is based upon a speculative enquiry into the empirical question of how language is used), and the general accuracy of his conclusions, they do not seem to apply when moral right is defined as above.
99. L. Wittgenstein, *Tractatus Logico-Philosophicus* Routledge and Kegan Paul, 1961, 5.632. See also, 5.633–5.641.
100. Detmold, *op. cit.*, pp. 135–136.
101. Detmold, *op. cit.*, p. 135.
102. '*Classes are not like individuals*, even if we admit that they behave nearly like individuals so long as there are *two* classes who are joined in battle.' K. Popper,

The Open Society and its Enemies: Vol II Routledge and Kegan Paul, (5th ed., 1966) p. 138.

103. E. Kamenka, *The Ethical Foundations of Marxism* Routledge and Kegan Paul, 1972, p. 64.

104. Kamenaka, *loc. cit.*

105. I Corinthians 12: 12–13. See also, I Corinthians 12: 14–27. For discussion of the ethical significance of this passage, in the context of the early Church, see C. Dodd, *Gospel and Law* Cambridge University Press, 1951, pp. 32–39.

106. R. Flathman, *The Practice of Rights* Cambridge University Press, 1969, p. 5.

107. E. Kamenka, 'The Anatomy of an Idea' in E. Kamenka and A. Erh-Soon Tay (eds), *Human Rights* Edward Arnold, 1978, p. 6.

108. Lyotard, *op. cit.*, p. 15.

109. P. Mondoza and Gabriel García Márquez, *The Fragrance of Guava* Verso, 1982, p. 23. The sentiment is not a new one. Gore Vidal, quoting Augustine, has written that, 'every human heart is closed to every other human heart'. (G. Vidal, *Two Sisters* Heinemann, 1970, p. 117.)

110. Zhang Xianling, *Getting Used to Dying* Collins, 1991, p. 135.

111. M. Detmold, *The Unity of Law and Morality* Routledge and Kegan Paul, 1984, p. 106. (Love, here, is not Eros.) However, unlike Detmold, I would wish to distinguish love from friendship (Detmold, *op. cit.*, p. 130). As Raz argues, friendship is a reciprocal relationship which is 'to a considerable degree' culturally determined. (J. Raz, *The Authority of Law* Clarendon Press, 1979, pp. 253–258.) Love acknowledges the existential nature of another person There are, of course, cultural, and more specifically sexual, elements which are often associated with love. They, however, have nothing to done with the essence of the condition. It might well be that many more of our relationships than we suppose are more properly thought of in terms of love than friendship (or the reverse may be true).

112. Plainly an individual's autonomy can be effected by a sanction. Prison, for example, restricts one's ability to move. However, radical autonomy is untouched by the experience by prison. The self remains unaltered. Thus we are able to say that we put a person in prison. The person remains even though we have placed restrictions on their corporeal body.

113. T. Campbell, *Justice* Macmillan, 1988, pp. 23–25.

114. Detmold, 1989, *op. cit.*, pp. 113–114.

115. Detmold, 1989, *op. cit.*, p. 112.

116. It may be that in describing or applying these strong rights to particular situations I make judgements which reflect the particular melange which constitutes my personal cultural background. If so, then such judgements are thereby invalidated. However, such mistakes, of themselves, do nothing to invalidate the general theorem that there is culturally neutral notion of humanness.

117. A distinction is arbitrary if either it is unreasoned or if the reasoning can be shown to be false. As will be seen in later chapters it may be a matter of dispute whether the reasoning for a distinction is false or not. This will mean that individuals differ about whether a rule can or cannot be said to be illegitimate because of its challenge to radical autonomy. In itself, this shows no more than that some individuals err. There is, however, a distinction between reasoning which is false and reasoning which others may reject. On some questions there may be room for varying approaches. In such cases neither approach can be said to be arbitrary even though they produce very different results.

Part 2:

Examples

3 Marriage and family life

Introduction

Most people in Great Britain marry. More people now marry in Great Britain than did so in the Victorian era.[1] For many, marriage and family life are religious duties. The instruction, 'Be fruitful, and multiply', found in Genesis, is in a book sacred in three separate religious traditions.[2] The importance of family life can be found repeated in texts venerated by Hindus, Sikhs and numerous other disparate faiths. Within Islam, some schools of law consider marriage to be obligatory for certain individuals.[3] For Hindus, marriage is a crucial point in their lives.[4] A faithful religious life and family life is often inseparable. For this reason, it is of prime importance for the idea of religious freedom in Great Britain that one of the most oft-cited cases concerning the impartiality of the British courts to religion, *Re Carroll*, is a family law case.[5]

The ceremonial aspects of family life, inherent in the public institution of marriage, are stressed by most of the religious traditions to be found within Great Britain as a start to, or necessary stage in, family life. Moreover, for an adherent the religious rites required by their religion may be of greater importance than the formalities required by civil law.[6] Thus, if religious freedom and the right to family life is to be recognised within the law, the first thing to investigate is the attitude of the law towards the marriage ceremony and the relationship between that law and the varying marriage rites required by different religions.

Domestic law prescribes rules which delineate the necessary form of the marriage ceremony and dictate who can take part in that marriage ceremony. Either of these two kinds of rules can conflict with religious requirements.

Marriage formalities

Marriages in Great Britain can be divided into two main categories. These are religious marriages and legal or civil marriages; that is those conducted according to the tenets of a particular faith and those recognized by the domestic legal rules of the British legal systems. Any individual example of a marriage will usually fall into one or both of these categories.[7]

To be recognized for the purposes of civil law a marriage ceremony must conform with the Marriage Acts 1949 to 1990. These Acts lay down a series of

rules which set out where a marriage may take place, who can solemnize the
marriage, what vows must be taken, at what time the marriage can be held and
so forth. These rules are more than value-free, bureaucratic procedures. They
both reflect and reinforce the social mores of the time at which they were
created. It is consistent with ideas of religious freedom that one of the
intentions of these laws is to allow 'those who wish to associate with their [civil]
marriage the religious rites of their particular faith' to fulfill their wishes.[8]

Legal marriages within Great Britain can take one of four different forms.
First, the marriage may simply be according to civil form. In this case the
marriage, which is *per verba de praesenti*, can be held either in the office of the
Suprintendant Registrar or in any building which is certified as a place of public
religious worship under the Places of Religious Worship Act 1855.[9] If the
marriage is to be conducted in the latter then the building must be registered as a
place for the solemnisation of marriage by the Registrar General.[10]

This first form of marriage, as well as allowing for a purely civil form of
marriage, allows a religious ceremony of marriage to be recognised for civil
purposes. A purely religious ceremony of marriage has no effect in law.[11]
However, if a faith has its place of worship certified and registered under
section 41 of the 1949 Act then the civil ceremony of marriage can be
incorporated into or added on to the religious ceremony of that faith. Since the
civil ceremony is very simple, requiring no more than an exchange of vows,
this is something which is comparatively simple to effect.[12] Such a provision
would appear to reconcile the needs of the municipal legal system and the needs
of the different religions to be found in Great Britain. This conclusion is,
however, belied by the operation of the law.

The first step for any faith to have its marriage ceremonies recognised under
the Marriage Act 1949 is to have its place of worship certified as a place of public
religious worship under the 1855 Act. This statutory requirement presumes that
a religious community has both a sufficient degree of organisation and finance
such as to have a settled place of worship. Small or new religious communities
may lack both and thus be unable to satisfy this elementary criteria. For
example, whilst there was significant Hindu migration in to Great Britain from
1941[13] onwards the first Hindu temple was not opened until 1969.[14] Although,
at present, there is no large scale immigration into Great Britain bringing new
religious groups, the process of schism and the establishment of new religions,
ensures that there will always be faiths unable to even begin the process of
unifying the civil form of marriage with their religious ceremony. Equally,
even when there is an established place of worship, a religion may not require
marriage ceremonies to be at that site. Thus, for example, Hindu marriages
may be celebrated either at temples or in local buildings hired especially for the
purpose.[15]

Under the original requirements of the 1949 Act a building could only be
registered as a place for the solemnisation of marriage if it was a 'separate
building' for religious worship.[16] This requirement made it difficult for some
faiths to have their buildings registered. The tenets of some faiths require or
encourage buildings to be used for purposes other than worship. Sikh
gurdwaras commonly have lodging houses attached to them.[17] Muslim
mosques may also be schools.[18] For religions, such as Islam, which stress the

centrality of a place of worship to the whole life of the community and do not distinguish religious and secular spheres, the separate building rule was a significant impediment to certification and thus to reconciling civil and religious forms of marriage.[19] In 1958 an exception to the general rule was made for the case of Roman Catholic chapels.[20] In introducing the Marriage Acts Amendment Bill 1958, Somerville Hastings described the provision in the then extant law requiring 20 householders to certify that they had used somewhere as their place of worship for the previous 12 months as 'a serious disability' for newly established Non-Conformist and Roman Catholic chapels.[21] The subsequent Act made an exception for Roman Catholic chapels not only in respect of this provision but also in respect of the 'separate building' requirement. Later the Law Commission reported that the 'separate buildings' test was unnecessary.[22] (At the same time the Law Commission cautioned against creating special rules for new religious groups on the grounds that they might not 'have long-standing traditions or [might] have traditions which are different to ours'.)[23] Finally, in 1990, a White Paper, *Registration: Proposals for Change*,[24] recommended the abolition of the 'separate building' requirement; a recommendation given subsequent statutory effect by the Marriage (Registration of Buildings) Act 1990. The White Paper recommending the abolition of the 'separate building' requirement made no mention of the needs of religious minorities as a reason for that abolition. However, at Committee stage in the House of Commons and on its presentation to the House of Lords, the Government made it clear that the change was necessary in order to help religious minorities.[25] The change has, if belatedly, removed one obstruction to people jointly celebrating a religious and civil marriage. Others, however, still, remain.

A place of worship may only be open to adherents. This will prevent a building being regarded a place of *public* religious worship. In *Church of Jesus-Christ of Latter-Day Saints* v. *Henning (Valuation Officer)*, where a Mormon could only enter a temple to worship if he had a 'recommend' from his local bishop, public worship was said to mean a place that was open to all those who were properly disposed.[26] It was not enough for the worshippers to regard it as a public as opposed to a private place.[27] The temple was not a place of public religious worship. In *Broxtowe Borough Council* v. *Birch* this interpretation was extended to exclude a meeting hall of the Exclusive Brethren from the definition of a place of public worship on the grounds that it was not obvious from the design of the building or from any other sign that it was open for the public to worship there.[28] Nor will it be enough for the applicants to regard their building as a place of worship. For example, the courts have refused to accept that Scientology is a religion and have therefore refused to certify their buildings as places of religious worship.[29]

The result of the restrictions above is that, with the exception of those religions below whose ceremonies receive special legal recognition, despite the abolition of the 'separate buildings' requirement, those who wish to have both a religious and civil marriage are still forced into having two separate ceremonies, a procedure described as 'cumbersome and unattractive' 20 years ago.[30]

Plainly, this first form of marriage, under the 1949 Act, does create greater problems for some religions than for others. Broadly, the rules presume an established faith with a separate specialist religious function for its place of worship. This is something appropriate to the structure and history of many, though as has been seen above not all, Christian churches but is largely inappropriate for non-Christian religions. The accommodations for the particular needs of religious minorities that have been made are, especially if that minority is non-Christian, perfunctory and grudging. Indeed, the situation is so conceptually confused that the rules relating to the formalities of a legal marriage ceremony for religions not specifically exempted in the 1949 Act are so tightly drawn that, were it not for the special status separately accorded to Church of England marriages under the 1949 Act, it seems doubtful that Church of England marriages could meet the tests of the Act. The courts have held that there is no authority for the proposition that anyone may take part in worship in an Anglican church[31] and canon law holds that only those who 'give due reverence to the name of the Lord Jesus' can attend divine service.[32] Neither of these propositions seem entirely compatible with the test of public worship laid down in *Henning* and *Broxtowe Borough Council*. If the Church of England cannot meet such tests why should any other religion be required to do so?

Whatever problems there might be with the implementation of this first form of civil marriage, it does have the perhaps dubious advantage of largely being overtly neutral as between different religions.[33] The remaining three forms of marriage plainly discriminate between different kinds of religion.

The other three forms of marriages recognised in British law are all religious forms. Marriages according to the rites of the Church of England, the Quakers and the Jewish faith will all receive special recognition in British law.[34] The law allows for the full incorporation of the civil and religious forms of marriage. With respect to these particular religions such special rules, giving civil effect to religious ceremonies, can be seen as an example of religious tolerance and a recognition of the need to allow believers to follow the dictates of their faith. However, by recognising these religions and not others, these three forms of marriage become at the same time an example of religious intolerance; a failure to accept the special needs of believers. If the needs of Jews can be specially dealt with, why not Sikhs? If Quakers receive recognition, why not Muslims?

Historically, the answers to the questions above are easy to give. The three special forms of marriage which relate to religious ceremonies are all to be found in the earliest statute relating to the marriage ceremony, Lord Hardwicke's Act of 1753. Lord Hardwicke's Act was passed to prevent clandestine marriages by ensuring that marriage was a public matter.[35] However, even if it is still necessary to prevent clandestine marriages, itself a moot point,[36] none of the religious forms of marriage which find it difficult to meet the test for certification or registration seem any more clandestine, either in theory or practice, than those allowed for first in the 1753 Act and now in the Marriage Acts of 1949 to 1990. It is of course necessary for it to be clear whether someone is married or not. Equally, by declaring that they wish to be married an individual is accepting that level of formality necessarily inherent in the existence of such a public institution. However, once again, it is not clear why the formalities of the religions which find it difficult to meet the current tests give rise to greater uncertainty than those that can comply with the tests.

There are two obvious differences between those religions which receive special treatment and those which do not. First, there is the length of time that adherents have been found in significant numbers in Great Britain. Thus, for example, there have been significant numbers of Muslims in Great Britain for less time than there have been significant numbers of Quakers in Great Britain. Thus the problems of Muslims have been given less consideration than the problems of Quakers. Although this question of time may be an historical explanation for the difference in treatment, it is not a justification for it. The second difference between those religions which receive special treatment and those which do not is the degree to which those religions which do not receive special treatment are perceived as varying in their traditions from what is taken to be the British norm; in the words of the Law Commission, a difference between those who conform to 'our traditions' and those who do not.

The current registration system, contradictory though it is, tends to seek to impose on individuals a series of requirements which can be wholly at odds with what are, for them, the more important requirements of their religion.[37] Such attempted regimentation becomes impossible to justify when special exceptions are made for some religious groups and not for others. What is of prime importance with respect to this area of law is the needs of the individuals involved. Marriage is a public facility. The form that the marriage ceremony takes has virtually no effect on anyone other than the participants. The importance of the religious needs of Quakers must be exactly the same as the religious needs of Hindus or any other group. To treat the needs of, for example, a Muslim differently on the grounds they have traditions 'different from ours' is precisely to discriminate on grounds of religion.[38] Moreover, it is to do so on the basis of a wholly false proposition, that there is a 'we' who have traditions and that adherents to an unnamed number of religions are outsiders. Rather, there are simply individuals who wish to marry for reasons of religious duty, public status, financial advantage or private pleasure. There is neither a uniform procedure in English law for such marriages nor a uniform tradition within those different religions whose ceremonies are given preferential status in English law. Once the wish of one person is accepted, and once one person's religious scruples regarding marriage formalities are accepted as justifying special treatment, it becomes necessary to accept all such scruples. This argument is strengthened by comparing the tortured complexities of English law on this matter with the comparatively liberal regime found in Scotland. Under the Marriage (Scotland) Act 1977 marriages can be celebrated anywhere.[39] Moreover, any religious body can nominate a celebrant.[40]

Parties to marriage

The Matrimonial Causes Act 1973 sets out rules regarding who can marry whom.[41] In the case of the rules relating to the parties to a marriage, clear though usually unargued policy decisions have been made which conflict with the principles of some religions. The three main areas of conflict between legal and religious requirements in these rules lie in the issue of polygamous marriages,[42] the rules regarding the age of the parties[43] and the question of individual consent to the marriage.[44]

The 1971 report on polygamous marriages by the Law Commission and the Scottish Law Commission addressed the issue of capacity to contract polygamous marriages.[45] The report rests on the unspoken assumption that such marriages are *prima facie* unacceptable. It is merely an assumption and the matter is not discussed during the report. Such silence is typical of the treatment of polygamy in English law. In one standard text on English family law polygamy is not even indexed.[46] In the other standard text the effects of polygamous marriages are discussed but there is no examination of the reasons for forbidding polygamous marriages in this country.[47] Despite the large number of Muslims living in Great Britain, and despite the fact that polygamy is permitted within Islam, few attempts have been made to justify the complete failure to allow polygamous marriages to be celebrated in Great Britain.[48] Although Pearl may be right in arguing that the question of polygamous marriages is numerically less significant now than it was 20 years ago,[49] because fewer groups actually practise polygamy even where their religion permits it, the problem remains important conceptually.

It is difficult to envisage a form of argument which could show that a polygamous marriage is *per se* harmful to the individuals contracting it. For example, it might be possible to show that polygamous marriages were in general harmful to those who entered into them, because such marriages hindered the emancipation of women.[50] However, this would neither show why everyone should be prevented from doing something that some found harmful nor why people should be prevented from harming themselves.

When discussing whether English or Scottish domiciliaries should be permitted to contract polygamous marriages the Law Commission and the Scottish Law Commission argued that whilst England and Scotland were pluralistic societies they were not polygamous societies.[51] The conceptual opposition to polygamous marriages seems to be based solely upon the principle that they fall outside 'our traditions'. Poulter may well be right in asserting that 'the bulk of public opinion would find this [the legal recognition of polygamy] unacceptable for the white majority'.[52] However, on the basis of the arguments in chapter 2, it is difficult to see what right others have to interfere in individual choices which do not directly impinge upon them. Individual autonomy requires a respect for the choices of others. To prevent polygamous marriages simply on the basis that the majority do not, or are thought not, to like them comes very close to legislating on the basis of a whim. The fact, if it is a fact, that the whim is common to a large group of people has, in the context of the arguments in chapter 2, no special significance. To prevent polygamous marriages on such a basis provides a plain example of legislation whose results have a differential effect on different religions, something adherents will correctly see as resulting in religious discrimination. Both English and Scottish law permits serial polygamy, with parties consecutively marrying and divorcing a number of different parties.[53] There is no good reason in principle why these legal systems should not permit concurrent polygamy.

Nobody under 16 can go through a legal service of marriage in England and Wales.[54] As in the case of polygamous marriages, this legal rule imposes obligations that are more likely to be problematic for some religions rather than for others. The stress on the age of parties is at odds with the position in many religions. Thus, for example, within Islam the concern is generally with the consent of the individuals to the marriage and age is not directly an issue.[55] 'The orthodox Hindu view is that the daughter belongs to the family of her husband, hence age cannot come in the way of her marriage.'[56] Here, however, it is easier to see how the prohibition of under-age marriages might be justified notwithstanding its conflict with religious practices. Individual autonomy means that there must be individual consent to marriage. That consent rests on an individual understanding of the implications of marriage.[57] This necessitates a level of acumen which is usually only reached at a certain point in life. A legal system may follow one of two different paths. Either it may have tests for some level of minimal understanding of marriage or, with a view to reducing the costs of the system, it may have age barriers which are presumed to be indicative of such understanding. If the latter course is taken the choice of the particular age is necessarily pragmatic, and to some extent arbitrary. However, the fact of an age limit merely reflects the necessity of individual choice. Nevertheless, the comparatively high age required before marriage can be undertaken may reflect considerations which go beyond an assessment of individual understanding. The courts have said that, the contract of marriage is a very simple one, which does not require a high level of intelligence to comprehend'.[58] If so, it is difficult to see that an average person of considerably less than 16 is incapable of understanding the implications of the contract. It seems more likely that the age limit reflects a notion of 'our' traditions of family life.

The prohibition of polygamy and the restriction on the age of those who can marry represent comparatively uncontroversial areas of law where the content of the rules is relatively clear. The final conflict between legal requirements and religious needs is a much more unclear area of law.

English law requires individual consent to marriage.[59] The legal effect of that consent will be lost if, *inter alia*, it is given due to duress. If there is duress the marriage will be voidable. Where a marriage is voidable the law regards the marriage as valid, having all the same effects as a properly constituted civil marriage, until the marriage is challenged by one of parties, at which time the court will then award a decree of nullity (as opposed to a decree of divorce) invalidating the marriage.[60] This requirement for individual consent is problematic for some religions where marriages are customarily arranged by families.[61] Assessing the impact of the law on such religions is made more difficult because the precise test for duress is in itself uncertain.

In a line of cases, which started with *Singh* v. *Singh*,[62] the Court of Appeal adopted the view that a person could only show that their consent to marriage had been given under duress if they could show that there had been a threat to life, limb or liberty. Threats of social ostracism, loss of job or purely psychological pressure were not seen as sufficient to constitute duress.[63] In discussing the reasons for this conclusion the judges referred to the social effects of the various rulings that they could make and were concerned about the effect of the ruling on immigrant communities.[64] The necessity of showing a threat to life, limb or liberty reduced the number of potential applicants. However, latterly, the Court of Appeal has ruled in *Hirani* v. *Hirani* that the test for duress is simply whether the mind of the applicant has in fact been overborne, howsoever that was caused.[65] This more liberal interpretation opens the way to a much wider number of cases. However, the test in *Hirani* is incompatible with the earlier line of reasoning.[66]

An insistence on individual autonomy in the marriage ceremony will result in a law which has a discriminatory effect on different religions since not all interpretations of all religions regard individual consent as necessary in marriage.[67] If the law enforces individual consent, such religions will not be able to coerce those whom they treat as their adherents into obedience. However, here, such discrimination is justified by the priority of the value of individual autonomy. If individual believers wish to treat themselves as creatures of another's will then, because of their autonomy, that is their right. Nor does the civil law on the basis of the interpretation in *Hirani* prevent them contracting civil marriages. Since only the parties to a voidable marriage can challenge the status of the marriage and since, if they accept the particular religious traditions, they will never wish to do so, the law will continue to treat their marriage as valid even though it is voidable. The law merely prevents those who do not accept the importance of individual autonomy from enforcing their view on parties marrying.

The situation would be different if lack of consent made the marriage ceremony void as it did in *Singh* which was decided before the Nullity of Marriage Act 1971. In the case of a void marriage ceremony the status of the apparently married parties can be challenged in court by any 'interested party'.[68] Thus, even if the parties were content with the religious traditions, an outsider might challenge their relationship. Such a challenge, since it would represent an attempt to impose one person's view of what constituted a proper marriage on another, fails to respect the autonomy of the married person. So long as duress makes a marriage voidable the Court of Appeal's interpretation of what constitutes duress in *Hirani* is preferable to that in *Singh* because it maximises the freedom of different religious groups to pursue their own marriage traditions whilst, at the same time, recognising the priority of individual will.[69]

The care of children

Historically, English law has seen religious belief as an important factor in assessing the quality of parenting. In the nineteenth century, both the poet Shelley and the socialist campaigner (and later leading member of the Theosophy movement) Annie Besant lost custody of their children because of their atheism.[70] This history is not without its present effect. In English law a parent still has a right to determine his or her child's religion.[71] Moreover, this concern with a parent's religion and the parent's right to select the religion of his or her child is reflected in a series of provisions giving priority to that right. Thus, for example, when a parent gives up his or her child for adoption, an adoption panel must take account of the wishes of the parent as to the religious upbringing of that child, insofar as that is practicable, when placing the child for adoption.[72]

English law sets a minimum standard of parenting, providing, for example, compulsory schooling. However, the courts are usually only called upon to assess the quality of parenting when families break up. Parents must then decide how they are to share the future care of their children. If the parties are divorcing the court will have to agree any arrangements the parties draw up. In any event the court will have to settle any disputes between parents about custody of their children.[73] The dominant academic view is now that, 'the question of religious upbringing will have little bearing on custody'.[74]

In a number of custody cases judges have expressed their lack of interest in the religion of the parents before them. Thus, in *Re Carroll*, Scrutton LJ noted that, 'the Court is perfectly impartial in matters of religion'.[75] Similarly, in *Re T* Scarman LJ observed that, '[i]t is not for this court…to pass any judgement on the beliefs of the mother or on the beliefs of the father'.[76] There are other examples of such dicta.[77] However, final determinations of disputes made by some courts suggest that such comments do not fully explain the attitude of the courts.

In *Buckley* v. *Buckley* the dispute about custody was between a mother, who was a Jehovah's witness, and a father who had no particular religious affiliation.[78] The children at the centre of the dispute were three girls, aged eleven, ten and five. In deciding that the mother should lose custody of her children the court noted *inter alia* that if the children were brought up as Jehovah's witnesses they would be different from other children around them.[79] In *Hewison* v. *Hewison* the dispute was between a father, who was a member of the Exclusive Brethren, and a mother who had left the same sect. The three children at the centre of the dispute, two boys and a girl, were aged ten, seven and eight respectively. They had lived with their father for six years from the date of the parents' separation. In deciding that the father should lose his children the court referred to the 'harsh limitations' of the way of life of the Exclusive Brethren and to the fact that the Brethren taught children to see themselves as 'different and separate from the rest of children'.[80] The approach taken by the court has not altered since the nineteenth century. In *Re Besant* Jessel MR argued that Annie Besant had to be refused custody of her child not because she was an atheist but because of the effect that being an atheist had on her social position.[81]

It is difficult not to over-emphasise the importance that religion, or the social usages inherent in the practice of some religions, takes on in the two cases above. This factor assumes a determinant importance, leading the court to ignore other matters it would normally have regarded as conclusive as to the decision that it should make. In both *Buckley* and *Hewison* the decision of the court meant that the children moved from the custody of the parent with whom they had been staying to that of the other. A study of 855 custody cases by the Oxford Centre for Socio-Legal Studies found that the *status quo* as to custody of the child was altered in only seven cases. The study concluded, unsurprisingly, that there was a 'general disposition of the courts against intervention and in favour of maintaining the *status quo*'.[82] Although there are no rules determining the outcome of custody disputes, over and beyond the statutory principle that the decision be made in accordance with the welfare of the child concerned,[83] commentators have identified certain principles which courts normally adhere to when making decisions. Of these, one of the firmest is that custody of young children in general and girls in particular is normally awarded to mothers.[84] *Buckley* conflicts with this principle.[85]

In one respect *Buckley* and *Hewison* do not reflect the usual outcome of custody cases where a parent's religion becomes a factor. In *Buckley* and

Hewison the parents concerned lose custody of their children, at least in part, because of that religion. More typical of the effect of a parent's religion is *Re H*.[86] In this case the mother was a Jehovah's witness; the child, the subject of the dispute, a boy aged five. In rejecting a magistrate's decision that the mother should lose custody of her child because of her religion, Hollings J commented that the mother was 'moderate in her beliefs'.[87] The mother was prepared to give undertakings that the child would be allowed to take part in school activities and that he would not be taken 'witnessing' with her. She was also prepared to allow him to celebrate his birthday and enjoy Christmas and Easter, events not normally recognised by Jehovah's witnesses.[88] On this basis the mother was allowed to retain custody of the child. This case reflects a pattern of judgements where parents are given custody of their children or allowed access to them but only on the basis that they are 'moderate' members of their faith and that they are prepared to make undertakings that they will not bring the child up in the ways of their faith.[89] In *Re T*, Scarman LJ observed that it was reasonable that the mother, a Jehovah's witness 'should wish to teach her children the beliefs and practices' of her faith.[90] Nevertheless, the award of custody of the children to the mother by the court was made only on the basis that the mother would allow the children to go to the father for Christmas and birthdays and not take the youngest child to meetings of Jehovah's witnesses. In *Wright* v. *Wright*, when the father refused 'to give any sort of undertaking which might reassure the mother that he would not actively indoctrinate' the child, the father was refused access to his child.[91] In *Wright*, Ormrod LJ in the Court of Appeal quoted with approval the first instance judge's comment that,

> [w]hat it really boils down to is not a matter of the faith of the Jehovah's witnesses being wrong or right…it is the matter of the custodial parent holding one set of views and the non-custodial parent holding a conflicting set of views and the conflict causing damage to the child.[92]

Whilst it is clear that the fact that parents hold conflicting value-systems may be damaging to a child, it is noticeable that in judgements it is consistently the parent who differs from that which the judge regards as the average in society who has to accommodate the wishes of the other parent.

In *C* v. *C*, Balcombe LJ said that in making decisions about the custody of a child a judge should start from '…the basis that the moral standards which are generally accepted in the society are more likely than not to promote his or her welfare'.[93] Balcombe LJ did concede that moral standards might differ between different communities and that it might be appropriate to take into account these different standards.[94] However this does not mean that parents will necessarily be judged according to the mores of their own religious community. In his judgement in *Re T* Scarman LJ said that with respect to Jehovah's witnesses, '[i]t is conceded that there is nothing immoral or socially obnoxious in the beliefs and practice of this sect'.[95] This proviso is important. If a religion cannot pass this test the fact that parents live according to the mores of their community will be irrelevant and its adherents will have even more difficulty in retaining custody of their children than in the cases above.

In *Re B and G* a father, who was a Scientologist, sought to retain custody of his children.[96] The children, a boy aged ten and a girl aged eight, had been living with the father for the five years before the mother, who had been but was no longer a Scientologist, attempted to gain custody of them.[97] No evidence was produced to impugn the parental abilities of either the father or the children's step-mother. At first instance, Latey J said that in the absence of the fact that the father was a Scientologist, 'the scales would probably [have] come down in favour of not disturbing the *status quo*'.[98] However, his final decision, subsequently upheld by the Court of Appeal, was that care and control of the children should go the mother on the grounds that Scientology was 'immoral and socially obnoxious' and that it was 'corrupt, sinister and dangerous'.[99] Latey J's particular concern was the possibility that the children might be brought up as Scientologists. On the basis of psychiatric evidence about Scientology, and on the basis of documents produced by Scientologists, Latey J concluded that such an outcome would be 'disastrous' for the children.[100]

The argument that the courts are neutral as to matters of religion in settling custody matters rests on the basis that what the courts are concerned with is not the theological soundness of a faith but its social effects.[101] This is an accurate analysis of the court's attitude. However, the consequence of that judicial concern is that adherents to some religions will on occasion lose custody of their children or be denied the right to bring their children up in the manner of their religion precisely because of their religion. That is a peculiar kind of neutrality.

Noting the judicial concern with the social effects of different religions when deciding custody cases, Walsh concluded that,

> Discrimination between faiths may well be legitimate in the interests of the child, but it is important that such discrimination should not be, and should not be seen to be, arbitrary.[102]

Whether the discrimination in the cases above is made on a non-arbitrary basis seems open to question.

Courts are not ideal venues for assessing the social consequences of comparatively little-known religions. Nor are judges immune from popular conceptions and misconceptions of such religions. Thus, for example, it is noticeable that in cases such as *Roughley* v. *Roughley* and *Re M* the courts consider the 'religious instruction' and 'religious education' of the children involved.[103] In these two cases the relevant religion was the Roman Catholic faith. However, when cases involve Jehovah's witnesses the court's concern is whether or not the children will be 'indoctrinated' in the faith.[104] Nothing in the evidence in such cases justifies the pejorative term 'indoctrinate' rather than the more neutral 'instruction' or 'education'. Its use, despite the positive comments about the Jehovah's witness faith sometimes made at the same time, does seem indicative of an *a priori* assumption of the intrinsic lack of merit of the faith.

Even when the courts can rely upon expert testimony about religions the evidence offered might not be that which is most appropriate. In *Re B and G* the court relied in part upon psychiatric evidence.[105] Such evidence, by its very nature, tends to concentrate on the pathological side of a religion, whatever the religion under consideration might be.[106] A sociological analysis can take a broader perspective in analysing a religion. Thus, whilst Latey J was able to conclude straightforwardly that Scientology was 'immoral and socially obnoxious', Wallis, in his study of Scientology, took a more complex stance.

One of Wallis' conclusions was that Scientology might be in the process of taking on the same sort of respectable standing as Christian Science, with its religious status being accepted without any widespread belief in 'its claims to therapeutic efficiency'.[107]

The distinctions between different religions made by the courts rests on comparatively weak evidence and argument. Thus, for example, in the case of Jehovah's witnesses, the difficulties of measuring the degree to which a child may be affected by, for example, not celebrating the traditional Christian festivals are manifest. The difficulty of ascertaining to what degree a child benefits from being brought up in a religion where the family unit has a special sanctity and where there is a particular 'plurality of supportive social groups' is also equally obvious.[108] Jehovah's witnesses do not encourage the pursuit of higher education, because it is seen as being necessary only for worldly advancement, 'but basic skills and knowledge offered by the school[s] are highly-valued'.[109] How does a court judge whether a religion's rejection of 'worldly advancement' is disadvantageous to a child?

Giving absolute priority to the right of parents to bring their children up in the religion of the parent's choosing would result in the death of some children. In the nineteenth century case, R v. Wagstaffe, parents refused to get medical assistance for their sick child because of their religious beliefs, relying instead on prayer. The child died.[110] There have been similar more recent cases, both in this country and abroad. To take just one year, 1990, in the USA, a Christian Scientist couple were convicted of the manslaughter of their two-year-old child after relying on prayer to cure their child when he was suffering from an intestinal obstruction.[111] In the same year, in Great Britain, a Jehovah's witness couple attempted to prevent their child, who was suffering from leukemia, from being given a blood transfusion which was said by doctors to be necessary to save the child's life.[112] Finally, again in Great Britain, a Muslim father killed his daughter because she planned to become a Jehovah's witness.[113] Plainly a theory of individual autonomy would not permit parent's to exercise their rights in such a manner. Children are people too. Yet, given that parents are still permitted to make decisions for their children, given that this does not of itself neglect the child's autonomy a close reading of Wagstaffe does not suggest that it is easy to decide when a parent should be allowed to impose their religious beliefs on their child and when they should not.[114]

In Wagstaffe, according to a medical witness who gave evidence in that case, instead of prayer the proper treatment for the child should have been leeching and small doses of antimonial wine.[115] Modern rationalist understanding might find it rather difficult to distinguish between the inefficacy of prayer and the inefficacy of the use of leeches. With regard to more recent cases, although the Jehovah's witness objection to blood transfusions, which is often cited as a reason for not allowing them custody of their children or for attaching conditions to that custody, rests upon theological propositions, they also advance rational objections to such procedures based upon the risks involved and the availability of alternative treatment.[116] Parents regularly take decisions which result in the death of their children, permitting or encouraging them to engage in life-threatening activities. At a less dramatic level, parents regularly make decisions which subsequently can be seen to have been detrimental to their child's best interests. To choose the least detrimental parent for the child, and at the same time to be seen not to be arbitrary by treating as rational parenting that which is commonly accepted as the norm for parenting, puts a heavy burden on the courts. Where the law is perceived to fail in discharging this burden the result is that, as in the 1990 Jehovah's witness leukemia case, the result is described as 'religious persecution'.[117]

The present relative scarcity of cases where religion is an issue is merely a reflection of the small place that religion holds in the lives of most British people. In the case of mainstream Christian churches in Great Britain membership is predominantly nominal. As the membership of other religions, where this is not so, rises so an increase in the number of custody cases where religion is a live issue might be expected. Thus, for example, as the number of Muslims increases so we might reasonably expect an increase in the number of cases involving Muslim parents contesting custody of their children. In such cases the parents may be divided in their religious attitudes, with one being less Westernised or traditional in their values than the other. One, for example, may want to send the children to an independent Muslim school. The other may not. Such schools have been criticised by Her Majesty's Inspectorate for Education for failing to fully develop the potential of their pupils.[118] However, such schools remain legal and sending a child to such a school fulfils a parent's legal duty to ensure the education of their child. Faced with such cases the courts will either have to follow the principles above and deny custody to the less Westernised parent or accept that a child can be brought up to follow Muslim precepts. If they make the former choice a large religious group will regularly see its more devout members lose custody battles. If they make the latter choice it will raise the question why children can be brought up as Muslims but not as Exclusive Brethren.[119]

Conclusion

To describe the law as being neutral to matters of religion when it is concerned with family life is, from the above, inaccurate or, at least unhelpful. The religion to which one adheres will influence the attitude the law takes in a series of important areas of family law both in England and Wales on the one hand and Scotland on the other.[120] In some instances the policy decision that lies behind the different treatment is clear as, for example, in the case of custody decisions or the necessity of consent for marriage. In other cases, however, the different treatment seems almost inadvertent as, for example, in the case of the formalities necessary for a civil ceremony of marriage.

It is not surprising to find that the failure of legal rules in Great Britain to take account of the intricacies of faith has been a major source of concern to believers. Thus, for example, in the Muslim Institute's, *The Muslim Manifesto*, one of the major reforms suggested by the Institute is the introduction of a system of Muslim personal law into Great Britain with Muslims being bound in matters of family law and inheritance by the *sharia*, Muslim legal rules, rather than normal British municipal law.[121] The radical nature of this suggested reform is indicative of many religious group's perception of the scope of the problem. For members of such groups, whilst much can be done by piecemeal, small-scale reforms, such measures cannot go to the heart of the matter. For some believers their religion represents

> ...a total integrated system based on sources divinely revealed [and this makes]...it extremely difficult to accept anything other than a separate system of family law, with its own autonomous judiciary.[122]

In this area of law individual autonomy and complete freedom of religion are incompatible. Some religions will demand a right to impose obligations on those whom they take to be their community. In such instances the priority of individual autonomy outlined in chapter 2 justifies religious discrimination. In other instances, however, legal rules can quite properly facilitate the wishes of individuals whose religious demands do not involve disturbing the autonomy of others. Thus, for example, a personal law system into which believers can opt if they wish to do so is entirely compatible with the demands of personal autonomy. Indeed, such a system of personal laws might be seen as the logical result of family law reforms in Great Britain over the past two decades which have increasingly sought to provide a legal structure within which individuals can create the type of relationship that suits them.[123]

The failure to take account of the needs of adherents to a variety of faiths sometimes seems to be due to an ignorance of the results of adherence. Sometimes it is based upon a weakly argued imposition of communal values which are enforced simply because they are, or are said to be, communal values. In some areas of law, whilst the legal tests involved are justifiable on ground of individual autonomy, though clearly discriminatory in their effect, their application seems to be based upon superficial evidence and thus discriminatory and unjustifiable.

What matters with respect to legal rules relating to the family and marriage, as in other areas of law, is that the rules should be founded on principles which are rational and articulated and that they should be applied in the same manner. Faced with criticism from those with a strong religious faith, the concern is that these basic conditions have not been met by either the English or the Scottish legal systems.

Notes

1. R. Fletcher, *The Family and Marriage in Britain* Penguin Books, (3rd ed., 1973) pp. 117–122.
2. The quotation is from Genesis 1:28. The books of what Christians call the Old Testament are sacred in Christian, Islamic and Jewish traditions.
3. Abdur Rahman I Doi, *Shariah: The Islamic Law* Ta Ha Publishers, 1984, p. 118.
4. W. Menski, 'Legal pluralism in the Hindu Marriage' in R. Burghart (ed.), *Hinduism in Great Britain* Tavistock Publications, 1987, p. 185.
5. [1931] 1 KB 317, CA. See particularly Scrutton LJ at p. 336.
6. See, for example, *A* v. *J* [1989] 1 FLR 110, FD.
7. Other types of marriage do occur. One example would be marriages between homosexuals. In his biography of Oscar Wilde, Richard Ellman records one such instance of a ceremony which appears to have been both secular and, of necessity, without legal formality. (R. Ellman, *Oscar Wilde* Hamilton, 1987, p. 369.)

8. *Law Commission Report on Solemnisation of Marriage* Law Commission No. 65 (1973) para. 78.
9. Marriage Act 1949 s 44.
10. Marriage Act 1949 ss 41.
11. *R. v. Bham* [1966] 1 QB 159, CA.
12. The vows required are to be found in SI 1986/1442. The legal requirement for the civil ceremony is much less extensive than the form of words which is customarily used in registry offices. This latter form of words, which often contains, *inter alia*, the Hyde formula describing marriage as being between one man and one woman for life (*Hyde* v. *Hyde* (1866) LR 1 P & D 130), has, in so far as it goes further than the necessary vows, no legal authority.
13. The great majority of Hindu immigration into Great Britain culminated in an exodus from East Africa following the Africanisation policies of Kenya and Tanzania. (D. Bowen, *The Sathya Sai Baba Community in Bradford* Community Religions Project, University of Leeds, 1988, pp. 15–17.) A typical example of Hindu immigration into particular cities is that of Leeds. Hindus first arrived in Leeds in the 1940s but a trust to collect funds for the purchase of a temple was not set up until 1968 and the actual temple was only opened in 1970. (K. Knott, *Hinduisim in Leeds* Community Religions Project, University of Leeds, 1986, pp. 37, 53 and 62.)
14. Knott, *op. cit.*, p. 10.
15. Menski, *op. cit.*, p. 189.
16. Marriage Act 1949 s 41(1).
17. W. Cole and P. Sambhi, *The Sikhs* Routledge and Kegan Paul, 1978, p. 143.
18. See, for example, S. Barton, *The Bengali Muslims of Bradford* Community Religions Project, University of Leeds, 1986, p. 178. Badawi notes that '[t]he Mosque is not just a place of worship but is an educational and cultural centre for the whole community'. (Z. Badawi, *Islam in Britain*, Ta Ha, 1981 p. 24.)
19. In 1986, the last year for which figures are available, 52 mosques and 86 gurdwaras were registered as places for the solemnisation of marriage. (*Marriage and Divorce Statistics Office of Population and Census Surveys*, 1986, Table 3.11b.) Either these buildings are atypical examples of their kind or they are illegally so registered.
20. Marriage Acts Amendments Act (1958) s 1(2).
21. *Hansard*, HC, Vol 581, col 1577, February 7, 1958.
22. *Law Commission Report on the Solemnisation of Marriage* Law Commission No. 65 (1973) para. 79.
23. Law Commission No. 65, *op. cit.*, para. 73.
24. *Registration: Proposals for Change* Cm 939 (1990) para. 3.33.
25. Standing Committee C, 13 June 1990; *Hansard*, HL, Vol 521, col 75, July 9, 1990.
26. [1946] AC 420, HL per Lord Evershed at p. 435.
27. *per* Lord Pearce at p. 440.
28. [1983] 1 WLR 314, CA per Oliver LJ at p. 319.
29. *R. v. Registrar General ex parte Segerdal and another* [1970] 2 QB 697.
30. D. Pearl, 'Immigrant Marriages: Some Legal Problems' (1972/73) 2 *New Community* 67 at p. 67.
31. *per* Parcq J in *Cole* v. *Police Constable 443A* [1937] 1 KB 316, KBD p. 331.
32. Canon B9, paras 1,2.
33. Even here there is the exception of Roman Catholic chapels. See n. 18 above.
34. Under, respectively, Marriage Act 1949 Part II, s 47 and s 26(1)(d).
35. P. Bromley and N. Lowe, *Bromley's Family Law* Butterworths (7th ed., 1987) p. 36.
36. Though something the Law Commission continued to regard as important in its report on the solemnisation of marriage. See Law Commission No. 65 *op. cit.*, para. 73.

37. See, for example, Menski, *op. cit.*, p. 194.
38. Whether the reason for this discrimination is intended to be on grounds of religious, racialist, nationalistic bias or whatever is not, here, to the point. It is sufficient to note that such discrimination is, *inter alia*, discrimination on grounds of religion.
39. s 6(5).
40. s 8(1). See further, J. Thompson, *Family Law in Scotland* Butterworths (2nd ed., 1991) pp. 10–12.
41. ss 11, 12. Matrimonial Causes Act 1973.
42. s 11(d) MCA 1973.
43. s 11(a)(ii) MCA 1973.
44. s 12(c) MCA 1973.
45. *Private International Law: Polygamous Marriages: Capacity to Contract a Polygamous Marriage and Related Issues* Law Commission No. 42 and Scottish Law Commission No. 96 (1971).
46. S. Cretney and J. Masson, *Principles of Family Law* Sweet and Maxwell, (5th ed., 1990).
47. P. Bromley and N. Lowe, *op. cit.*
48. Polygamy was also permitted in some situations by the Hindu sages. However, the Indian Parliament abolished Hindu polygamous marriages in India when it passed the Hindu Marriage Act 1955 (see D. Srivastava, 'Personal Laws and Religious Freedom' (1976) 18 *Journal of the Indian Law Institute* 551 at pp. 573–574). In theory Hindus might want to marry polygamously in Great Britain but the prevailing social mores and legal rules in India make this less likely in practice.
49. D. Pearl, *Family Law and the Immigrant Communities* Family Law Publications, 1986, p. 39.
50. D. Pearl, *A Textbook on Muslim Personal Law* Croom Helm (2nd ed., 1987) p. 78.
51. *Polygamous Marriages: Capacity to Contract a Polygamous Marriage and the Concept of the Potentially Polygamous Marriage* Law Commission Working Paper No. 83 and Scottish Law Commission Working Paper No. 56 para. 5.5, para. 6.4. The argument seems curious since the question at issue in the Working Paper was whether domicilaries should legally be permitted to contract polygamous marriages and the existence of individuals within Great Britain who thought such marriages proper was a plain matter of fact.
52. S. Poulter (1986) *op. cit.*, p. 58. Poulter's book contains one of the few discussions of the policy implications behind the non-recognition of polygamous marriages.
53. S. Poulter, '*Hyde* v. *Hyde* – A Reappraisal' (1976) 25 *International and Comparative Law Quarterly* 475 at p. 507.
54. s 11(a)(ii) MCA 1973.
55. Abdur Rahman I Doi *op. cit.*, p. 123. Pearl (1987) *op. cit.*, pp. 42–43.
56. Srivastava, *op. cit.*, p. 75.
57. *Re Park deceased* [1954] P 89, P at p. 99.
58. *per* Sir J. Hannen (President) in *Durham* v. *Durham* (1895) 10 PD 80 at p. 82.
59. s 12(c) MCA 1973.
60. s 16 MCA 1973.
61. See, for example, Poulter, *op. cit.*, p. 30.
62. [1971] P 226.
63. *per* Karminski LJ at p. 231H.
64. In *Singh* Megaw LJ, in the course of argument before the court, asked (at p. 228B) whether a finding of duress in the instant case would mean that all 'arranged or Sikh marriages' were *a priori* void. He received an incorrect affirmative answer. The term 'arranged marriages' does not refer to a discrete social category so *Singh* would have determined the law only in respect of, at most, Sikh marriages.

Nevertheless this answer may well have been important in his later judgement. In his judgement (at p. 232E) he noted that other cases were waiting for the judgement in *Singh* to be handed down. In the later case of *Singh* v. *Kaur* ((1981) 11 Fam Law 152, CA) Ormrod LJ argued (at p. 152) that it was necessary to have 'a rigorous standard of proof' with respect to the test for duress because of the incidence of arranged marriages within 'Asiatic' and 'European' communities.

65. (1984) 4 FLR 232, CA.

66. See *contra* Cretney and Masson, *op. cit.*, pp. 58–60. The court in *Hirani* could have argued that the original test in *Singh* was no longer binding on the court since in *Singh* lack of consent led to a marriage being void whereas by *Hirani* lack of consent led to a marriage being voidable. The court, however, did not do this completely failing to mention any of the previous authorities. It is therefore possible to argue that the decision in *Hirani* was made *per incuriam*. See further, A. Bradney, 'Arranged Marriages and Duress' [1984] *Journal of Social Welfare Law* 278, [1985] *Journal of Social Welfare Law* 2.

67. Pearl (1987) *op. cit.*, p. 43.

68. *per* Baron Parke in *Sherwood* v. *Ray* (1837) 1 Moore 353 at p. 396. See further, J. Jackson, *The Formation and Annulment of Marriage* Butterworths (2nd ed., 1969) pp. 100–102.

69. This does create the conceptual problem that if an individual's consent to marriage is deemed necessary its absence should logically mean that the marriage is void, i.e. that no legal relationship between the parties has been created at all. This was the case in English law prior to the Nullity of Marriage Act 1971.

70. *Shelley* v. *Westbrooke* (1817) Jac 266, *Re Besant* (1879) 11 Ch D 508. For a history of Shelley's case see L. Schutz Boas, *Harriet Shelley* Oxford University Press, 1962, chp 8. For a history of Besant's case see A. Nethercot, *The First Five Lives of Annie Besant* Rupert Hart-Davis, chp 8 and A. Taylor *Annie Besant* Oxford University Press, 1992, chp 12. During the nineteenth century atheism had the same place in British society as that now occupied by some new religions. Even the '"mad, bad" Lord Byron objected to his daughter being brought up by the Shelleys because he did not wish her to be taught to believe that there is no Deity' (quoted in E. Barnard, *Shelley's Religion* Russell and Russell, 1964, p. 17). As late as 1974 Samuels was arguing that the 'devout parent should be preferred to the indifferent or casual parent' and that 'Christianity is to be preferred to atheism' when determining custody disputes between parents. (A. Samuels, 'Custody and Access: Law, Principles and Practice' (1974) 4 *Family Law* 141 at p. 143). In Scottish law, which adopts the same basic test for determining custody disputes but applies it somewhat differently, an even greater attention is paid to the religious attitudes of parents. In Scottish law it is still said that, 'it may be difficult for an atheistical spouse to obtain custody if the other spouse is prepared to provide a religious upbringing'. (Thompson, *op. cit.*, p. 188.)

71. *per* Sir G. Mellish LJ in *Andrews* v. *Salt* (1873) 8 Ch App 622 at p. 638. In this case the right was expressed as a father's right. Since the Guardianship Act 1973, in the case of legitimate children, the right has been one held equally by mother and father. This right, as with all parental rights, is subject to the principle that a 'parental right yields to the child's right to make his own decision when he reaches a sufficient understanding' (*per* Lord Scarman in *Gillick* v. *West Norfolk and Wisbech Area Health Authority* [1986] AC 112, HL at p. 186).

72. s 7 Adoption Act 1976. Under the previous provision, s 4(3) Adoption Act 1958, a parent giving up their child for adoption could make a condition regarding the religious upbringing of their child. For other similar provisions see Boarding-Out Regulations 1955 regulation 19 and s 2(3) Child Care Act 1980.

73. More rarely the disputes will involve parties other than parents.

74. Bromley and Lowe, *op. cit.*, at p. 330. A similar view is to be found in the other main family law text, Cretney and Masson, *op. cit.*, at p. 533. See also Poulter (1986) *op. cit.*, at pp. 135–136.

75. [1931] 1 KB 317, KBD, at p. 336.

76. (1981) 2 FLR 239, CA, at p. 245.

77. See, for example, Ormrod LJ in *Re C* ([1978] Fam 105, CA, at p. 119).

78. (1973) 3 Fam Law 106, CA.

79. The court also referred to the mother's difficult financial situation and the fact that she had no family in England.

80. (1977) 7 Fam Law 207, CA.

81. *Re Besant* (1879) 11 Ch D 508 at p. 513. In upholding this judgement in the Court of Appeal, James LJ also referred to work that Annie Besant had published on physiology, medical science and economics, including in particular a book on birth control, as being matters which were likely to exclude Besant from society as a whole (see p. 520).

82. *Custody after Divorce* Oxford Centre for Socio-Legal Studies, 1977, p. 74.

83. For most reported cases regarding religion and custody disputes this rule is to be found in s 1 Guardianship of Minors Act 1971. This re-enacts the same formula found in the Guardianship of Minors Act 1925 which is in turn a codification of the previous common law rule. In *Poutney* v. *Morris*, Dunn LJ said that, 'there is only one rule; that rule is that in consideration of the future of the child the interests and welfare of the child are the first and paramount consideration. But within that rule, the circumstances of each individual case are so infinitely varied that it is unwise to rely upon any rule of thumb...' ([1984] FLR 381, CA, p. 384) The Children Act 1989 changes the statutory formula that 'first and paramount consideration be given to the welfare of the child', removing the word paramount. (s1 Children Act 1989) It also adds a checklist of matters to take into account when determining what is in the child's best interests (s 1(3) Children Act 1989). Neither change is likely to have any effect on the way in which the court takes into account religious belief in determining custody disputes.

84. Lowe and Bromley, *op. cit .*, pp. 323–325.

85. Similarly, in Scottish law aetheism has been a factor which has overridden other factors which would usually determine a custody case. Custody of a nine year old boy was awarded to an adulterous mother, at a time when such adultery would normally have debarred a parent from custody, simply because the father was an atheist and, in accordance with his principle, refused to allow his child 'the opportunity to be brought up in the generally accepted religious beliefs of the society' in which he lived (*per* Lord-Justice-Clerk Thompson in *M'Clements* v. *M'Clements* [1958] SC 286 at p. 289). Thompson continues to regard this case as likely to be a good illustration of the prevailing view in the Scottish courts. (Thompson, *op. cit.*, p. 188.)

86. *Re H* (1981) 2 FLR 253, FD. Scottish law adopts a similar approach to Jehovah's witness custody cases as that taken in English law. See *McKechnie* v. *McKechnie* (1990) SLT (Sh C) 75.

87. *Re H op. cit.*, at p. 258.

88. A. Rogerson, *Millions Now Living Will Never Die* Constable, 1969, p. 116.

89. In the same fashion, in Scottish law atheists may be allowed custody of their children if someone else will give the children religious instruction. *Mackay* v. *Mackay* (1957) SLT (Notes) 17.

90. *Re T* (1981) 2 FLR 239, CA, at p. 245.

91. *Wright* v. *Wright* (1981) 2 FLR 276, CA.

92. *per* Ormrod LJ at pp. 277–278.

93. [1991] 1 FLR 223, CA, at p. 230.

94. *C* v. *C, op. cit.*, p. 231.
95. (1981) 2 FLR 239, CA, at p. 244.
96. *Re B and G* [1985] FLR 134, FD, [1985] FLR 493, CA.
97. Scientology discourages its members from using courts, having its own dispute resolution procedures. Only when the mother ceased to be a Scientologist was she free to pursue an action for custody of her children in the courts. (see *Re B and G*, FD, *op. cit.*, p. 137.)
98. [1985] FLR 134, FD, at p. 138.
99. *op. cit.*, at p. 157.
100. *op. cit.*, at p. 159.
101. See, for example, Poulter (1986), *op. cit.*, p. 135.
102. B. Walsh, 'Religious Considerations in Custody Disputes' (1988) 18 *Family Law* 198 at p. 200.
103. *Roughley* v. *Roughley* (1973) 4 Fam Law 91, CA, at p. 92. *Re M* [1967] 3 All ER 1071, CA, at p. 1073.
104. See, for example, Stamp LJ In *T* v. *T* (1974) 4 Fam Law 190, CA, at p. 191 and Hollings J in *Re H* (1981) 2 FLR 253, FD, at p. 260. Latey J used the same term with respect to Scientology in *Re B and G* [1985] FLR 134, FD, at p. 157.
105. The court also considered documentary evidence and the testimony of Scientologists.
106. The use of such evidence also tends to 'medicalise' a religion making membership a mental health matter. See further, T. Robbins and D. Anthony, 'Deprogramming, Brainwashing and the Medicalisation of Deviant Religious Groups' (1982) 29 *Social Problems* 283.
107. R. Wallis, *The Road to Total Freedom* Heinemann Educational, 1976, p. 254.
108. J. Beckford, *The Trumpet of Prophecy* Basil Blackwell, 1975, at p. 53 and p. 178.
109. R. Homan, 'Teaching the Children of Jehovah's Witnesses' (1988) 10 *British Journal of Religious Education* 154 at p. 155.
110. *R* v. *Wagstaffe* 10 Cox Crim Cases 531.
111. See the *Independent*, 17 April 1990; *The Times*, 6 July 1990; the *Guardian*, 7 July 1990.
112. *The Times*, 14 June 1990.
113. *The Times*, 5 July 1990.
114. The notion of parental rights in English law has to be seen in the context of the gradual acquisition by the child of its own legal autonomy. *Gillick* v. *West Norfolk and Wisbech Area Health Authority, op. cit.*
115. *Wagstaffe, op. cit.*, at p. 532.
116. Rogerson, *op. cit.*, p. 187. There are, of course, risks involved in any medical treatment and, in almost every case, some possible alternative. The selection of treatment is based upon an assessment of the relative degree of risk and likely success of the treatment.
117. This was the Religious Correspondent of *The Times*, Clifford Longley's, description of the treatment of the couple who attempted to prevent their child receiving blood transfusions (*The Times*, 16 June 1990). Subsequent correspondents disagreed with his analysis of the case (*The Times*, 22 June 1990).
118. See pp. 69-70 below.
119. The latter choice was made in the unreported 1980 Court of Appeal case *Malik* v. *Malik*. (A full report of this case is on LEXIS.) In *Haleem* v. *Haleem* ((1975) 5 Fam Law 184) custody of two boys, aged one and six, was awarded to an agnostic mother rather than a Muslim father.
120. Nor are these the only areas which might be considered though they serve to establish the point.
121. K. Siddiqui (ed.), *The Muslim Manifesto* The Muslim Institute, 1990, p. 35.

122. J. Nielsen (ed.), *Islamic Family Law in the UK: Report of a seminar held at Woodbrooke College* Centre for the Study of Islam and Christian–Muslim Relations, Selly Oak Colleges, 1985, p. 3. The comment was made in relation to Muslims but it could equally well be made with respect to adherents to a number of different faiths.
123. Personal law systems raise many practical problems. When does one decide to opt into a particular system? Is that decision final? Should the personal law systems be totally unconstrained by the state? However, the former British Empire was replete with examples of such systems. India, both before and after independence, offers but one example of such a system (see, Srivastava, *op. cit.*).

4 Education

All parents in Great Britain have a legal duty to ensure that their children, between the ages of five and sixteen[1] 'receive efficient full-time education suitable to [their]...age, ability and aptitude...either by regular attendance at school, or otherwise'.[2]

In England and Wales if parents do not comply with this duty school attendance orders may be issued.[3] If an initial school attendance order is not obeyed the local education authority is required to order that the child concerned become a registered pupil at a named school.[4] Any parent who fails to comply with such orders is guilty of a criminal offence[5] and may be fined.[6] Alternatively, in the event of failure to obey school attendance orders, proceedings for an education supervision order may be instituted and, eventually, the child may be removed from the care of its parents.[7] Similarly, in Scotland, where a parent, having been asked to provide information regarding the education of their child,[8] fails to satisfy the education authority that their child is being given an efficient education, attendance orders may be issued requiring the child to attend a named school.[9] Failure by a parent to obey an attendance order is a criminal offence.[10] As in England and Wales, a child who fails to attend a school without a reasonable excuse may be taken into care by a local authority.[11]

As a corollary of the parental duty to provide for the education of their children, local education authorities are required to provide sufficient schools to enable parents in their area to discharge their duty to ensure education.[12] In England and Wales the education in these schools must comply with that specified in the National Curriculum.[13]

There is no legal requirement that the children attend a school which is funded by the state.[14] Children may attend private, independent schools. However, if a school offers full-time education, even though it receives no state funding, it is still liable to inspection by Her Majesty's Inspectorates of Education. Reports made by the Inspectorate analyse the suitability of the school premises, the competence of the staff and the efficiency of the education provided.[15] An adverse report on an independent school can lead to it being removed from the registers of independent schools.[16] Operating such a school is a criminal offence.[17]

At the same time, alongside these legal duties, adherents to different religions may find that one of the duties of their faith is to educate the children under terms laid down by that faith. Parents may be under a duty to educate their children. All the members of a religious community, whether they personally have children or not, may have a duty to ensure that there are institutions in being which will enable such education to take place.[18] The precise nature of the adherent's duty will vary from religion to religion. It may relate to matters of the content of the curriculum or the character of the teachers. Whatever its content however, education, in one form or another, will normally be central to the practice of a religion, for it is, in part, by education that a religion perpetuates itself.[19] Thus the area of education provides an opportunity to test the meaning of the terms 'religious freedom' or 'religious tolerance' within Great Britain.

The education 'Concordat'[20]

Given the nature of education in Great Britain it is not surprising to find the view that, '[e]ducation in Great Britain...prepares the individual for a society free from religion' is expressed.[21] In England and Wales religious education is part of the basic curriculum but not the core curriculum.[22] Thus, because the acquisition of skills and knowledge in the core curriculum but not the basic curriculum is tested, religious education is arguably devalued.[23] There is a shortage of religious education teachers which successive Governments have done little to try to alleviate.[24] Even in schools run by Christian churches, where admission policies give priority to children of church-going parents, such children are usually in a minority.[25] The majority of time in most schools is given over to secular education. Even in church schools most time is given over to secular study. This can be seen from, for example, the fact that Roman Catholic bishops have recently said that Roman Catholic voluntary-aided schools should, notwithstanding the pressures of the core curriculum, devote 10 per cent of their time to religious education.[26] However, whatever the effect of legislation, the intention in the minds of the majority of those who have framed British education law has not been to divorce religion from education. Rather, this has been one area of law where there has been a conscious attempt to give Christianity a dominant place in legislation.

The Education Act of 1944 was designed to be a major piece of educational reform for England and Wales. Prior to its passage, '[i]t was clear that agreement on the religious issue must precede any measure of large-scale educational reform. Half the schools in the country were still church schools...'.[27] Nevertheless, by the 1940s, it was true that, 'the Anglican contribution to the national provision had much diminished' when compared with previous decades.[28] The number of Anglican schools had diminished and pupils in such schools represented a steadily decreasing proportion of the school population taken as a whole.[29] Because of the level of financial support for those schools, many Anglican church schools were in a poor state to perform their educational function.[30] The Board of Education commented at the time that church schools failed to provide 'large numbers of children' with 'healthy and decent school conditions'.[31] Roman Catholic schools at this date were better supported by their parent church but, partially because of their success compared with Anglican schools, could not rely on ecumenical support for their continued existence.[32]

Notwithstanding the comparative financial and political weakness of the churches in 1944, the legislation of that year deliberately created a system which strengthened the place of Christianity and the churches in the educational system. The Act provided, for the first time, for compulsory religious instruction and worship in all primary and secondary schools which received direct assistance from state funds.[33] It also provided for a system of voluntary-aided schools which could be under denominational control but receive partial state funding.[34] In cases where such funding proved to be insufficient the Act also provided for a system of voluntary-controlled schools, which were entirely state funded, where denominational religious instruction would continue if parents so desired, and where a small number of teachers would be appointed on the basis of their 'fitness and competence' in giving such instruction.[35] Although, as a number of MPs noted during the passage of the Bill,[36] the 1944 Act made no reference to 'Christianity', instead referring to 'religion', there can be little doubt the Act was designed to encourage Christianity. The Government stated that both religious instruction and worship under the Act were intended to be Christian.[37] There was a preponderance of Christian church schools at the time of the passing of the 1944 Act which then became voluntary schools under the Act. More importantly, the religious instruction which was made compulsory by the Act had to be given according to an agreed syllabus drawn up by local conferences.[38] The Act laid down that membership of these conferences had to include, *inter alia*, representatives from the Church of England.[39] Agreement as to the syllabus by the committee had to be unanimous giving the Church of England a veto over the content of each syllabus.[40]

The financial support for church schools given in the 1944 Act can be attributed to government recognition that, given the contribution of church schools to the nation's education and given the school's parlous financial state, there was little alternative to state funding. The introduction of religion into the curriculum and into the school day, however, seems to have owed more to a desire to increase the spiritual content of schooling. This in turn reflected a concern about the need to promote the place of religion and religious values in post-war Britain.[41]

In Scotland a settlement between the churches and the state had been reached much earlier; and on terms even more favourable to the churches. Under the Education (Scotland) Act of 1918 the churches had been allowed to transfer their schools into the state sector.[42] The Act gave the Churches a right to scrutinise the religious convictions of prospective teachers in schools which were formerly church schools.[43] 'Most important of all, the time spent in religious instruction and observance and the methods used were to conform to use and wont".'[44] In return the schools received full state funding.

In England and Wales, despite the fact that, as the Church of England Council for Education noted, many churchmen believed that, in the 1944 Education Act, 'the State was being very generous in relieving [the Church] of financial responsibility', in fact, during the next few decades, the financial burdens of voluntary-aided schools proved too much for both the Church of

England and the Roman Catholic church.[45] Rising costs led both churches to call for a reassignment of the financial burdens of such schools.[46] The need for the State to give the Churches extra financial help was accepted by successive governments.[47] In the Education Acts of 1959, 1967 and 1975 the percentage of the costs of voluntary-aided schools met by the Government was gradually raised to a level of 85 per cent of the full costs.[48] State financial support for church schools was officially seen as a necessary concomitant of religious tolerance.[49] Education was a matter for co-operation between the churches and the state.[50]

Both the concordat in England and Wales and the settlement in Scotland created some difficulties with religious and secular groups. The arrangements involved the State making payments to some religious bodies (those that had voluntary or denominational schools) but not to others. Thus, for some citizens, their taxes were being used to support faiths they did not support or towards whom they felt outright hostility. Thus, for example, Middleton and Weitzman note a 'traditional antipathy between Nonconformists and Roman Catholics'.[51] Equally, in England and Wales, religious worship and instruction had become a compulsory part of the school's provision (though some attempt was made to mitigate any difficulties by the insistence that such worship and instruction should be 'non-denominational' in county schools).[52] Both these matters were discriminatory, favouring some groups rather than others, though, as will be seen below, the actual degree of discrimination was decreased by the way in which the law was put into effect. Even within the broad Christian church the settlement was not wholly welcomed. '[M]any in the Free Churches found it difficult to stomach the legalising of so much influence by the Established Church.'[53]

Conscience clauses

Whilst Christianity, and more precisely certain mainstream Christian churches, clearly dominated the structure of education first set up in Scotland under the 1918 Act and in England and Wales under the 1944 Act, it is important to note the various conscience clauses which were enacted in the self-same legislation that established that domination.

The Education (Scotland) Act of 1918 permitted parents to withdraw their children from any religious instruction that was given.[54] The Act also repeated the previous provisions of the Education (Scotland) Act of 1872 which prevented children being excluded from schools maintained from public funds on the grounds of their religion.[55]

The provisions for England and Wales contained in the Education Act of 1944 were more complicated. Children could be withdrawn from religious worship or instruction by their parents.[56] In county schools, if the parent wished, and if convenient arrangements could be made, the children could be sent to some other place to receive alternative religious instruction.[57] Boarders at county or voluntary schools had to be given the opportunity to attend the form of worship and religious instruction that their parents wished on either Sundays or any other such day set aside by their religion as a special day, provided that such attendance did not involve the local education authority in expense.[58] Finally, teachers were given protection from discrimination on the grounds of their religion. They were also given the right not to attend any act of religious worship or to give religious instruction.[59]

The existence of this battery of conscience clauses may be less impressive in practice than it seems. First, the clauses gave rights to parents or, in some cases, teachers. Children, who were the subjects of the enforced instruction and worship, had no such rights. This is in accordance with the general pattern of British law which does not normally treat children as independent creatures. However, if the ethical imperative is one of individual autonomy, the fact that the law conforms to a uniform pattern is of no account, if the child should be treated as a separate individual and the law fails to do that.[60] Second, in assessing the importance of the conscience clauses, it is necessary to distinguish between the formal status of the clauses and their actual operation. It is not clear to what extent parents have ever been aware of their right to withdraw their children from religious instruction or worship. In 1969, 25 years after the 1994 Act had been passed, a National Opinion Polls survey found that 64 per cent of declared non-believers were unaware that religious education was compulsory in schools; 73 per cent were unaware that an act of worship was compulsory.[61] Awareness of the compulsory nature of something seems a prerequisite to awareness of a conscience clause which allows children to be withdrawn. Nevertheless, no education authority appears to have systematically informed parents of their rights to withdraw their children from religious instruction or worship.[62] Moreover, even when parents have been aware of their rights, they have sometimes been persuaded not to exercise that right.[63] Finally, parents have sometimes felt that the exercise of the right of withdrawal would damage their child's place in the school community.[64] To the extent that any or all of these have been the case, the existence of the conscience clauses has had that much less effect on the operation of the law.[65]

The implementation of the legislation

The difference between the formal existence of a legal rule and its actual operation is of importance when examining not only the conscience clauses but also the relationship between religion and education law generally. In form, the Education Act of 1944 and, to a lesser extent, the Education (Scotland) Act of 1918 had clearly given Christianity a dominant place. Schools were some of the few communities in England and Wales where an act of worship was legally mandatory.[66] However, even that which was mandatory did not always occur.

The early years of the legislation seem to have largely reflected the intentions of the Act's progenitors.[67] The main content of agreed syllabuses was based on the Christian Bible.[68] Moreover the syllabuses adopted what the Swann Committee called 'a confessional approach' seeking to provide 'intellectual and cultic indoctrination'.[69] Even much later, when writing in 1974, a Department of Education and Science Staff Inspector for Religious Education felt able to argue that, '[u]ntil comparatively recently it would have been assumed that religious education was synonymous with teaching Christianity'.[70] However, the late 1960s saw a change in approach to the position of religion in school. It began to be argued that, '[r]eligious education is no longer [there] to foster or nurture faith in any particular religion; it is to promote a sympathetic but critical understanding of religions'.[71] Agreed syllabuses no longer placed the same emphasis on Christianity.[72] The syllabuses sought to, 'give children the opportunity to reflect about themselves and their relationships and the world in which they live'[73] rather than foster commitment to a particular religion. Similar changes occurred in the practice of holding school assemblies. Thus, for example, a 1982 survey of schools in Hampshire found that only half of all county secondary schools studied and two-thirds of county primary schools held Christian assemblies on a regular basis.[74] In O'Keefe's 1986 sample of schools only just under 11 per cent of county school pupils attended a daily assembly,[75] and 39.4 per cent of assemblies in O'Keefe's sample had no Christian content.[76] This change in the educational approach occurred without any corresponding change in the legislation. These changes, in their more extreme manifestations, plainly constituted a breach of the 1944 Act.

The Swann Committee report

The preparation of the 1985 Swann Committee report on the 'contribution of schools in preparing all pupils for life in a society which is both multi-racial and culturally diverse...' gave an opportunity to reconsider the relationship between religion and education.[77] The Committee argued that, in a pluralist, multicultural society, '[a] major task in preparing *all* pupils for life...must...be to enhance their understanding of a variety of religious beliefs and practices'.[78] In order to achieve this end the Committee felt that religious education should take a phenomenological approach, seeking to promote understanding through the empathetic experience of a variety of religions.[79] In recommending this approach the Committee saw itself as doing no more than authorising what was already the general trend in educational thinking and practice.[80] The Committee went on to suggest that if there was a phenomenological approach to religious education neither agreed syllabuses nor rights of withdrawal were necessary since there would be no devotional content to that which was taught.[81]

Although the Government generally welcomed the findings of the Swann Committee it pre-emptorily rejected those parts of the report which suggested changes in the law on religion and worship in schools, giving neither reasons nor arguments in support of this rejection.[82]

The Education Reform Act 1988

As can be seen from the above, in England and Wales the period between 1944 and 1988 was one marked by a gradual movement away from the imposition of Christianity through the educational system. The Education Reform Act 1988, in form at least, reversed this process, 'Christianising' state educational provision.[83]

The provisions in the 1988 Act relating to religious education and worship owe their origins to a series of backbench amendments to the Education

Reform Bill introduced by Baroness Cox and the then Bishop of London, Dr Graham Leonard. These amendments sought to 'secure the centrality of Christian education in religious education'.[84]

As with the previous provisions of the Education Act 1944, the measures contained in the 1988 Act are complex, varying in their content depending on the status of the school under consideration. Under the Act, in all maintained schools[85] pupils are required to take part in a collective act of worship.[86] This, however, is subject to a parent's right to withdraw a child from such an act of worship.[87] The Act allows for separate acts of worship by pupils in different age groups or school groups.[88] In the case of county schools arrangements for worship are to be made by the head teacher after consultation with the school's governing body.[89] In voluntary schools the reverse is the case.[90] In the case of county schools the act of worship has to be of 'wholly or mainly of a broadly Christian character'.[91]

It is in the fact that 'for the first time Christianity is specifically mentioned' that the 1988 Act differs most greatly from previous legislation.[92] An act of worship is of a 'broadly Christian character' if 'it reflects the broad traditions of Christian belief without being distinctive of any particular Christian denomination'.[93] Not all acts of worship must be of a broadly Christian character but most must be so.[94] Schools may vary the content and character of the act of worship they provide, taking into account the age, aptitude and background of their pupils.[95] However, in varying the act of worship, the school must still continue to comply with its duties under s 6(1) and s 6(3) of the 1988 Act.[96] The only exception to the general rule about the provision of acts of worship occurs in the case of schools where a local standing advisory council on education (SACRE) has determined, either in relation to the school as a whole or in relation to some class or description of pupils at the school, that an act of worship need not be of a wholly or mainly Christian character or should not be distinctive 'of any particular Christian or other religious denomination'.[97]

The 1988 Act makes religious education part of the required basic curriculum in all maintained schools.[98] Under s 8(3) of the Act agreed syllabuses have to reflect the 'fact' that the religious traditions of Great Britain are in main Christian though the syllabuses must also take account of the other principal religions in Great Britain.[99]

Whilst the Act provides for a form of education in which Christianity is the dominant religion, the 1988 Act also continues the practice of the 1944 Act and provides conscience clauses for those parents who do not want their children to be brought up in this way. Children must be excused from attending classes in religious education if their parents so wish.[100] Parents also have a right to send their children to receive religious education elsewhere if religious education of the type desired by the parent is not available in the school they are attending and if the child cannot reasonably be sent to a maintained school providing such education.[101] As with worship, some of the provisions regarding religious education in the curriculum vary depending on the type of school concerned. Boarding pupils in maintained schools can be withdrawn to attend worship on religious days set aside by the religious body to which they adhere if their parents so wish.[102] Parents may also have boarders given religious education of the kind the parent's desire in the school itself providing such education does not entail the local education authority in any expense.[103] The Secretary of State has also suggested that religious leaders be allowed on to school premises to lead minority worship or education. The Act does not give any parents or others rights in this respect.[104]

As with previous legislation, the formal content of the 1988 Act regarding religious education and worship and its actual impact are separate matters. The legislation is still relatively recent, some of its relevant provisions not having come into force until 1 August 1990. The interpretation and implementation of sections is a matter of uncertainty.[105]

Readings of the 1988 Act suggested by some writers would mean that schools need to make relatively few changes in their practices because of the new legislation. Thus, for example, writing about the new act of worship, Hull has argued

> All that is necessary to constitute a broadly Christian act of worship is that the broad traditions (note the plural) of Christian belief shall be reflected. We are not told that these traditions of Christian belief shall be affirmed, presented, acknowledged, proclaimed, made the basis of worship or any other of the dozens of similar expressions which might with clarity have been used. School worship is merely to reflect them. This is a distant and muted expression...[106]

Hull is not alone in his approach. The IQRA Trust's guide, *Meeting the Needs of Muslim Pupils*, states that worship, 'does not have to be uniquely Christian, and can concentrate on those aspects different faiths have in common'.[107] Other writers have produced more cautious, less liberal interpretations of the Act.[108] However, early evidence suggests that the Act may have been read in a loose way, producing results far removed from those intended by the authors of the original amendments.[109]

In their 1991 report on the curriculum, the Her Majesty's Inspectorate noted that the quality of work in religious education 'was generally unsatisfactory' and that '[m]any assemblies contained no explicit religious references'.[110] The former finding does not suggest that the centrality of religious education let alone Christianity in education has in fact been secured. The latter finding seems difficult to reconcile with the content of the legislation.

The Act lays down mechanisms for parents to test whether duties under the Act have in fact been complied with. Each local education authority is required to set up a local complaints machinery to consider, amongst other things, complaints about religious education and worship.[111] Complaints about the operation of the 1988 Act have already reached the Secretary of State.[112]

In its most recent statement on education the Government noted that upwards of two-thirds of Local Education Authorities had not reviewed their agreed syllabuses for religious education in the light of the changes introduced by the 1988 Act.[113] At the same time the Government announced that it intended to compel Local Education Authorities to engage in such reviews.[114] Whether in practice the Government will be able to enforce this policy, and whether such reviews will result in any changes to actual educational practice, remains to be seen.

Church schools

In the state maintained sector of education voluntary schools (whether aided or controlled) in England and Wales and their counterpart in Scotland, denominational schools, have long been a mechanism whereby the state could partially support religious groups who felt that the normal state educational provision was incompatible with their religious ethos. Both types of schools were created because, *inter alia*, individual religious groups were not able to provide adequate financial support for their own private schools.[115]

Church schools have always provided a different kind of education to that found in other state maintained schools.

> ...a Church school is attempting to offer something specific and special in the teaching and nurturing of the young. Within a Christian ethos, schools' governors, headteacher, staff, parents and children share a common philosophy. They work to build up and sustain a Christian community in which religious education, worship, Christian values and their source, have high priority.[116]

Not unexpectedly, church schools have offered a more overtly 'religious' education. Thus, in O'Keefe's 1986 survey of schools, in contradistinction to her findings for county schools, she found that '[i]n 69 per cent of church schools Christian nurture continues to be an important aim'.[117]

Church schools have not been unaffected by changes in educational practice or by social trends generally. The number of children in church schools who come from a Christian background has, over the years, significantly dropped in line with the general decrease in Christian observance.[118] A survey of Anglican primary schools in the London diocese, published in 1991, showed that, despite the fact that nearly all the schools surveyed gave top priority to admission to children whose parents attended Anglican churches, only 16 of the 100 schools surveyed had more than half of their pupils in this category.[119] Moreover, in the same survey, there were six schools where Muslims constituted 50 per cent or more of the school population.[120] In this kind of context, it is not surprising to find that some church schools now see their role as being one 'to teach about religion, not to indoctrinate'.[121] However, others, even those with a high percentage of pupils from a non-Christian background, still see the role of their school in the context of '[t]he vocation of the Church ...to bear witness to the truth concerning God and man'.[122] Despite doubts about the continuing viability of church schools, those who still argue for their existence see them, at least in part, as providing 'a specifically Christian form of education'.[123]

Although denominational and voluntary schools are usually thought of as serving Christian needs (and although this has normally been the case), such schools have never been limited by law to Christian groups. In 1979 there were twenty Jewish voluntary-aided schools in England and Wales.[124] In 1987 there was one Jewish denominational school in Scotland.[125] Given the religious ethos of church schools, and given that the schools are not legally limited to the Christian community, it is not surprising that other religious groups have sought to create them for their communities.

As Hull has noted

> Since Christians, mainly Roman Catholics and Anglicans, are allowed their own aided schools, and the Jewish community is similarly supported, it is inevitable that Muslims and perhaps others will seek the same advantages. These generous and tolerant provisions by the state offer security, acceptance and financial support to

religious groups concerned about the threat which pluralism presents to religious community life.[126]

Voluntary-aided status is perceived by Muslim parents as allowing their children to have access to the same level of general education as that enjoyed by the population at large whilst, at the same time, permitting the preservation of distinctive community values.[127] *Prima facie*, simple justice, treating like cases alike, seems to mean that this demand for voluntary-aided status must be met.[128] However, in practice, although there are Church of England, Jewish, Methodist and Roman Catholic church schools, other religions have consistently failed to meet the legal tests to receive state assistance.[129] The largest number of applications for voluntary-aided status from any religion not already having such a school has been from Muslims.[130] No school has been turned down on the grounds that it was a school catering for Muslims. Rather, rejection has been on procedural or technical grounds.[131] Thus, for example, the application of the Zakaria primary school for voluntary-aided status was turned down on the grounds that the school was too small.[132]

It has been argued that, such is the desire to reject Muslim applications for voluntary-aided status on technical grounds, the government has changed its policy, withholding money from existing Church of England and Roman Catholic voluntary-aided schools and so preventing their expansion, in order to produce conformity with the technical reasons that have been given to rejected Muslim applicants for voluntary-aided status.[133] Even if it is accepted that there is no intentional discrimination against Muslim schools, the continued adherence to a policy of judging new applications for voluntary-aided status in the light of spare pupil spaces in the extant maintained and voluntary-aided sector will necessarily tend to perpetuate the exclusion of Muslim schools from voluntary-aided status.[134] The Government announcement, allowing St Joseph's Catholic Primary School to expand, using government money, despite the existence of spare spaces in other local schools may indicate a reversal of this policy which, in turn, will allow Muslim and other schools to achieve voluntary-aided status.[135]

Even if Muslims or others were successful in getting voluntary-aided status for their schools they might be disappointed in the results. Although voluntary-aided schools are able to offer religious education in accordance with the trust deeds of the school, it does not follow that in voluntary-aided schools all forms of religious education are permissible.[136] Thus, for example, for children who are eight years old or more there must be at least four hours secular instruction in every day.[137] Since Islam does not distinguish between religious and secular education and Muslims 'only accept as education education that leads to Islam', this would be a severe difficulty.[138] A matter of equal difficulty is the National Curriculum, for '[f]rom the Muslim perspective...the main problem is that the curriculum is secularist and utilitarian and is based on a fragmentary view of reality'. The National Curriculum is as integral to the life of the voluntary-aided school as it is to that of a county school.[139] Indeed, the Education Reform Act 1988, taken as a whole, may be seen as making voluntary-aided status less attractive to religious groups. One commentator has argued that, in the case of Roman Catholic voluntary-aided schools the Secretary of State's increasing ability to determine educational policy, which is a feature of the 1988 Act, 'undermines the very reason for their existence'.[140] If this is so in the case of Roman Catholic schools it is likely to be still more the case in the instance of Muslim and other schools where the desired educational provision differs more radically from that which is normal in the state-maintained sector.

Granted-maintained status (created under Chapter IV Education Reform Act 1988) offers attractions and problems similar to voluntary-aided status for religious groups wishing to withdraw from the full state sector. Whilst such a school is 100 per cent state funded,[141] has special representatives on SACREs[142] and must be consulted about any changes to agreed syllabuses for religious education,[143] the powers of the governing body of a grant-maintained school are limited to conducting a school of 'the same description' as that which it was immediately before it became grant-maintained.[144] The governing body of the school can only make changes to its character after approval by the Secretary of State.[145] However, the Government has recently indicated that it intends to change the law in order to allow any Grant-maintained school to teach according to any local education authority agreed syllabus for religious education.[146]

Independent schools

As has been noted above, whilst parents are under a duty to educate their child, they are under no duty to send the child to a state-maintained school.[147] The independent, private schools have long offered an alternative for those parents who are dissatisfied with the schooling offered by the state. Schools offering education suitable for a particular religious ethos have always formed part of this independent sector.

A wide range of independent, religious schools now exists in Great Britain.[148] They serve a number of different communities. Many reflect the long-standing religious traditions of Great Britain, being for those who want education in established denominations such as those of the Anglican, Roman Catholic or Quaker persuasions. Others, however, have been set up more recently to serve religious traditions new to Great Britain. Given the religious composition of Great Britain it is not surprising to find that a significant number serve the Muslim population.[149] Schools for Orthodox Jews also exist.[150] There are also a group of schools which have been set up for fundamentalist Christians.[151] Finally there are a number of individual schools which have been set up to serve smaller religious faiths; for example, the Chaitanya College set up for the children of the supporters of the International Society for Krishna Consciousness.[152]

Many of these schools, set up to serve religious traditions which have only arrived, or achieved any prominence, in Great Britain relatively recently, have, despite their diverse religious affiliations, suffered similar problems to each other in their relationship with the state.[153]

HMI reports on such schools have tended to make adverse comments on two areas of the school's life.[154] First the HMI have criticised the curriculum offered by the schools. These criticisms have touched on both the content of the curriculum and the manner in which it has been delivered. Thus, for example, in reports on Jewish and Muslim schools the HMI have reported on the lack of music in the curriculum.[155] Similar remarks have been made about the insufficient provision of physical education.[156] Schools have been criticised for the amount of time spent on religious as opposed to secular education. In their report on the Oholei Yossef Yitchok School, the HMI recommended that the school 'should give urgent consideration to meeting the minimum requirement [for secular education] recommended for schools in the maintained sector' even though the appropriate regulations for the maintained sector, the Education (Schools and Further Education) Regulations 1981, are explicitly not binding on independent schools.[157] Equally important has been the criticism of the way in which material has been taught. Thus, for example, in a series of reports on fundamentalist Christian schools, all of which were using the Accelerated Christian Education programme, the HMI criticised the schools for offering an education that was 'exceedingly narrow in its approach to learning and [that] gives very little scope for them [the children] to exercise initiative or think problems out for themselves'.[158] HMI objections to teaching centred on any approach which, in their view, gave insufficient attention to 'the value of allowing [pupils]...more independence, the place of talking as an aid to learning and the desirability of a wide range of writing activities.'[159] Alongside comments on the curriculum, the HMI have also frequently made adverse comments on the qualifications of some of the teachers in the schools. Being new and usually small, such schools cannot offer all the professional and career advantages to be found within the state system or within some larger independent schools. Teachers employed are likely to be relatively junior. Such schools often put a high premium on teachers being 'good devotees'.[160] They may value qualifications which are important for the faith they serve, even though they are unrecognised by the state.[161] Finally, the HMI have criticised the physical facilities offered by some of the schools, commenting on poor provision of toilet facilities and the like.[162]

All of the above criticisms have posed great difficulties for religious groups seeking to set up independent schools to serve the needs of their community. Such groups are likely to be small and will find it difficult to finance physical premises which the HMI will judge adequate.[163] Moreover the conflicts on teacher qualifications, teaching style and curriculum content are often about matters central to the very *raison d'être* of the schools. The individualistic, Aristotelian approach of the HMI to education is antithetical to that of those who wish the education of their children to be primarily directed towards inculcating the child into the their religious community, and who 'place considerable emphasis on learning by example'.[164] Whilst independent, religious schools for new religious minorities continue to exist, they do so in a climate which is hostile to their aims.

Conclusion

Education, whatever its form, cannot negate the fact of a child's autonomy. However, education can assist the individual in their use of their own autonomy. As has been seen in chapter 2 once the individual makes the (by no means necessary) speculative leap which accepts others as human beings they are then committed to treating those others as themselves. [165] Just as they consider their own needs, desires and wants when acting, so they must consider (though, as with themselves, not necessarily bow to) the needs, desires and wants of others. They are thus under a duty, and others may take it as a right, to bear those others' needs in mind when making their wholly autonomous choices. An individual's decision which bears upon another must be considered in the sense of being thought out. A decision which is made without being thought out is one which is made in bad faith because it either treats the person deciding as someone who is not responsible for their act (who thus does not need to think out their decision because they are a mere automaton, a creature of another or are driftwood, driven by currents over which they have no control) or treats those who are effected by the decision as being unworthy of the decision being thought out (as being less than the decision-maker). Education assists individuals in making a decision – one which is thought out. Thus, individuals can expect, as a matter of right, that others acquire education, as they themselves are duty-bound to acquire education. However, that education must be a matter of instruction not indoctrination, seeking to enable the individual to facilitate their own ends rather than to determine what those ends are. [166] This duty to acquire education is not one which is fulfilled simply by schooling at some particular age; rather, it is a life-long habit which speaks of a way of life.

The approach to religious education which began in the 1960s, and which was developed in schools during the 1970s and 1980s, was more in accord with both the principles of freedom of religion and individual autonomy than the approach which had first been followed when the 1944 Act was implemented. By not placing so much emphasis on a particular religion (or a particular interpretation of a particular religion) education was made less discriminatory. By concentrating on teaching about religion and by centring the subject on the child as learner rather than religion as subject, the teaching did more to develop the child's awareness of its own autonomy.

The Education Reform Act 1988 has the potential to alter the nature of religious education in England and Wales. '[R]eligious education in Britain is, once again, in the melting pot.'[167] By focusing religious education on Christianity, the legislation has alarmed religious minorities who, at best, seek 'clarification' of the legislation[168] and, at worst, see the legislation as leading to the indoctrination of their children into an alien faith. [169] Such a perception in turn increases the pressure for voluntary-aided or denominational schools or for a relaxation of the official attitude towards independent schools. Moreover, the 'Christianisation' of large parts of the maintained sector has weakened the argument for opposing such schools. [170] At the same time, by insisting on an attempt to inculcate most children into one religion, Christianity, chosen simply because it represents supposed community values, the 1988 Act has diminished the state educational system's ability to encourage children's own discovery of themselves.

The Swann Committee was able to reject the case for separate schools for ethnic minorities, on the grounds that such schools would constitute 'a real manifestation of the psychological barriers and divisions which undoubtedly do exist in our society'. [171] However, this rejection was in the context of

Committee proposals which would have introduced non-denominational religious education and ended religious worship in schools.[172]

Notwithstanding the provisions for withdrawal on the part of pupils and opting-out on the part of schools in the 1988 Act, the insistence on the Christian religion in the Act underlines the case for separate schools for religious minorities. If the state sees religious values as an important part of education and the state also regards religious tolerance as an important value then, as in the past, how in equity can the state not support such separate schools? The specific history of voluntary and denominational schools further fuels the case for support for the Muslims, Orthodox Jews and others. Given that voluntary and denominational schools were first allocated state funding because their own churches could no longer sustain the financial burden of maintaining them, given the HMI's comments on the poor physical facilities on offer in the independent religious schools (this being a consequence of the financial straits of the communities they serve), given the fact that the schools are (despite the HMI's criticisms) judged to offer suitable and efficient education under the 1944 Act and, finally, given that funding voluntary and denominational schools was officially seen as being a concomitant of religious tolerance, the case for state funding of such schools seems overwhelming. Ranged against these arguments there is little except the notion that, 'by their very nature religious schools are divisive'.[173] Whilst this might be so, there does not seem to be any evidence to suggest that there is anything uniquely divisive about those schools which are now unsucessfully applying for voluntary-aided status.[174] The only possible problem with these schools is whether the education on offer in such schools is compatible with the existential demands noted above.

Differences in teaching styles in religious schools have been noted above, as has the HMI's adverse comments on those differences. Such differences can be exaggerated. Whilst some differences are due to differences in educational philosophy, others are more the result of underfunding of independent religious schools. Thus Ibrahim Hewitt, one of the strongest proponents of separate Muslim schools, has written, 'Muslims are well aware that their children must compete in the open market for university places and jobs and that a good command of English is essential'.[175] Yet the differences between religious and secular schools do persist. Secular schools, unlike some religious schools, will not see education as 'training for life and after-life'.[176] Different valuations of higher education, different attitudes towards the role of men and women, different perceptions of the relative place of the material and the spiritual worlds are some of the things that mark out religious schools. And if religious schools, whatever their attitude to the National Curriculum or whatever, were not different how could they be religious schools?

Insofar as religious schools set out to educate their pupils to be members of a particular religious community, they fail to fully acknowledge their pupil's autonomy for they treat their pupils as though they have a given essence – they assume their pupils are, or are putative, Muslims, Jews, etc. On this basis the 'education' they offer is inappropriate for the pupil's full development. But this failing is no different in kind (though it may be different in degree) to that found in the maintained sector. In the maintained sector the law requires the pupils to be treated as though they were essentially 'British' and, usually, essentially Christian. In both cases education is designed to fit a child for a mould.[177] If religious schools are treated differently then the underlying reason must be something other than their failure to recognise individual autonomy.

Notes

1. s 35 Education Act 1944, s 31 Education (Scotland) Act 1980.
2. s 36 Education Act 1944, s 30 Education (Scotland) Act 1980.
3. s 37 Education Act 1944.
4. s 37(2) Education Act 1944.
5. s 39(2) Education Act 1944.
6. s 40(1) Education Act 1944 as amended by Schedule 15 Children Act 1989.
7. ss 36 , 31(1)(a) Children Act 1989.
8. ss 36(1), 37(1) Education (Scotland) Act 1980.
9. ss 36(2), 37(2) Education (Scotland) Act 1980.
10. s 41 Education (Scotland) Act 1980.
11. s 32(2)(f) Social Work (Scotland) Act 1968.
12. s 8 Education Act 1944.
13. s 2 Education Reform Act 1988.
14. Or, indeed, a school at all; education may be 'otherwise' (s 36 Education Act 1944, s 30 Education (Scotland) Act 1980).
15. s 71(1) Education Act 1944, s 99(1) Education (Scotland) Act 1980. Independent schools, however, need not comply with the dictates of the National Curriculum. The Education (Schools) Act 1992 details the role of the Inspectorates.
16. There are separate registers for England and Wales on the one hand and Scotland on the other.
17. s 70(3) Education Act 1944, s 98(2) Education (Scotland) Act 1980.
18. Thus, for example, Raza comments that, 'the teaching of Islamic education rests with Muslim parents or the Muslim community' (M. Raza, *Islam in Britain* Volcano Press, 1991, p. 57).
19. 'All cultures depend for their vitality in large extent upon the effectiveness of their transmission from one generation to the next through the medium of education.' Poulter, *op. cit.*, p. 161.
20. I owe the use of this term to Robilliard. See Robilliard, *op. cit.*, p. 151.
21. Raza, *op. cit.*, p. 56.
22. s 2(1)(a) Education Reform Act 1988.
23. ss 3,4 Education Reform Act 1988.
24. The Durham Report concluded that eighteen years after the commencement of compulsory religious worship and instruction in schools in England and Wales there was too few qualified Religious Education teachers (*The Fourth R: The Durham Report on Religious Education* National Society and the SPCK, 1970, p. 18). The consistent undersupply of teachers has lead some to suggest that there is a deliberate underfunding of the supply of Religious Education teachers (*Times Educational Supplement*, 15 March 1991). Some governments have said that increasing the number of Religious Education teachers is one of their priorities (*Times Educational Supplement*, 16 December 1988).
25. See, for example, *Times Educational Supplement*, 5 July 1991.
26. *Times Educational Supplement*, 1 February 1991.
27. M. Cruickshank, *Church and State in English Education* Macmillan, 1963, p. 158.
28. J. Murphy, *Church, State and Schools in Britain* Routledge and Kegan Paul, 1971, p. 114.
29. Cruickshank, *op. cit.*, p. 140.

30. Murphy, *op. cit.*, p. 114.
31. *Education After the War* Board of Education, para. 128. (This report is reprinted as an appendix in N. Middleton and S. Weitzman, *A Place for Everyone: A History of State Education from the Eighteenth Century to the 1970s* Gollancz, 1976.) 541 of the 753 primary schools on the Board of Education's blacklist of condemned schools were voluntary schools (Middleton and Weitzman, *op. cit.*, p. 226).
32. Anglican schools constituted 85 per cent of the non-provided sector. Cruickshank, *op. cit.*, p. 140.
33. s 25(1)(2) Education Act 1944. Parents could withdraw their children from both instruction and/or worship if they so wished (s 24(4)).
34. s 15(2) Education Act 1944. The managers or governors of a voluntary-aided school are responsible for external repairs and for any alterations made to the school buildings. The local education authority is responsible for all other costs. The State makes a contribution towards those costs that the managers or governors are responsible for. (See n. 42 below)
35. s 27(1)(2) Education Act 1944. There was also the category of 'special agreement schools', first introduced under the Education Act of 1936. Under this local authorities were empowered to make grants for the building of denominational schools. Under the 1944 Act local authorities were once again given the power to make such grants with the control they exercised over such schools being similar to that in the case of voluntary-aided schools. Other schools, run directly by the local education authority, which were in the majority, were called 'county schools'.
36. See, for example, *Hansard*, HC, Vol 397, col 2423 and col 2427, March 10, 1944.
37. See, for example, the Earl of Selbourne's remarks in the House of Lords (*Hansard*, HL, Vol 132, col 336, June 21, 1944).
38. s 26, 29(1) Education Act 1944.
39. 5th Sched. para. 2 Education Act 1944. This provision did not apply to Wales or Monmouthshire. The local education authority was also required to appoint, having regard to the circumstances of the area, representatives of other denominations to the conference.
40. 5th Sched. para. 5 Education Act 1944. If the conference was unable to reach a unanimous view as to the content of the syllabus the Minister was required to appoint a 'body of persons' to prepare a syllabus (para. 10).
41. See, for example, the leading article in *The Times*, 17 February 1940. Taylor attributes these provisions to a fear that Christian devotion in parents and teachers could no longer be relied upon. (A.J.P. Taylor, *English History: 1914–1945* Clarendon Press, 1965, p. 568.)
42. s 18 Education Act (Scotland) 1918. Such transfers now take place under s 16(1) Education (Scotland) Act 1980.
43. s 18(3) Education (Scotland) Act 1918.
44. J. Scotland, *The History of Scottish Education: Volume 2* University of London Press, 1969, p. 45.
45. Quoted in Murphy, *op. cit.*, p. 118.
46. See, for example, the Archbishop of Canterbury's statement in *The Times*, 20 April, 1950.
47. See, for example the statement that, 'the Goverment recognise that the Churches may need some further help' (in *Secondary Education for All* Cmnd 604 1958 para. 32).
48. s 3 Education Act 1975. The same percentage applies to special agreement schools.
49. See, for example, the statement by the then Parliamentary Secretary to the Minister for Education (*Hansard*, HC, Vol 474, col 2044, May 4, 1950).
50. See, for example, *Secondary Education for All*, Cmnd 604, 1958 para. 22. This was even more the case in Scotland where there was a 'tendency to make education the handmaid of religion' (Scotland, *op. cit.*, p. 271).

51. Middleton and Weitzman, *op. cit.*, p. 249. Complaints about having to support, through the tax system, religious instruction and worship that taxpayers did not believe in continued through the years (see, for example, *Hansard*, HC, Vol 474, col 2002, May 4, 1950).

52. s 26 Education Act 1944.

53. *A Future in Partnership*, The National Society (Church of England) for Promoting Religious Knowledge, 1984, pp. 13–14.

54. s 7. The Act did not make such instruction mandatory.

55. s 7 Education (Scotland) Act 1918 incorporating s 68 Education (Scotland) Act 1872. Both these provisions are now found in s 9 Education (Scotland) Act 1980.

56. s 25(4) Education Act 1944.

57. s 26 Education Act 1944.

58. s 25(7) Education Act 1944. For the present provision in Scotland see the similar s 10 Education (Scotland) Act 1980.

59. s 30 Education Act 1944. This protection was limited in some cases. In the case of voluntary schools religion might be made a condition of employment. If a teacher in a voluntary-aided school failed to give religious instruction in accordance with the agreed syllabus that teacher could be dismissed (s 28(2) Education Act 1944).

60. See chapter 3 above. Several MPs in debate on the 1944 Act queried whether it was appropriate not to allow children the benefit of a conscience clause pointing out that once the children reached the age of fourteen and fifteen many mainstream Christian denominations expected them to make independent decisions regarding their confirmation in the faith of their birth (see *Hansard*, HC, Vol 397, cols 2420–2422, March 7, 1944). The National Head Teachers Association has recommended that pupils aged between sixteen and nineteen should have a personal right to withdraw from religious education and worship (*The Times*, 28 December 1988).

61. Quoted in *Religious Discrimination in Schools* National Secular Society/Humanist Teachers' Association, 1969, p. 5. All such evidence is, of course, open to debate. For example, the Plowden report cited evidence that 80 per cent of parents approved of the arrangements for religious education and worship contained in the 1944 Education Act (*The Plowden Report: Children and their Primary Schools* Department of Education and Science, 1967, para. 558). This might imply knowledge of the arrangements.

62. The Plowden Report recommended that parents should be told about their right to withdraw children when the children were first admitted to a school (Plowden Report, *op. cit.*, para. 577).

63. The National Secular Society and Humanist Teachers' Association argued that both parents and teachers had great difficulty in practice in exercising their rights under the 1944 Act (see *Religious Discrimination in Schools, passim*). The Plowden Report concluded that teachers did not always exercise their right of withdrawal either because of the inconvenience which such exercise would cause to the school or because the teachers feared that such exercise would cause professional disadvantage (Plowden Report, *op. cit.*, para. 564). O'Keefe, in her survey of maintained schools, noted that in her sample of church schools, '[a]lthough there was a small percentage of children who were not Christians, their parents were asked not to withdraw them from assembly' (B. O'Keefe, *Faith, Culture and the Dual System* Falmer Press, 1986, p. 77).

64. See D. Attar, 'No Easy Choice' *Times Educational Supplement*, 4 November 1988 for an account of the potential difficulties of such withdrawal. Halstead and Khan-Cheema notes that Muslim parents prefer to exercise their right of withdrawal only as a last resort because, 'to withdraw the child for whatever reason is tantamount to saying that the child is not a member of the group' (J. Halstead and A. Khan-Cheema, 'Muslims and Worship in the Maintained School' in L. Francis and A. Thatcher, *Christian Perspectives for Education* Gracewing, 1990, p. 201).

65. A study by the Institute of Christian Education concluded that the right of withdrawal was exercised in 10 per cent to 20 per cent of all schools and even then only in the case of a negligible number of children (*Religious Education in Schools* Institute of Christian Education, 1954, pp. 11–12).

66. One of the few other examples is that Christian prayers are said at the beginning of each Parliamentary day in the House of Commons and House of Lords (C. Boulton (ed.), *Erskine May's Treatise on the Law, Privileges, Proceedings and Usage of Parliament* Butterworths, (19th ed., 1976) pp. 317, 309).

67. Although the emphasis here should be on the word 'largely'. There is anecdotal evidence to suggest that the terms of the Act were sometimes not implemented at all (see, for example, W. Owen Cole, 'Holy Orders' in *Times Educational Supplement*, 16 December 1988).

68. *Religious Education in Schools, op. cit.*, p. 39.

69. *Education for All: Report of the Committee of Inquiry into the Education of Children from Ethnic Minority Groups* (Swann Committee) Cmnd 9453 (1985) p. 471.

70. W. Earl, 'The Place of Christianity in Religious Education' (1973/74) 13 *Learning For Living* 132 at p. 132.

71. J. Hull, 'Introduction: New Directions in Religious Education' in J. Hull (ed.), *New Directions in Religious Education* Falmer Press, 1982 p. xiv.

72. Hull, *loc. cit.* Poulter (1986) *op. cit.*, p. 167. The Swann Committee regarded the 1975 Birmingham agreed syllabus as being a watershed in the changing nature of syllabuses (Swann Committee *op. cit.*, chp. 8 para. 3.3 p. 485). It should, however, be noted that even these new syllabuses, including the Birmingham syllabus, were criticised in some quarters on the ground that they continued to constitute religious indoctrination (see, for example, J. Hull, *Studies in Religion and Education* Falmer Press, 1984, p. 35).

73. S. Hewitt, 'Primary Purposes', *Times Educational Supplement*, 16 December 1988.

74. P. Souper and W. Kay, *The School Assembly in Hampshire* University of Southampton, Department of Education, 1982, pp. 28–29. The survey also notes that one headmaster reported that he 'would not use the term 'act of worship' to describe any of our assemblies' (p. 6). Souper and Kay concluded that, 'the experience of assembly is less common in secondary than in primary schools which is far from the declared intention enshrined in the Act of 1944' (p. 18).

75. O'Keefe, *op. cit.*, p. 70.

76. O'Keefe, *op. cit.*, p. 72.

77. Swann Committee Report, *op. cit.*, terms of reference.

78. Swann Committee Report, *op. cit.*, p. 466 (emphasis in original).

79. Swann Committee Report, *op. cit.*, p. 474.

80. Swann Committee Report, *op. cit.*, p. 471.

81. Swann Committee Report, *op. cit.*, chp 8 p. 498. The Committee also argued that an act of worship should no longer be mandatory (p. 497).

82. *Hansard*, HC, Vol 75, col 452, March 14, 1985.

83. A. Stillman, 'Legislating for Choice' in M. Flude and M. Hammer (eds), *The Education Reform Act 1988* Falmer Press, 1990, p. 88.

84. Bishop of London, *Hansard*, HL, Vol 498, col 638, June 2, 1988.

85. Which, for the purposes of religious education are defined as (a) any county or voluntary school and (b) any grant-maintained school (s. 6(7), s 25(1) Education Reform Act 1988).

86. s 6(1) Education Reform Act 1988. The local education authorities and school governing bodies are under a duty to exercise their functions with 'a view to securing' such attendance. A head teacher is under a duty to secure such attendance (s 10(1)(a) Education Reform Act 1988).

87. s 9(2)(a) Education Reform Act 1988.

88. s 6(2) Education Reform Act 1988.

89. s 6(3)(a) Education Reform Act 1988.

90. s 6(3)(a) Education Reform Act 1988.

91. s 7(1) Education Reform Act 1988.

92. J. Hull, 'School Worship and the 1988 Education Reform Act' (1989) 11 *British Journal of Religious Education* 119 at p. 119.

93. s 7(2) Education Reform Act 1988.

94. s 7(3) Education Reform Act 1988.

95. s 7(5) Education Reform Act 1988.

96. s 7(4) Education Reform Act 1988.

97. s 7(6) Education Reform Act 1988. In such a case the Act does permit the worship to be distinctive of a particular faith.

98. s 2(1)(a) Education Reform Act 1988.

99. As with religious worship, the local education authority and the governing body of schools have a duty to exercise their functions, 'with a view to securing' the provision of religious education and a head teacher is under a duty to secure such provision (s 10(1)(b) Education Reform Act 1988).

100. s 9(3)Education Reform Act 1988.

101. s 9(4)(b) Education Reform Act 1988. The child must only be sent for such periods of time as are reasonably necessary.

102. s 9(7) Education Reform Act 1988.

103. s 9(7), s 9(8) Education Reform Act 1988.

104. Department of Education and Science Circular 3/89 para 42.

105. N. Slee, 'Conflict and Reconciliation Between Competing Models of Religious Education: Some Reflections on the British Scene' (1989) 11 *British Journal of Religious Education* 128 at p. 128.

106. J. Hull, 'School Worship and the 1988 Education Reform Act' (1989) 11 *British Journal of Religious Education* 119 at p. 120. See also J. Hull, *The Act Unpacked* University of Birmingham, School of Education, 1989, *passim* and the same writer's comment that, since the balance of the content of the agreed syllabus has to reflect, *inter alia*, the local composition of a community, it would not be inconsistent with the Act for some schools to present a syllabus based largely upon Islam (*Times Educational Supplement*, 20 September 1991).

107. *Meeting the Needs of Muslim Pupils* IQRA Trust, 1991, p. 24.

108. See, for example, E. Cox and J. Cairns, *Reforming Religious Education: The Religious Clauses of the 1988 Education Reform Act 1988* Kogan Page in association with the Institute of Education, University of London, 1989, chps 4–9 where, *inter alia*, Cox suggests that it would be 'pedantic' to make much use of the word 'reflect' in the Act (p. 47).

109. It should be noted that the intentions of the two leading progenitors of the relevant amendments, Baroness Cox and the Bishop of London, may not have been the same. Colin Alves, General Secretary of the General Synod Board of Education, of which the Bishop of London was Chairman at the time of the passage of the Education Reform Act 1988, has argued that the final amendments, introduced by the Bishop of London, had a more limited purpose than those introduced but not pressed by Baroness Cox. He has concluded,

    What the Act has achieved is the establishment of religious education (including the provision of school worship) as an essentially educational activity, an entirely appropriate part of the basic curriculum for every school, incorporating within the *one* curriculum for *all* pupils a proper explanation of *all* faiths. If it happens thereby to contribute to nurture in one particular faith, well and good, but that cannot, must not, be its prime purpose.

    C. Alves, 'Just a Matter of Words? The Religious Education Debate in the House of Lords' (1991) 13 *British Journal of Religious Education* 168 at p. 174 (emphasis in the original).

110.   Her Majesty's Inspectorate of Education, *The Implementation of the Curriculum Requirement of the ERA*, 1991, p. 6.

111.   s 23(1) Education Reform Act 1988. This provisions supplements the right of parents to make a complaint to the Secretary of State under ss 68 and 99 of the Education Act 1944. Parents may also, of course, take action for judicial review.

112.   See, for example, *Times Educational Supplement*, 29 March 1991 (a complaint about an agreed syallabus which was accepted) and *Times Educational Supplement*, 2 August 1991 (a complaint about worship which was rejected).

113.   *Choice and Diversity: A New Framework for Schools* Cm 2021, 1992, para 8. 6.

114.   *Choice and Diversity: A New Framework for Schools, loc. cit.*

115.   Middleton and Weitzman, *op. cit.*, p. 303, Scotland, *op. cit.*, pp. 44–45.

116.   R. Green, *Church of England Church Schools: A Matter of Opinion* London and Southwark Diocesan Board of Education, Schools Division, 1982, p. 4.

117.   O'Keefe, *op. cit.*, p. 99.

118.   Church schools are entitled to select children on the basis of their religious affiliation even when this conflicts with the principle of parental choice in education introduced by the Education Reform Act 1980. Section 6(6) of the 1980 Act enables the local education authority to make admission arrangements with the governors of a voluntary-aided school so as to preserve the school's 'character'. Even if this has not been done the school may still use religious criteria in its admission policy providing this is done to avoid over-crowding (*Choudhury* v. *Governors of Bishop Challenor Roman Catholic Comprehensive School*, the *Guardian*, 17 June 1992. A full report of this case is available on LEXIS.)

119.   J. Gay *et al*, *A Role for the Future* Culham Educational Foundation, 1991, p. 36.

120.   Gay, *op. cit.*, p. 33. However, in *Choudhury* v. *Governors of Bishop Challenor Roman Catholic Comprehensive School*, *op. cit.*, it was said that only 11.5 per cent of the 701,000 pupils in Roman Catholic voluntary-aided schools were non–Catholic.

121.   *Church, School, Education and Islam* Manchester Diocesan Council for Education (no date) p. 5.

122.   *Church, School, Education and Islam, loc. cit.*

123.   G. Duncan, *The Church School* National Society for the Propagation of Religious Education, 1991, p. 7. Doubts about the viability of church schools have concentrated on two areas of concern. First, some have suggested that with, for example, the decreasing number of Roman Catholic pupils and teachers in Roman Catholic voluntary-aided schools there is no longer a market for such schools (*Times Educational Supplement*, 18 October 1991). Second, it has been argued that the increasingly centralised control of the curriculum is incompatible with the independence of church schools (J. Arthur, 'Catholic Responses to the 1988 Education Reform Act: Problems of Authority and Ethos' (1991) 13 *British Journal of Religious Education* 181 at p. 188).

124.   *Statistics of Education* Department of Education and Science, 1979, Volume 1, Table 14, p. 29.

125.   *The Law in Scotland* Scottish Consumer Council, p. 78.

126.   Hull, 1984, *op. cit.*, p. 48.

127.   J. Halstead, *The Case for Muslim Voluntary-Aided Schools* Islamic Academy, 1986, pp. 15–16.

128.   S. Mason, 'Islamic Separatism?' (1986) 8 *British Journal of Religious Education* 109 at p. 112.

129.   Applications by Orthodox Jews for voluntary-aided status have failed (the *Guardian*, 15 November 1988). Similarly, an attempt by Sikhs to set up a voluntary-aided school in 1980 also foundered (Swann Committee Report *op. cit.*,

p. 500). Although there is one Sikh denominational school in Scotland (*The Law of the School* Scottish Consumer Council, p. 78) Muslims have also failed to get denominational status in Scotland (the *Guardian*, 9 July 1991).

130. *Times Educational Supplement*, 17 January 1992. It is important to remember that Islam is not a monolith. There are differences of opinion within Islam about what constitutes the best educational provision just as there would be in any large religious group. Thus, the Swann Committee noted that all representatives from the Turkish Muslim community that they met disassociated themselves from any call for 'separate' schools (Swann Committee Report *op. cit.*, p. 503 fn). A 1990 survey of Muslim Bangladeshi parents in Tower Hamlets concluded that there was, 'no overt support [amongst parents] for separate Muslim school' (see S. Tomlinson and S. Hutchinson, *Bangladeshi Parents and Education in Tower Hamlets* ACE, 1991, p. 46. Even those Muslims who support separate schools are not united in what they think those schools should teach. Murad observes that only 'paucity of resources' prevents 'a Barelvi school, a Deobandi school, or a Salafi school cropping up at the same place' (K. Murad, *Muslim Youth in the West* Islamic Foundation, 1986, p. 12).

131. *Times Educational Supplement*, 17 January 1992.

132. The *Guardian*, 22 February 1989. One Muslim school, the Ismalia school, continues to be the subject of an application for voluntary-aided status; an application which has the support of the relevant local education authority, the Brent Education Authority. An attempt by the Secretary of State to turn down the application was rejected by the courts on the grounds of procedural unfairness. (*R. v. Secretary of State for Education and Science ex parte Islam*. This case is unreported but is available on LEXIS.)

133. *Times Educational Supplement*, 1 July 1991.

134. *The Times*, 6 June 1992.

135. The *Guardian*, 22 February 1992.

136. s 28(1) Education Act 1944.

137. Education (Schools and Further Education) Regulations 1981 SI 1981/1086 Reg. 10(3).

138. Y. Zaki, 'The Teaching of Islam in Schools: A Muslim Viewpoint', (1982) 5 *British Journal of Religious Education* 33 at p. 34. See also *Guidelines and Syllabus on Islamic Education* Union of Muslim Organizations for the United Kingdom and Ireland, 1976, for a general statement on the nature of Islamic education.

139. Shaikh Abdul Mabud, 'A Muslim Response to the Education Reform Act 1988' (1992) 14 *British Journal of Religious Education* 88 at p. 91. Similar remarks could be made in respect of Orthodox Jewish or Fundamentalist Christian groups (see, for example, the HMI report on the Talmud Torah Machzikei Hadass School, Hackney, 20–24 June 1983 and the HMI report on the Life Christian School, Battersea, 28–31 January 1985 for descriptions of the educational practice of such schools).

140. Arthur, *op. cit.*, at p. 188. For similar concerns from a Jewish perspective see Cox and Cairns, *op. cit.*, p. 95. These comments take on added weight when they are read in the light of the Religious Education Council's comment that the National Curriculum Council's work is producing an increasingly secularised curriculum (*Times Educational Supplement*, 20 September 1991).

141. s 79 Education Reform Act 1988 and s 102 Education Act 1944.

142. s 11(3)(b) Education Reform Act 1988.

143. s 88(2) Education Reform Act 1988.

144. s 57(1) Education Reform Act 1988.

145. s 89 Education Reform Act 1988.

146. *Choice and Diversity: A New Framework for Schools*, *op. cit.*, para 8.8.

147. See p. 59.
148. Discussion here is of schools which have been set up to provide full-time education. There are also a much larger number of schools which have been established to provide supplementary education, meeting at weekends or in the evenings (see, for example, J. Nagra, 'Asian Supplementary Schools: a Case Study in Coventry' (1981/82) 9 *New Community* p. 431).
149. *Times Educational Supplement*, 17 January 1992.
150. *Times Educational Supplement*, 16 August 1991.
151. A list of these schools is to be found in an appendix to R. Deakin, *The New Christian Schools* Regius Press on behalf of the Christian Schools' Trust, 1989.
152. HMI Report on Chaitanya College, 24–25 May 1983, p. 2.
153. Some Muslim schools put more emphasis on the quality of education, assessed in terms of a teacher's western qualifications, than on the Islamic ethos of the school. In these schools there may be as small a percentage of Muslim teachers as might be found in a state-maintained school (P. Dooley, 'Muslim Private Schools' in G. Walford (ed.), *Private Schooling* Paul Chapman Publishing Ltd, 1991, pp. 104–106). Such schools are, however, in a minority.
154. For a more detailed account of HMI reports of independent schools for new religious minorities, see A. Bradney, 'Separate Schools, Ethnic Minorities and the Law' (1987) 13 *New Community* 412.
155. Report on Muslim Girls' High School, Bradford, 29 September–1 October 1986, p. 3; Report on Zakariya Girls' High School, Batley, 19–22 March 1984, p. 4; Report on Talmud Torah Machzikei Hadass School, Hackney, 20–24 June 1983, p. 8; Report on Oholei Yossef Yitchok School, Salford, 5–7 November 1984, p. 6.
156. Report on Beis Rochel D'Satmar School for Girls, Stamford Hill, London, 18–21 May 1987, p. 6; Report on Muslim Girls' High School, *op. cit.*, p. 6.
157. Report on Oholei Yossef Yitchok School, *op. cit.*, pp. 5–6.
158. Report on Life Christian School, Battersea, London, 28–31 January p. 27. See also, Report on Coventry Christian Academy, Coventry, 24–27 January 1983; Report on Shekinah Christian School, Tower Hamlets, London, 25–28 February 1985; Report on Faith Christian Academy, Bromswell, Suffolk, 28–31 January 1985; Report on New Court Christian School, Finsbury Park, London, 11–14 February 1985. Similar remarks have been made about schools serving other religious faiths. See, for example, Report on Darul Uloom Islamic school, Birmingham, 26–29 November 1990, p. 10.
159. Report on the Institute of Islamic Education, Dewsbury, West Yorkshire, 7–10 May 1985, p. 7.
160. See, for example, Report on Chaitanya College, *op. cit.*, p. 8.
161. See, for example, Report on Darul Uloom Islamic School, *op. cit.*, p. 8; Report on Coventry Christian Academy *op. cit.*, p. 6.
162. See, for example, Report on Talmud Torah Machzikei Hadass School, *op. cit.*, p. 2. Despite criticisms in the reports noted above, only one Notice of Complaint against a school has been issued by the Department of Education and Science. This was subsequently withdrawn after court action by the school (the *Guardian*, 11 September 1989).
163. It is, for example, not the Muslim community or the Jewish community which sets up a school of the type discussed in this section but, rather, a group within either of these communities. It is these groups which find the financing of the schools difficult. This in turn leads to the applications for voluntary-aided status discussed above.
164. Halstead and Khan-Cheema, *op. cit.*, p. 206.
165. Although they must, of course, bear in mind Shaw's dictum, '[d]o not do unto others as you would have them do unto you. Their tastes may not be the same

(G.B. Shaw, 'Maxims for Revolutionists' in G.B. Shaw, *Man and Superman* Archibald Constable, 1909, p. 227).

166. Mill, in his essay 'On Liberty', argues that the State may legitimately require its citizens to have a general education but that this education must be limited to matters of fact rather than attempts to influence opinion (J.S. Mill, 'On Liberty' in J.S. Mill, *Utilitarianism, Liberty, Representative Government* J.M. Dent and Sons, 1972, pp. 160–162). Substituting the individual for the state as the base unit the argument above takes the same form.

167. Slee, *op. cit.*, p. 128.

168. See, for example, the Hindu and Muslim responses in Cox and Cairns, *op. cit.*, at pp. 88–89 and p. 97 respectively. Here a distinction might appropriately be drawn between the response of particular associations and groups within a community and the response of the community as a whole. Thus, for example, a survey of Bangladeshi parents in Tower Hamlets showed that 90 per cent of mothers and 40 per cent of fathers questioned knew nothing at all about the Act (Tomlinson and Hutchinson, *op. cit.*, p. 28); 96 per cent of mothers and 90 per cent of fathers said that they had not heard about the Act's new arrangements for assemblies (Tomlinson and Hutchinson, *op. cit.,* p. 32). However, 42 per cent of mothers and 46 per cent of fathers thought that their children should only be taught about Islam in religious education (Tomlinson and Hutchinson, *op. cit.*, p. 31). There is, in this sense, no discrete Muslim reaction to the 1988 Act just as there is no Muslim, Christian, Jewish or other group reaction to any issue. Equally, Hiskett may be right in arguing, 'that the first-generation Muslim on the street" is somewhat more eclectic in his attitude than the rhetoric of the ulama [Muslim scholars and leaders] suggests'. (M. Hiskett *Schooling for British Muslims* The Social Affairs Unit (no date) p. 9.)

169. *Times Educational Supplement*, 12 July 1991.

170. Even without those provisions which seek to give Christianity a central part in the life of the school the 1988 Act would still be offensive to some religious communities. Thus, for example, Muslims have a range of objections to matters relating to sex education, physical education and so forth (see *Meeting the Needs of Muslim Pupils* IQRA Trust, 1991, *passim*) whilst the Exclusive Brethren have objected to the possibility of their children being taught the use of computers (the *Guardian*, 5 October 1989).

171. Swann Committee Report, *op. cit.*, at p. 510.

172. Swann Committee Report, *op. cit.*, at pp. 508–509 and pp. 518–519, respectively.

173. Lord Dormand, *Hansard*, HL, Vol 526, col 1275, March 4, 1991.

174. Moreover, the Education Reform Act 1988 has, in some senses, turned all state-maintained schools into religious schools.

175. I. Hewitt, 'The right to be on their own', *Times Educational Supplement*, 22 July 1988.

176. *White Paper on Education* The Muslim Parliament of Great Britain, 1992, p. 7.

177. 'The moulded, conditioned, disciplined, repressed child – the unfree child, whose name is Legion, lives in every corner of the world...He sits at a dull desk in a dull school; and later, he sits at a duller desk in an office or on a factory bench.' A.S. Neill, *Summerhill* Penguin Books, 1968, p. 95.

5 Blasphemy, heresy or whatever means the good

Introduction

Writing in 1949, the then Sir Alfred Denning stated that '...the offence of blasphemy is a dead letter'.[1] At that time the remark appeared uncontroversial. Denning himself instanced *Bowman* v. *Secular Society Ltd* as evidence of the English legal system's abandonment of blasphemy.[2] This seems to be a misreading of that case. The decision in *Bowman*, itself a case dealing with the legality of an charitable bequest, simply clarified the definition of what blasphemy was, holding that the matter complained of had to include an element of vilification to count as blasphemy in law, rather than rejecting the concept of blasphemy altogether.[3] Nevertheless, it is true that no successful prosecution for blasphemy had been recorded in the 27 years which preceded Denning's essay.[4] Nor was there successful prosecution after his essay until *Whitehouse* v. *Lemon* some 30 years later.[5] Two prosecutions in 57 years seems indicative of an anachronism; a hangover from past times. Because of this, five years ago to write a chapter about the law of blasphemy in a book of this kind might of smacked of a makeweight; something added to provide the book with bulk. Salman Rushdie's *The Satanic Verses* has changed all that. Now, not to write of blasphemy would be an absurdity.[6]

The crime of blasphemy

Analysis of blasphemy and its place in British society should start by clearly stating the nature of the crime. Here, however, is the first point of difficulty. The Law Commission, in their Working Paper on blasphemy, said that '...it is hardly an exaggeration to say that whether or not a publication is a blasphemous libel can only be judged *ex post facto*'.[7] To say precisely what constitutes the law of blasphemy is difficult if not impossible. Yet to commit blasphemy is to breach the criminal law laying the offender open to fine or imprisonment.

The statutory offence of blasphemy was abolished in 1967.[8] Blasphemy is now just a common law offence. Common law crimes are described and defined by reference to judicial statements. But it is this patina of authorities that the law relating to blasphemy lacks. Cases on blasphemy are few. Those that exist are often briefly (and possibly inadequately) reported in old series of reports.[9] Their precedent value is sometimes dubious. For example, the report in Gathercole's case, recently regarded by the Divisional Court as an authority for the proposition that the law of blasphemy does not extend to protect Islam and often cited in text books, is a report of a judge's summing up to a jury at York Summer Assizes.[10] In most areas of the common law the analysis is of the latest Court of Appeal or House of Lords decision. In discussion of the law of blasphemy the analysis is of decisions which would, in other areas of law, be treated as legal history. There is still only one twentieth century House of Lords decision where the criminal law of blasphemy is the matter for decision and one other twentieth century House of Lords case where the criminal law of blasphemy plays a part in the decision.[11]

In their report on the law of blasphemy the Law Commission concluded that, '[t]here is no single, comprehensive definition of the common law offence of blasphemy'.[12] Rather than being defined, the offence is more usually described by example. Any such description must be divided into two parts. First there is the question of the nature of the act, the *actus reus*, which will constitute a blasphemy. In *R. v. Ramsay and Foote*, Lord Coleridge held that, 'the mere denial of the truth of Christianity is not enough to constitute the offence of blasphemy'.[13] Instead Lord Coleridge held that,

> [a] wilful intention to pervert, insult, and mislead others, by means of licentious and contumelious abuse applied to sacred subjects, or by wilful misrepresentations or wilful sophistry, calculated to mislead the ignorant and unwary is the test of guilt.[14]

The manner in which views are expressed determines whether or not they may be said to constitute a blasphemy.[15] In *Bowman* v. *Secular Society Ltd* Lord Parker of Waddington held that for there to be blasphemy at common law, 'there must be an element of vilification, ridicule, or irreverence as would be likely to exasperate the feelings of others'.[16] In *R. v. Gott* the content of the material complained of, freethinking periodicals and pamphlets, was illustrated by quoting a passage which described Christ entering Jerusalem, 'like a circus clown on the back of two donkeys'. The Court of Appeal held that such expressions were 'offensive to anyone in sympathy with the Christian religion, whether he be a strong Christian, or a lukewarm Christian, or merely a person sympathizing with their ideals'.[17]

Both *Bowman* and *Gott* suggested that blasphemous material would be likely to occasion a breach of the peace.[18] Whether this likelihood continues to be a necessary feature of the offence is now a matter for doubt. In *Whitehouse* Lord Scarman commented that,

> [t]he true test is whether the words are calculated to outrage and insult the Christian's religious feelings: and in the modern law the phrase "a tendency to cause a breach of the peace" is really a reference to that test. The use of the phrase is no more than a minor contribution to the discussion of the subject.[19]

For Lord Scarman the phrase, 'occasion a breach of the peace', is a reminder of the kind of manner in which the material complained of should be presented rather than a separate test in itself.

Words such as 'vilification', 'scurrilous', 'abusive' are, because of their inherent vagueness, difficult to apply objectively. They become even more

difficult to apply when they have to be interpreted in the context of a Christian
sensibility. It is difficult to see that they are capable of any coherent application
when it is remembered that the decision as to whether something is
blasphemous or not is one which is made by members of a jury who,
statistically, are likely to have little personal idea of Christianity.[20]

A good example of the difficulty of operating the test for the act of
blasphemy is to the jury's decision in one of the few twentieth century cases, the
Whitehouse case. The material complained of was a poem and an illustrative
drawing. The poem, by Professor James Kirkup, used the analogy of religious
and sexual feelings which is recurrent in many different forms of art from
Bernini's sculpture of Saint Teresa to the poetry of George Herbert. In Stephen
Spender's words, the poem which was at the centre of the case, 'expresses the
transformation, within the inner life which is his [Kirkup's] individual
imagination, of those experiences which make up for him the external and
public world'.[21] It recalls in its approach other earlier work by Kirkup.[22] The
poem's title is a deliberate misquotation of a line from Alfred Lord Douglas's
earlier poem 'Two Loves' where Douglas wrote of, 'the love [homosexual love]
that dares not speak its name'. And it is in this that the poem's only slightly
unusual feature lies. The poem transforms the increasingly banal use of
heterosexual sexual imagery in relationship to religious themes into more vivid
homosexual sexual imagery. One thing the poem was intended to do, indicated
as much by its place of publication, '*Gay News*' as by its content, was to claim a
place for homosexuals in the Christian tradition. The then editor of '*Gay
News*', Denis Lemon, later commented that the poem was intended to show 'the
absolute universality of God's love'.[23] The effect of the imagery in the poem is
to quicken the reader's reaction, giving much more a sense of the same shock to
the senses that would have been found in the original reaction to Bernini's
sculpture; a reaction now coarsened and jaded by the familiarity of the
metaphor.

In Anthony Burgess's novel, *Earthly Powers*, a prosecution for blasphemy
occurs. The fictional incident appears to have owed its origins to the *Gay News*
case. In Burgess's novel, his central character says of the prosecuted book,

> [t]his book of poems is a sincere expression of an image of Christ very comforting to
> homosexuals but totally forbidden by a Christian Church hostile, sometimes
> hypocritically so, to what it regards as a wilful aberration. It is not a wilful aberration.
> It is as natural a tropism as the other.[24]

The same defence could be made of Kirkup's poem. Despite this, the jury
found the poem to contain 'vilification' and to be 'abusive' and 'scurrilous'.
Bernini, presumably, they would have acquitted. From such a jury verdict, as
the House of Lords noted, no appeal is likely to be successful.[25] In predicting
the possibility of conviction, this leaves one wondering, in any future case,
what random predjudice will determine a jury's application of those words that
describe the *actus reus* of blasphemy.

The *actus reus* of blasphemy is only one side of the crime. There is also the
question of what mental intent, what *mens rea*, is necessary. This seems
relatively clear. Following *Whitehouse* v. *Lemon* all that is necessary for a
blasphemy to have been committed is for a person to have intended to publish

that which was published. There is no need for the publisher to intend to publish a blasphemy.[26]

The Satanic Verses

In 1988 Salman Rushdie published his fourth novel, *The Satanic Verses*. Criticism was voiced almost immediately although initially little mention of this appeared in the national media. After requests from various Muslim groups to the Penguin group, the publishers of *The Satanic Verses*, to withdraw the book had not succeeded in their object, protests were made to the Government.[27] Demonstrations, both in the United Kingdom and abroad, followed. Muslim commentators condemned the book as blasphemous.[28] Perhaps most notoriously on 14 February 1989 the Ayatollah Khomeini issued a *fatwa*, an opinion, stating that Rushdie and all those involved in the publication of the book who were aware of its contents were under a sentence of death under Islamic law. The Ayatollah went on to ask Muslims everywhere to execute that sentence.[29]

The hostile Muslim reaction to *The Satanic Verses* is largely to the content of those two sections of the book set in Jahilia. Neither Mecca nor the Prophet Muhammad are named in these sections. Instead the novel tells of their counterparts Jahilia and Mahound. Jahilia is the Islamic name for Mecca prior to the Muslim era and means 'ignorance'.[30] According to the Oxford English Dictionary, Mahound has five meanings, all of them, to one degree or other, derogatory. The term is variously linked with the 'false prophet' Muhammad (imagined also as a god), with a monster, as an alternative name for the Christian devil and so forth. In all its forms the term is one of abuse.

Rushdie's use of the names 'Jahilia' and 'Mahound' provide a starting point for the Muslim critique of *The Satanic Verses*. Neither name is one used in ordinary western conversation. The average western reader of the novel would be unlikely to understand the names. Certainly they would not comprehend the connotations suggested by the words. Thus, argue Muslim critics, western readers can never fully understand the offence caused by the book because such readers constantly misread the book, being unaware of the context of the names, terms and stories used or parodied by Rushdie.[31] Moreover, such critics add, western readers understand *The Satanic Verses* in the context of the 'orientalist' depiction of Islam that permeates modern western culture.[32] Edward Said has argued that the depiction of oriental, and specifically Muslim, civilization in western culture is not a neutral one. Rather, there is a constant distortion and belittlement of this civilization which has the effect of enhancing the ostensible authority of western cultural values.[33] For the West, the Orient 'represents all that Europe considers to be evil and depraved, licentious and barbaric, ignorant and stupid, unclean and inferior, monstrous and ugly, fanatic and violent.'[34] In this context *The Satanic Verses*, insofar as it also vilifies Islam, conforms with and is acceptable to the western reader's unconscious predjudices resultant from the prevalent orientalism.

Qureshi and Khan list as the major causes of Muslim discontent with *The Satanic Verses* its insult of divine revelation, to historical personalities of Islam, to Muslim women from the household of the Prophet and to the Prophet Muhammad himself. Those passages in the novel which are taken to link material which is sexually explicit with figures from the history of Islam have caused particular offence.[35] Islam is not a discrete entity and it would be wrong to treat all Muslim critics as though they speak with a single voice. In criticising Rushdie and *The Satanic Verses* there has been, and is, division on the precise points complained of, the specific offence under Islamic law and the appropriate remedy and punishment for the offence. Nevertheless, Qureshi and Khan's list captures the substance of most Muslim complaints.[36]

The very title of the novel is illustrative of the matters which caused Muslim complaints.[37] The phrase 'the satanic verses' refers to the suggestion that when God gradually revealed the Koran to Muhammad through the medium of the angel Gabriel, because of the difficulties Muhammad had in presenting the monotheistic message of the Koran to the polytheistic people of Mecca, Satan was able to induce Muhammad to include verses in the Koran which gave a continuing intercessory status to three of the existing goddesses previously worshipped in Mecca. According to the legend, having done this, Muhammad was then rebuked by Gabriel. Muhammad then repudiated the verses.[38] For Muslims the legend raises the problem that the Koran may have been influenced and manipulated by Satan. If the legend is true might there not be verses which were suggested by Satan which Muhammad did not subsequently repudiate?

> The accusation cuts at the very root of Muslim belief that the Qur'an is the unique revelation of God preserved in the same language and diction as was revealed to the Prophet through the agency of the Angel Gabriel....[39]

Rushdie's Mahound goes through the same experiences as Muhammad does in the legend of the satanic verses. However, argue Muslim critics, Rushdie's particular offence is to use something which has been rejected in Islamic tradition and then make it a central element in what is seen as his attack on Islam. Although the satanic verses were reported by some early Muslim chroniclers, the legend is now regarded by Muslim historians 'as a spurious invention that does not form part of the authentic [Muslim] tradition'.[40]

> Ordinary readers in the West who have no knowledge about the story do not realize that Rushdie by naming his novel *The Satanic Verses* has tried to kill, as it were, two birds with one stone – firstly, to discredit the Prophet and secondly, to make Muslims question their belief in the authenticity of the Qur'an, and so undermine the very basis of Islam. It needs an ingenious but malicious mind like that of Rushdie's to conjure up a plot like this![41]

It is important to note that Muslim complaints about *The Satanic Verses* are not based upon the fact that Muslims interpret the novel as a denial of the truth of the Muslim revelation. As Rabana Kabbani writes, the objections to *The Satanic Verses* arose not because of its subject but because it was 'read by Muslims not as a serious critique but as frivolous mockery'.[42] Moreover, the objections were not based upon the fact that the book was a work of fiction. In criticising Rushdie's novel Akhtar contrasts it with Naguib Mahfouz's novel, *The Children of the Man of the Mountain*, a novel where, the successive heroes of his

[Mahfouz's] imaginary Cairo alley relive unawares the lives of Adam, Moses, Jesus and Mohammed'.[43] Whilst denouncing Rushdie's novel, Akhtar describes Mahfouz's work as 'a landmark in the history of reverent scepticism about Islamic conviction'.[44] Muslims' complaints centre on the tone and the language of The Satanic Verses.

Several attempts were made to prosecute the publishers of the The Satanic Verses. However, in R. v. Chief Metropolitan Magistrate ex parte Choudhury, the Divisional Court ruled that the criminal law of blasphemy did not extend so as to protect the Islamic religion.[45] The Government had already previously said that it did not intend to introduce legislation to extend the law of blasphemy to cover Islam.[46] An attempt to prosecute the publishers under s 4(1) Public Order Act 1986 also failed.[47]

As Muslim criticism grew so criticism from other quarters developed. Individual Christian leaders said they saw the pain caused by the book and some called for it to be withdrawn.[48] The then Prime Minister, Margaret Thatcher, and the then Foreign Secretary, Geoffrey Howe, said that they understood why Muslims were deeply offended by the book.[49] Although most literary figures supported Rushdie, some attacked him.[50] A number of critical accounts of Rushdie's stance by non-Muslims were published.[51] Despite all this the book continued in production and translations were produced. Finally, in March 1992, the book was given mass distribution when a paperback edition of The Satanic Verses was produced in the United States, copies being immediately imported into the United Kingdom.[52]

Offence and The Satanic Verses

That the publication of The Satanic Verses resulted in offence and distress to many people is not a matter which can sensibly be disputed. However, notwithstanding the criticism noted above, whether the book caused any of this offence and distress and what the proper reaction to such distress should be, are more difficult questions.

Rushdie himself has written that, '[i]t has been bewildering to learn that people, millions upon millions of people, have been willing to judge The Satanic Verses and its author, without reading it...'.[53] It is clear that many of those who have taken part in demonstrations against the novel have done so without having first read the book. '[M]any Muslim leaders have not read the whole book...'.[54]

That there has been offence is self-evident; that it is the novel itself that has caused this offence is not necessarily obvious. A valid reaction to Muslim complaints about the novel demands an understanding of the novel itself. This is necessary in order to see how far the criticism of the The Satanic Verses is accurately based upon the novel itself or how far it is founded on a chimera. This is still more the case because some of the criticism of The Satanic Verses has been based in part upon doubts about the sincerity of Rushdie's purpose in writing the novel. Akhtar describes the 'dominant intention' of the novel as being 'unprincipled abuse' and Qureshi and Khan write, 'the writer's intention was clear...instead of being critical he was being insulting'.[55] Indeed some critics seem to have thought that Rushdie's dominant motive in his choice of subject matter and literary method was a desire to enhance his royalties.[56]

The Satanic Verses is a complex novel which does not admit of an easy reading. It develops themes in form and content already found in Rushdie's earlier work. In his first novel, *Grimus*, one of Rushdie's characters observes that, 'the limitations we place upon the world are imposed by ourselves rather than the world'.[57] All of Rushdie's novels have been concerned in part with the way in which each individual constructs his or her own reality. In *Midnight's Children* he writes, '[e]ven a baby is faced with the problem of defining itself'.[58] For Rushdie's characters, at least for those who learn how to be human, life is a constant quest to allocate meaning where each person must wrestle with the fact that, '[w]hat's real and what's true aren't necessarily the same thing'.[59] Moreover, the quest is always personal. '[N]o sane human being ever trusts someone else's version more than his own.'[60]

At issue in the quest for meaning is the very nature of language itself. 'Our names contain our fates...we are also the victims of our titles.'[61] For Rushdie, '[a] poet's work....[is] [t]o name the unnameable, to point at frauds, to take sides, start arguments, shape the world and stop it from going to sleep'.[62] But the tool available to Rushdie, the English language,

> like many other bequests [to the former colonies] is tainted by history...The language, like much else in the newly independent colonies, needs to be decolonized, to be remade in other images...[63]

Language is a central determinant in the construction of both societies and the individuals who live in those societies. Who controls the language is of vital importance. 'They describe us...That's all. They have the power of description and we succumb to the picture they construct.'[64] Others have noted how Rushdie has 'successfully liberated the English language [and] invested it with an Indian accent'.[65] Of his own aim in his work Rushdie has written, 'reclaim the metaphor'.[66] Rushdie is not Jane Austen nor would want to be. His novels twist history, mix time and warp geography. Language is 'bent and kneaded' until it speaks in a voice Rushdie can regard as his own.[67]

The size of the task Rushdie sets himself is self-evident. Roger Burford Mason, in comparing Rushdie's novels to other examples of the contemporary English novel, talks of the, 'grand panorama as opposed to the little square of embroidery'.[68] With this size comes risks. In *Shame*, his third novel, Rushdie writes that, '[i]t is the true desire of every artist to impose his or her vision on the world...'.[69] This desire is a necessary accompaniment to the interpretative act that each person is involved in. In *Midnight's Children* Rushdie had already noted that, '[i]t's a dangerous business to try and impose one's view on others'.[70]

There is an obvious analogy between the creative role that Rushdie sees for each individual and the role of a god in most theocratic systems. And indeed, for Rushdie, it is more than an analogy. 'A man who sets out to make himself up is taking the Creator's role, according to one way of seeing things...'[71] Any individual act of self-creation sets itself up against all religious systems (and against all political or philosophical systems). As the scribe and poet, Salman the Persian says of the prophet, Mahound, '[i]t's his Word against mine'.[72] For Rushdie this conflict is unavoidable. Yet, despite his acceptance of the deistic equivalence of the individual's role, Rushdie remains sceptical about people's strength of vision. '[H]uman beings do not perceive things whole; we are not gods but wounded creatures, cracked lenses, capable only of fractured perceptions.'[73] 'Reality is built on our predjudices, gullibility, and ignorance, as well as knowledge and analysis.'[74]

'The element of fantasy is very strong in all of Rushdie's work.'[75] Although only two out of his five novels are set in wholly fantastical worlds all of the other three distort the 'true histories' they are based on. Thus, *Shame* is about the Pakistan of President Bhutto and General Zia. And it is not about the Pakistan of President Bhutto and General Zia. 'My story, my fictional country exists, like myself, at a slight angle to reality...My view is that I am not writing only about Pakistan.'[76] Part of the reason for Rushdie's use of fantasy lies in his concern with the subjective creation of reality. In *Midnight's Children* Rushdie writes,

> I have discovered an error in chronology. The assassination of Mahatma Ghandi occurs, in these pages, on the wrong date. But I cannot say now, what the actual sequence of events might have been; in my India, Ghandi will continue to die at the wrong time.[77]

History is personal. 'Morality, judgement, character...all starts with memory' says Rushdie and memory, 'selects, eliminates, alters, exaggerates, minimizes, glorifies, and vilifies also; but in the end it creates its own reality'.[78]

Fantasy also has other purposes for Rushdie. In *Haroun and the Sea of Stories* Haroun knows that, 'the real world was full of magic, so magical worlds could easily be real'.[79] Rushdie's consciousness is as a writer who is part of the Indian diaspora.[80] '[T]he techniques of the novel "Midnight's Children" reproduce the traditional techniques of the Indian oral narrative tradition.'[81] Shifts between the surreal and the prosaic, the mythical and the natural and the secular and the religious are all part of the weft and warp of Rushdie's narrative structure. But, though purposefully included by Rushdie, such diverse elements are also merely part of the ordinary experience of his Indian heritage. The discourse of Indian culture does not separate out these various elements in the same way that secular, rational, western culture does.

Rushdie is sometimes linked with the magical realism school of writing emanating from Latin America. Of this type of writing Gabriel García Márquez has observed, '[e]veryday life in Latin America proves that reality is full of the most extraordinary things'.[82] As with Latin America so with India. Malise Ruthven suggests that most Western readers will see an episode in *The Satanic Verses* where a prophetess leads her followers to drown in the Arabian sea as 'surrealistic fantasy'. However, as Ruthven goes on to point out, the episode in based upon an actual event at Hawkes Bay in Karachi in February 1983 when 38 people entered the sea expecting it to divide for them.[83] Whilst the surreal is an important element in Rushdie's work not all that appears fantastical to the Western reader is in fact surreal.

One final element in Rushdie's writing is important in assessing *The Satanic Verses*. In *Shame* Rushdie says, 'I, too, like all migrants, am a fantasist, I build imaginary countries and impose them on the ones that exist'.[84] That Rushdie is not simply an Indian, writing in an Indian tradition, is important to him.[85] For him, his perspective of 'cultural displacement [means that I am forced] to accept the provisional nature of all truths, all certainties'.[86] The position of the migrant seeking to create his or her own personal reality is paradoxical. 'In exile all attempts to put down roots look like treason, they are admissions of defeat'.[87] The migrant is not of his or her lost home nor his or her new world. Yet their personal world must come from somewhere. 'Nothing comes from nothing...no story comes from nowhere; new stories are born from old – it is the combination that makes them new.'[88] Migrants are forced to create a new world for themselves. In doing so they use, and in using change, the material from their old world. 'Displaced people are like that, you know. Always counterfeiting roots'.[89] But, for Rushdie, we are all 'displaced people'. Thus the migrant status becomes a metaphor for and a mirror of the modern human condition.[90]

The Satanic Verses comes naturally from the above.

> Standing at the centre of the novel is a group of characters most of whom are British Muslims, or not particularly religious persons of Muslim background, struggling with....problems of hybridization and ghettoization...*The Satanic Verses* celebrates hybridity, impurity, intermingling, the transformation that comes of new and unexpected combinations of human beings, cultures, ideas, politics, movies, songs. It rejoices in mongrelization and fears the absolutism of the Pure. *Melange*, hotchpotch, a bit if this and a bit of that is *how newness enters the world*. It is the great possibility that mass migration gives the world, and I have tried to embrace it. *The Satanic Verses* is for change-by-fusion, change-by-conjoining. It is a love-song to our mongrel selves.[91]

The Satanic Verses is about faith and doubt.[92] And, as *Shame* is about Pakistan, *The Satanic Verses* is about Islam.[93] One of the questions that Rushdie's attempts to answer in the novel is, 'if we accept that the mystic, the prophet, is sincerely undergoing some sort of transcendent experience, but we cannot believe in a supernatural world, then *what is going on?*'.[94] Another subject the book meditates upon is,

> [w]hen a great idea comes into the world, a great cause, certain questions are asked of it...What manner of cause are we? Are we uncompromising, absolute, strong, or will we show ourselves to be timeservers, who comprise, trim and yield?[95]

Rushdie's answers to these questions are framed by a sensibility that believes that, '[n]o aesthetic can be a constant, except an aesthetic based on an idea of inconstancy, metamorphosis, or, to borrow a term from politics, perpetual revolution.'[96] The resultant clash with an Islam, for which any attempt to create an alternative world is inimical, was all but inevitable.[97]

Rushdie has said, 'I cannot censor. I write whatever there is to write.'[98] His novels are an attempt to be one of those writers 'whose voices are fully and undisguisably their own, who, to borrow William Gass's image, *sign every word they write*'.[99] Thus, in dealing with the subject matter he chose, at the time when he wrote it, no book other than *The Satanic Verses* was possible for Rushdie. The historical distortions, the scatological language and the refusal to accept the traditional modes of writing are all an inevitable result of the way in which Rushdie has developed as a writer and a person. Indeed, if we accept that he writes in good faith (to take the title of another of his essays on *The Satanic Verses* and to use it in the context of the analysis in chapter 2 of this book), *The Satanic Verses* was, to a very great extent, already part of Rushdie before it was written. As it stands, each word and image is Rushdie.[100] The precise words, images and structure are, or at least were at the moment of writing, Rushdie's reaction to religion, migration and the other themes of the novel. No other words, no other arrangement of words, could have constituted that reaction.

The novel described above probably bears little relationship to book understood by the average Muslim who has protested about, and been offended by, *The Satanic Verses*. For some such a reading as that above is wholly irrelevant to consideration of the demonstrations resulting from the publication of the novel. Sardar and Wyn Davies have argued that, '[w]hether The Satanic Verses is an original work of fiction or not is secondary to the fact that it fits neatly into, indeed is the logical culmination of, the well-known tradition of Orientalism...'.[101] For them it is important to take cognisance of the reading of the novel given to it by individuals within the Muslim community.[102] The offence lies in that reading and, as the reading is occasioned by the book's existence, the offence is caused by the book. However, just as it has been argued that the average Western reader, unfamiliar with the details of Islam, misreads *The Satanic Verses* because of that lack of knowledge so it can be argued that the average Muslim reader, unfamiliar with the history of Western literature, similarly misreads the novel. The title of *The Satanic Verses* may be taken from an incident in Islamic tradition but the epigraph to the novel is taken from Daniel Defoe's *The History of the Devil*, the models for its form are William Blake's *Marriage of Heaven and Hell* and Mikhail Bulgakov's *The Master and Margarita* and its first unacknowledged quotation on its opening page is taken from Brecht.[103] Indeed the importance of the sections set in Jahilia for the novel as a whole can be over-stated. Weatherby notes that, 'most British reviewers [of the novel]...paid little attention to the Islamic aspects of the novel'.[104] Although this may in part be due to limited knowledge about Islam on the part of the reviewers it remains the case that the Jahilia sections of *The Satanic Verses* are not the book; they are merely part of the book. The book criticised by Muslim critics simply does not exist.

Sardar and Wyn Davis argue that, 'one locates Salman Rushdie's writings to understand the artistic truth he provides'. For them he is a 'brown sahib' working in a tradition which consciously devalues the Orient.[105] Similarly, Feroza Juassawalla concludes that Rushdie, 'the anti-Orientalist has turned into an Orientalist'.[106] Locating *The Satanic Verses* in the context of Rushdie's other writings suggests a somewhat different reading to that given by such critics. There is a continuity in Rushdie's work. In the debate about whether personal identity is to be found through community or in self, whilst Islam opts unequivocally for the former, *The Satanic Verses* is part of a process whereby Rushdie is coming to opt more and more for the latter; to feel that, as he concludes in his latest book on the film 'The Wizard of Oz', 'there is no longer any such place *as* home: except, of course, for the home we make, or the homes that are made for us, in Oz'.[107]

Reforming the law of blasphemy

It is difficult to conceive of an intellectually respectable argument for the continued existence of the present common law offence of blasphemy. One of Lon Fuller's eight ways to fail to make law is to draft a law which is so obscure that neither ordinary citizen nor trained lawyer can understand what the law commands or forbids.[108] The present law of blasphemy is an example of precisely such a failure. The question is not should the law of blasphemy be reformed but, rather, how should the law of blasphemy be reformed and should that reform be the drastic step of abolition?

Publication of *The Satanic Verses* has led Muslims to call for an extension of the law of blasphemy so that it protects not just the faith of the religion established in England and Wales but Islam as well.[109] In turn such suggestions have heightened concern about the limitation on free speech that any law of blasphemy necessarily constitutes.[110]

In part Muslim demands are for something which would do no more than mirror the present practice of the law of blasphemy. Blasphemy is defined at common law by the fact that it is a scurrilous or offensive comment. Muslims simply seek to extend that protection to Islam. Yet, even if the law of blasphemy were extended to encompass Islam, it seems unlikely that any jury would convict a publisher of *The Satanic Verses*. The very opacity of the text, the length and difficulty of the book, general ignorance of Islam and a prevailing orientalist attitude towards the East are all factors that would make conviction unlikely. If Islam is to be protected by the law of blasphemy from works like *The Satanic Verses* more than a reversal of Gathercole's case is required. Islam has a higher regard for honour, whether personal, communal or religious, than is common in the West.[111] The law would need to endorse Islam's own attitude to what constitutes an offensive attack in order to accomplish the end desired by Muslims. But what would justify this change?

In one of his contributions to debate on the Rushdie affair, Bikhu Parekh has written that, 'like individuals, communities can only flourish under propitious conditions. They need a sense of their own worth…'[112] For him, 'the widespread belief that British society is made up of, and only values, self-determining individuals and cannot tolerate self-conscious communities is fundamentally mistaken.'[113] In the context of an assertion that the maintenance and propagation of diverse cultural values is an important feature of British society, the real purpose of the blasphemy law can be seen as being the protection of 'cultural identity'.[114] A properly constructed blasphemy law would allow religious communities to throw barriers round their sacred sites. Communities which were protected in this way would then feel more valued and thus more open to intercourse with other communities within British society. The recompense for a general limitation on free speech would be a richer cultural life in which all could grow.

Objections to such an argument for the extension of the law of blasphemy stem from several different sources. First, there is the difficulty of identifying the religious communities which are to be protected. This difficulty is one which strikes still deeper than the problem of identifying which religions are to be protected noted by the Law Commission in their working paper on blasphemy.[115] The problems described by the Law Commission were concerned with the difficulties of defining religion and the likely scope of potential definitions: what form of words would encompass both deistic and non-deistic religions and would it be right to extend such protection to all of the new religions which have recently developed in the West? Where the protection of religious communities are concerned, to such problems as are discussed by the Law Commission, is added the fraught issue of who, once a religious community is identified, is to be seen as the legitimate bearer of the values of that community. Who determines the tenets of the community when all such communities are divided amongst themselves? Not, surely, the legislature or judiciary with scarce or no knowledge of the matters at issue? Is the decision to be made by reference to the things which are most commonly held in the community or by reference to the things most strongly held? Do zealots decide, even if they are numerically a minority, or is it matter for the silent majority, even if they are weak in their faith? Secondly, there is the difficulty of dividing up the world's store of religious icons amongst the various religious communities. For whom is the figure of Christ to be seen as valuable: Christians, with his messianic status, or Muslims, with his prophetic status? In demonstrations against Rushdie, Muslims marched with banners saying, Rushdie is Satan. Do Satanists have their share of religious icons? Thirdly, there is the problem that religious icons are also cultural goods having value even for those without religious faith. '[I]s history to be considered the property of the participants solely. In what courts are such claims stated, what boundary commissions map out the territories?'[116] Such problems are pressing and genuine. But fourthly, and much more importantly, one must ask, by what right are such claims for communities made? Is the assertion of the value of communities anything more than an assertion? Can it become an argument and if it can, can it become an argument which will justify the subjugation of the individual? To answer that one needs to look more closely at what a law of blasphemy does.

Writing after judgement had been given in the *Gay News* trial, Geoffrey Roberston stated that, '[b]lasphemy is no longer a crime of disbelief: it may be committed with the profoundest religious intentions if Christian sentiment is expressed in an eccentric or shocking manner'.[117] One can go further. The hostile reaction to Professor Kirkup's poem is analogous to the same hostile reaction to the collection of essays entitled *The Myth of God Incarnate*, published at much the same time.[118] These essays, written by Christian academics, had denied the physical reality of Christ's resurrection. Both the poem and the essays are examples of the Arian heresy. The hostility to the two works is, amongst other things, to their denial, implicit or explicit, of Jesus Christ's consubstantiality with God the Father.[119] Kirkup had written of his poem, 'I wanted to portray strong, deep emotion and intense passion (in both senses of the word), to present a human earthly and imperfect Christ symbolising my own outcast state, and that of all outcasts in our society'.[120] In punishing *Gay News* and its editor for publishing these sentiments, whatever else it was, the *Gay News* trial also became a trial for heresy.

Attempts to bring *The Satanic Verses* within the ambit of the law of blasphemy also necessarily involve a limitation of free speech. Some Muslims have distinguished between a wish to censor what Rushdie says and the way in which he says it.[121] However, the passages in this chapter above make it clear that such a distinction is incapable of sensible application. Jeremy Waldron has distinguished between one-dimensional, two-dimensional and three-dimensional freedom of speech. One-dimensional freedom involves taking care to say nothing that would criticise or cut across the religious convictions of anyone else. Two-dimensional freedom permits criticism and discussion in the area of religious faith providing that criticism is serious, earnest, respectful, circumspect and inoffensive. Three-dimensional freedom leaves people completely free

> to address the deep questions of religion and philosophy in the best way they can in the modern world, that may mean the whole kaleidoscope of literary technique – fantasy, irony, poetry, word-play, and the speculative juggling of ideas.[122]

Muslims seem ready to grant Rushdie two-dimensional freedom but not three-dimensional freedom. Kirkup, too, may live in two but not in three dimensions. But the way in which both Rushdie and Kirkup challenge traditionally received values is part of their argument. To censor the method is to censor the message.

Rushdie himself has stated that a special freedom has to be given to the novelist. Citing Carlos Fuentes in his support, he has argued the novel has 'the *right to be the stage upon which the great debates of society can be conducted.*'[123] Such a statement stands in the tradition of those who would want to argue that,

> All serious art, music and literature is a critical act. It is so, firstly, in the sense of Matthew Arnold's phrase: 'a criticism of life'. Be it realistic, fantastic, utopian or satiric, the construct of the artist is a counter-statement of the world.[124]

In this tradition the role of the artist as creator and re-creator is such as to necessitate the right to take greater liberties than are permitted to the ordinary person. Three-dimensional freedom is demanded not because the artist will not mis-use it, hurting others without cause, but because such errors and pain are an inevitable result of the artist's role.[125] Such a view, which seems to cast the artist as romantic hero, suffers from the empirical difficulty of not being able to identify who the artist is. Plainly the distinction between artist and non-artist is not determined by the technical matter of publication since this would give a Jeffrey Archer or Barbara Cartland rights of free expression not granted to a nascent author. As George Steiner suggests, the concern is with the 'serious artist' not just with any writer, musician or whatever. But what makes someone a 'serious artist'? Such a question takes on a particular edge if we accept that, as Rushdie suggests, 'even a baby is faced with the problem of defining itself'; a view which chapter 2 above supports.[126] If we are all authors of our own being, in what sense is the novelist, the poet or the artist special?

The individual makes a better subject for Waldron's three-dimensional freedom of speech than the artist or the novelist. Since we are all, by virtue of our existence, bound to take a side in the debates to which Rushdie refers, we all need the freedom he demands for the artist. Indeed, we all have that freedom, whether it is recognised or not. A law of blasphemy which encompassed *The*

Satanic Verses would no more change Rushdie's views on the subject matter of his novel than prosecution of 'The Love that Dares to Speak its Name' changed Kirkup's view of the relationship between homosexual sexual acts and the love of God for man. All such law would do is seek to silence Rushdie in public discourse so that some people could pretend that views such as his did not exist.

Suggested reforms which extend the law of blasphemy seek to use individuals in the service of supposed communities. Communities may grow in self-esteem because their view of themselves is not challenged in ways they find distasteful. But such communities are no more than aggregates of the individuals within them. A law of blasphemy thus seeks to silence one person because their speech offends another person. To speak about the importance of communities is to subtly seek to alter the rhetorical weight of the argument by opposing persons and groups. How can one person, one blasphemer, such arguments ask, be more important than the group? More pertinent would be the question, how can one person legitimately ask another to pretend, through silence, to be the person they are not? Why would they see a value in acting out such a charade? To seek to silence someone who speaks in good faith is to pretend that the speaker is something that they are not; the act of censorship is in itself to act in bad faith.

Attempts to alter the ground of the debate by suggesting that, for example, limitations on free speech should be drawn up in the light of Great Britain's international law obligations similarly fail to address the appropriate argument.[127] Human speech follows from human existence. If I exist I must speak. In creating my world I am constantly engaged in an argument addressed primarily to myself. The justification for purported constraints of positive law, whether the positive law be an international or municipal law system, have to be viewed in the light of that fact. 'Free speech is the whole thing, the whole ball game. Free speech is life itself.'[128] Literally.

Many people have commented on the need to address the question of the responsibility of the writer rather than the right of the artist to free speech.[129] Free speech, however, does not bring with it responsibility except in the sense of saying what is truly, deeply felt. In speaking there is the demand that one does not speak trivially, frivolously or without thought. Speech, like life, must be exercised in good faith: hence the importance of assessing the integrity of Rushdie's work by looking at his other writing. Such a demand is not one which goes to style. Foote, in the nineteenth century blasphemy case, was right in arguing that his 'coarse language', expressed so because, 'I have not sufficient culture or education to cull my words carefully', did not negate his right to speak.[130] Nor does the demand for good faith go to form. Monty Python's *Life of Brian* may be seen by some as a light comedy and by others as blasphemy but, at least in Anthony Burgess's eyes, it is also 'a very fair interpretation of the lot of Jews under Roman rule'.[131]

Conclusion

The Rushdie affair has illustrated the depth of predjudice against Muslims in British society. Lecturing Muslims on their duties as British citizens, as the then

Home Secretary Douglas Hurd did in the Birmingham Central Mosque, is not an appropriate response to Muslim protests which have largely been conducted in accordance with the normal political processes of the country.[132] Describing the Koran as 'food for no-thought' is not an acute analysis of a work which has generated such a wealth of literature including, not least, *The Satanic Verses*.[133] Akhtar and Webster are surely right in thinking that the general liberal response to Muslim protests about the publication of *The Satanic Verses*, emphasising the importance of free speech, has been based upon a slight reading and consideration of the philosophical texts which bear upon the issue of free speech.[134] The judicial response to the Rushdie affair has been no less suspect than that of the Government or the media. In refusing to extend the law of blasphemy to cover Islam the Divisional Court held that, 'where the law is clear it is not the proper function of this court to extend it; particularly is this so in criminal cases, where offences cannot retrospectively be created'.[135] On 11 July 1991 the House of Lords refused leave to appeal against this judgement. Ten days before this the House of Lords had heard argument in *R. v. R.*[136] Giving judgement in this latter case, the court overturned the 100-year-old precedent exempting husbands from the crime of rape with respect to their wives. When it is remembered that the marital rape exemption had been reaffirmed by the courts in a series of cases throughout the twentieth century whilst the question of which religion the law of blasphemy protected had not been the subject of litigation since the nineteenth century, it is difficult not to compare these two decisions unfavourably and to see them as part of a prevailing pattern of hostile attitudes to Islam. But to accept the existence of these errors and prejudices is not the same thing as accepting that, because of them, the Muslim case thereby becomes stronger, still less unassailable.

The Islamic case against *The Satanic Verses* has constantly been misrepresented. Many of those who have written in favour of free speech might well be horrified by the realties of the implementation of such a principle. Nevertheless, important as these matters are, such difficulties are ones which go to the history of the affair and the personalities involved. They are not germane to the philosophical arguments themselves. The logic of the argument which runs through this book dictates the conclusion that the law of blasphemy, any law of blasphemy, is an unwarranted and indefensible attempt to limit an individual's expression of themselves. 'God or whatever means the Good', wrote Louis MacNeice; creeds, heresies, blasphemies and atheistic statements all lie on the same plane.[137] The self-same argument that justifies the importance of allowing an individual to express himself or herself through religious belief justifies acknowledging that others must express themselves by denying the validity of such religious beliefs.

In the light of the lack of prosecutions for blasphemy it might, nevertheless, be thought better to let the whole matter drop. Even if the law is incoherent, both in technical and moral terms, one might argue that, since it rarely leads to prosecutions, it has no real impact. Changing the law would undoubtedly be time-consuming. Such reforms might be seen as being pointless because it would undoubtedly anger and offend some but, arguably, because of the lack of prosecutions, help nobody. This seems to have been the view of the successive governments which have neither followed the Law Commission's recommendation to abolish the law nor complied with requests from Muslims to expand the law. However, such an approach is mistaken. The effect of a criminal legal rule is to be judged not just by an assessment of the prosecutions that it generates but also by looking at what people do to avoid such prosecution.

Assessing the hidden history of what has not been said because of the law of blasphemy is because of its very nature difficult. Some things have not been published because of the law of blasphemy. Thus, for example, Dom Moraes records that George Barker's *Collected Poems* was incomplete because Barker's publishers refused to include one poem on the grounds that it was blasphemous.[138] The result of this kind of effect of the blasphemy law is not necessarily a blanket prohibition on publication. Different publishers will take different views on what constitutes blasphemy. Barker's poem which was rejected by the publishers of his *Collected Poems*, 'The True Confessions of George Barker', had already been published by one press prior to the *Collected Poems* and was subsequently republished by another.[139] The result of the blasphemy law in that case was to restrict readership rather than prevent the poem being seen at all. Suppression, however, can be total. Thorensen's film about Christ was never made.[140]

Even a refusal to prosecute for blasphemy is a reminder of the possibility of prosecution. When, after due consideration, official decisions were taken not to prosecute either Michele Robert's novel, *The Wild Girl*, an account of a fifth gospel supposedly written by Mary Magdalene, or Martin Scorsese's film treatment of the Nikos Kazantzakis novel, *The Last Temptation of Christ*, the very fact that official thought had been given to the matter, rather than dismissing requests for such prosecution out of hand, indicated that a line did divide what might be written or what might be filmed from that which was forbidden.[141] *The Wild Girl* and *The Last Temptation of Christ* might be on the right side of that line but by how far? What should a publisher risk publishing?

Further effect is given to the law of blasphemy through the British Board of Film Classification's decision to use the law of blasphemy as part of their criteria for granting or withholding classification certificates for videos. In 1989 the Board refused such a certificate to a video entitled 'Visions of Ecstasy' which dealt with the mystical experiences of St Teresa of Avila on the grounds that it was blasphemous.[142] Refusal of a classification certificate prevents the commercial distribution of a video.[143]

The law of blasphemy remains a real constraint on freedom of speech. Moreover, by protecting only the tenets of the Christian church established in England, the law promotes religious discrimination favouring one religion against all others. Abolition of the law would not meet Muslim complaints. However, such abolition would mean that, at least in respect of this law, all religions and all individuals would be treated equally.

Notes

1. A. Denning, *Freedom Under Law* Stevens, 1949 p. 46.
2. *Bowman v. Secular Society Ltd* [1917] AC 406, HL.
3. See, for example, Lord Parker of Waddington in *Bowman v. Secular Society Ltd op. cit.*, p. 446.

4. The last successful prosecution had been in *R.* v. *Gott* (1922) 16 Cr App R 87.
5. *Whitehouse* v. *Lemon* [1979] 2 WLR 281, HL.
6. Blasphemy is an offence known to English law. The last reported prosecution for blasphemy in Scotland was in 1843 (*Henry* v. *Robinson* (1843 1 Brown 643). Some writers have argued that blasphemy may no longer be a crime in Scotland (see, for example, G. Gordon, *The Criminal Law of Scotland* W. Green (2nd ed., 1978) p. 998.) In any event, since Scottish law, unlike English law, requires a personal interest in a matter before there can be any private prosecution, and since the state is unlikely to want to prosecute for blasphemy, a prosecution, even if technically possible, is unlikely to occur (G. Maher 'Blasphemy in Scots Law' (1977) *Scots Law Times 257* at p. 260.)
7. *Offences Against Religion and Public Worship* Law Commission Working Paper No. 79 (1981) para. 6.1.
8. The Blasphemy Act 1697 was repealed by s 13, Schedule 4 Part 1 Criminal Law Act 1967.
9. Thus, for example, Kenny in his article on blasphemy notes that the case that he regards as the fount of the common law doctrine of blasphemy, *Taylor's Case*, is twice reported in the English Reports and that there is a significant, if small, variation in the reports (C. Kenny, 'The Evolution of the Law of Blasphemy' (1922) 1 *Cambridge Law Journal* 127 at pp. 129–130.) Neither of the two reports, *R.* v. *Taylor,* 1 Ventris 293 and 3 Keble 607, extends for more than 18 lines.
10. *R.* v. *Gathercole* (1838) 2 Lewin 237. The case was used by Watkins LJ in his judgement in *R.* v. *Chief Metropolitan Magistrate ex parte Choudhury* [1991] 1 All ER 306 at p. 313. The case is extracted in P. O'Higgins, *Cases and Materials on Civil Liberties* Sweet and Maxwell, 1980, pp. 65–66.
11. *Whitehouse* v. *Lemon op. cit.*, and *Bowman* v. *Secular Society Ltd op. cit.*
12. *Offences Against Religion and Public Worship* Law Commission No. 145 (1985) para. 2.1.
13. *R.* v. *Ramsay and Foote* (1883) 15 Cox CC 231 at p. 236.
14. *R.* v. *Ramsay and Foote loc. cit.*, The test, cited by Lord Coleridge, is taken from the 4th edition of *Starkie's Slander and Libel.*
15. *per* Viscount Dilhorne in *Whitehouse* v. *Lemon op. cit.*, at p. 295.
16. *Bowman* v. *Secular Society Ltd op. cit.*, at p. 446.
17. *R.* v. *Gott* (1922) 16 Cr App R 87 at pp. 89–90.
18. *R.* v. *Gott op. cit.*, p. 90, *Bowman* v. *Secular Society Ltd op. cit.*, at p. 446.
19. *Whitehouse* v *Lemon op. cit.*, at p. 312.
20. Expert evidence on theological matters cannot be used in blasphemy trials. (G. Robertson, *Obscenity* Weidenfeld and Nicholson, 1979, p. 240.) Alan King-Hamilton, the judge at first instance in *Whitehouse* v. *Lemon op. cit.*, subsequently explained his refusal to allow expert witnesses to be called with the comment that, 'conflicting theological opinions...would only serve to confuse the jury in what was, after all, a simple issue which twelve ordinary people ought to decide among themselves'. (A. King-Hamilton, *And Nothing But the Truth* Weidenfeld and Nicholson, 1982, p. 176.) If expert witnesses are in conflict the issue is presumably not as simple as King-Hamilton imagines.
21. *The Times*, 22 July 1977.
22. See his volume of early autobiography J. Kirkup, *I, of all People* Weidenfeld and Nicholson, 1988, at pp. 203, 207 and 212.
23. *Gay Times*, July 1992.
24. A. Burgess, *Earthly Powers* Hutchinson, 1980, p. 526.
25. *per* Viscount Dilhorne in *Whitehouse* v. *Lemon op. cit.*, at p. 291.
26. *per* Viscount Dilhorne, Lord Russell and Lord Scarman in *Whitehouse* v. *Lemon op. cit.* Given the difficulty that even a lawyer has in determining what is and what is

not a blasphemy the absence of specific intent is fortunate for the potential operative effect of the law.

27.   The main sequence of events is detailed in M. Ahsan and A. Kidwai (eds), *Sacrilege versus Civility* The Islamic Foundation, 1991, pp. 11–24. Several journalistic accounts of the affair have already been published. (See D. Pipes, *The Rushdie Affair* Carol Publishing Group, 1990; M. Ruthven, *A Satanic Affair* Chatto and Windus, 1990; and W. Weatherby, *Salman Rushdie: Sentenced to Death* Carrol and Graf, 1990.)

28.   See, for example, S. Akhtar, *Be Careful with Muhammad!* Bellew Publishing, 1989, pp. 70–79.

29.   The *Guardian*, 15 February 1989.

30.   Akhtar *op. cit.*, p. 14, Ahsan and Kidwai *op. cit.*, p. 149.

31.   See, for example, Sahib Mustaqim Blether and Ibrahim Hewitt, 'One man's blasphemy...', *Times Educational Supplement*, 24 February 1989 and S. Qureshi and J. Khan *The Politics of the Satanic Verses* Muslim Community Studies Institute, 1989, p. 2.

32.   See, for example, Z. Sardar and M. Wyn Davies *Distorted Imaginations* Grey Seal, 1990, *passim*.

33.   Said defines the term orientalism as 'a Western style for dominating, restructuring, and having authority over the orient'. (E. Said *Orientalism* Penguin Books, 1978, p. 3.)

34.   Sardar and Wyn Davis, *op. cit.*, p. 34.

35.   Qureshi and Khan, *op. cit.*, pp. 1–2. Samad has argued that the book has caused particular offence in Great Britain because of the dominance of the Brevli sect amongst Muslims in Britain; they being a sect who place great spiritual siginficance on the personality of Muhammad. (Y. Samad, 'Book burning and race relations: Political mobilisation of Bradford Muslims' (1992) 18 *New Community* 507 at pp. 507–508.)

36.   The best collection of such complaints is to be found in *Sacrilege versus Civility op. cit.* For an example of the division amongst those Muslims otherwise united in their distaste for Rushdie see Qureshi and Khan's description of one of the other Muslim critics of Rushdie, Ahmed Deedat, as 'a senile preacher' (Qureshi and Khan, *op. cit.*, p. 44).

37.   See Sardar and Wyn Davis, *op. cit.*, pp. 146–153 and M. Ahsan, 'The "Satanic" verses and the Orientalists' in Ahsan and Kidwai, *op. cit.*, p. 131.

38.   A. Guillaume, *Islam* Penguin Books (2nd ed., 1956) pp. 35–37.

39.   Ahsan and Kidwai, *op. cit.*, p. 28.

40.   Sardwar and Wyn Davis, *op. cit.*, p. 148.

41.   Ahsan and Kidwai, *op. cit.*, p. 29.

42.   R. Kabbani, *Letter to Christendom* Virago Press, 1989, p. 66.

43.   P. Stewart, 'Translator's Introduction' in N. Mahfouz *The Children of Gebelawi* Heinemann Educational Books, 1981, p. vii. However, in his home country, Egypt, Mahfouz himself has been the subject of a *fatwa* judging him to be an apostate because of the contents of his novel. (The *Guardian*, 10 December 1988; *The Times*, 19 December 1988.)

44.   Akhtar, *op. cit.*, p. 30.

45.   *R. v. Chief Metropolitan Magistrate ex parte Choudhury op. cit.*

46.   *The Times*, 7 March 1989.

47.   *R. v. Horseferry Road Metropolitan Magistrate ex parte Siadatan* [1990] 3 WLR 1006, QBD.

48.   See, for example, the remarks by the Bishop of St Albans, the *Guardian*, 22 March 1989.

49.   The *Guardian*, 4 March 1989. In July 1989 John Patten, the then Minister of State at the Home Office, sent a letter to Muslim leaders saying, *inter alia*, that the

Government understood the 'hurt and anxiety' caused by the book. (Ahsan and Kidwai, *op. cit.*, p. 321.)

50. See, for example, Roald Dahl's letter to *The Times*, 28 February 1989.

51. See, for example, S. Lee, *The Cost of Free Speech* Faber and Faber, 1990 and R. Webster, *A Brief History of Blasphemy* The Orwell Press, 1990.

52. The *Observer*, 22 March 1992; the *Guardian*, 10 April 1992.

53. S. Rushdie, 'In Good Faith' in S. Rushdie *Imaginary Homelands* Granta Books, 1991, Granta Books, 1992. The 1991 edition contains the essay 'Why I Have Embraced Islam'. In the 1992 edition this is replaced with the essay 'One Thousand Days in a Balloon'.

54. Akhtar, *op. cit.*, p. 13.

55. Akhtar, *op. cit.*, p. 35. Qureshi and Khan, *op. cit.*, p. 31. Not all such critics were Muslim. See, for example, the editorial in the *Spectator*, 4 March 1989.

56. See, for example, A. Vetta, 'A Contract with the Devil' in Ahsan and Kidwai, *op. cit.*, at pp. 102 and 103, and Roald Dahl's letter to *The Times*, 28 February 1989. The Muslim Institute stated that, '[t]he circumstantial evidence, eg. the size of the advance paid to the author, and the media and literary hype that accompanied its publication, leaves no doubt that *The Satanic Verses* is the result of a conspiracy'. (K.Siddiqui (ed.), *The Muslim Manifesto* The Muslim Institute, 1991, p. 28.)

57. S. Rushdie, *Grimus* Grafton Books, 1979, p. 52.

58. S. Rushdie, *Midnight's Children* Jonathan Cape, 1981, p. 129.

59. S. Rushdie, *Midnight's Children, op. cit.*, p. 79. Shabbir Akhtar quotes Rushdie as saying, 'When we are born we are not automatically human beings. We have to learn how to be human. Some of us get there and some of us don't'. (Akhtar, *op. cit.*, p. 31.)

60. Rushdie, *Midnight's Children, op. cit.*, p. 207.

61. Rushdie, *Midnight's Children, op. cit.*, p. 295.

62. S. Rushdie, *The Satanic Verses* Viking, 1988, p. 97.

63. S. Rushdie, 'The Empire writes back with a vengeance', *The Times*, 3 July 1982.

64. Rushdie, *The Satanic Verses, op. cit.*, p. 168.

65. M. Couto, 'The Search for Identity' in M. Butcher (ed.), *The Eye of the Beholder* Commonwealth Institute, 1983, p.62.

66. Rushdie, *The Satanic Verses, op. cit.*, p. 186.

67. In 'The Empire writes back with a vengeance' (*op. cit.*) Rushdie wrote that G.V. Desani's novel *All About H Hatterr*, 'showed how English could be bent and kneaded until it spoke an authentically Indian voice'.

68. 'Salman Rushdie interviewed by Roger Burford Mason' (1988) 15 *PN Review* No. 4 15 at p. 18.

69. S. Rushdie, *Shame* Jonathan Cape, 1983, p. 87.

70. Rushdie, *Midnight's Children, op. cit.*, p. 208.

71. Rushdie, *The Satanic Verses, op. cit.*, p. 49.

72. Rushdie, *The Satanic Verses, op. cit.*, p. 368.

73. S. Rushdie, 'The Indian Writer in England' in Butcher (ed.), *op. cit.*, p. 77.

74. S. Rushdie , '"Errata" Unreliable Narration in Midnight's Children' in B. Olinder (ed.), *A Sense of Place* Goteborg, 1984, at p. 100.

75. U. Parameswaran, *The Perforated Sheet: Essays on Salman Rushdie* Affiliated East–West Press, 1988, p. 56.

76. Rushdie, *Shame, op. cit.*, p. 29.

77. Rushdie, *Midnight's Children, op. cit.*, p. 164.

78. Rushdie, *Midnight's Children, op. cit.*, p. 207.

79. S. Rushdie, *Haroun and the Sea of Stories* Granta Books, 1990, p. 50.

80. Something he, himself, says he first came to terms with in writing *The Satanic Verses* (See 'Salman Rushdie interviewed by Roger Burford Mason' *op. cit.*, at pp. 15–16.

81. B. Ashcroft, G. Griffiths, H. Tiffin, *The Empire Writes Back: Theory and Practice in Post-Colonial Literatures* Routledge and Kegan Paul, 1989, p. 183.

82. P. Mendoza and Gabriel García Márquez, *The Fragrance of Guava* Verso, 1982, p. 35. See T. Brennan, *Salman Rushdie and the Third World* Macmillan, 1989, pp. 65–70 for an analysis of the relationship between the writing of Márquez and Rushdie.

83. Ruthven, *op. cit.*, pp. 44–45. The incident is discussed in A. Ahmed, 'Death in Islam: The Hawkes Bay Case' (1986) 21 *Man* 120.

84. Rushdie, *Shame, op. cit.*, p. 87.

85. This is not to say that Rushdie has not acknowledged a debt to Indian writers writing in India; he has (see, for example, his praise of G. V. Desani's *All About H Hatterr* in his article, 'The Empire writes back with a vengeance' *op. cit.*). His concern has been to distance himself from the idea of any school of regional writers, 'Indian Writers Writing in English'. (See Parameswaran *op. cit.*, p. 13 and S. Rushdie, 'Commonwealth Literature Does Not Exist' in Rushdie, *Imaginary Homelands, op. cit*).

86. S. Rushdie, 'The Indian Writer in England' in Butcher (ed.), *op. cit.*

87. S. Rushdie, *The Satanic Verses, op. cit.,* p. 208.

88. Rushdie, *Haroun and the Sea of Stories, op. cit.*, p. 86.

89. Rushdie, *Grimus, op. cit.*, pp. 81–82.

90. Rushdie, 'In Good Faith' in Rushdie, *Imaginary Homelands, op. cit.*, p. 394.

91. Rushdie, 'In Good Faith', *loc. cit.*

92. Rushdie, *The Satanic Verses, op. cit.*, p. 92.

93. Though, unlike Pakistan in *Shame*, Islam forms only a part of *The Satanic Verses*.

94. Rushdie, 'In Good Faith' in Rushdie, *Imaginary Homelands, op. cit.*, p. 408.

95. Rushdie, *The Satanic Verses, op. cit.*, p. 81.

96. S. Rushdie, 'Is Nothing Sacred?' in Rushdie, *Imaginary Homelands, op. cit.*, p. 418.

97. 'The desire to create an alternative world, to modify or augment the real world through the act of writing (which is one motive underlying the novelistic tradition in the West) is inimical to the Islamic world-view.' (E. Said, *Beginnings* Columbia University Press, 1975, p. 81.)

98. In an interview extracted in Ahsan and Kidwai, *Sacrilege versus Civility, op. cit.*, p. 62.

99. Rushdie, 'Is Nothing Sacred?' in Rushdie, *Imaginary Homelands, op. cit.*, pp. 425–426.

100. Many critics, as I have already noted, would not accept that Rushdie has written in good faith. To substantiate this charge, however, given the place that the novel has in his work as a whole, such critics have to show that all of his work is written in bad faith. Some seem happy to attempt this task. (See, for example, Sardar and Wyn Davies, *op. cit.*, chapters 5 and 6.)

101. Sardar and Wyn Davis, *op. cit.*, p. 3.

102. Sardar and Wyn Davis, *op. cit.*, p. 4.

103. For the novel's progenitors see Rushdie, 'In Good Faith' in Rushdie *Imaginary Homelands, op. cit.*, p. 403. The first quotation comes when, as Gibreel Farishita falls, he sings, 'I tell you, you must die, I tell you, I tell you'. The line is taken from Brecht's *Threepenny Opera*.

104. Weatherby, *op. cit.*, p. 125. Kumar has noted that, '[o]ut of the total pages of 507 of the novel, only 72 pages…are concerned with the early days of Islam.' (G. Kumar, *Censorship in India* Har-Anand Publications, 1990, p. 43.)

105. Sardar and Wyn Davis, *op. cit.*, p. 141.

106. F. Jussawalla, 'Resurrecting the Prophet: the Case of Salman, the Otherwise' (1989) 2 *Public Culture* 106 at p. 111.

107. S. Rushdie, *The Wizard of Oz* BFI Publishing, 1992, p. 57.

108.   L. Fuller, *The Morality of Law*, 1969, pp. 35–36.

109.   See, for example, *The Muslim Manifesto*, *op.cit.*, p. 12.

110.   See, for example, *The Crime of Blasphemy – Why it Should be Abolished* The International Committee for the Defence of Salman Rushdie and his Publishers, 1989, pp. 13–14.

111.   A A'la Mawdudi, *Human Rights in Islam* The Islamic Foundation (2nd ed., 1980) p. 24.

112.   B. Parekh, 'Britain and the Logic of Social Pluralism' in Commission for Racial Equality, *Britain: A Plural Society*, 1990, p. 72.

113.   Parekh, *op. cit.*, p. 68.

114.   Sardar and Wyn Davis, *op. cit.*, p. 2.

115.   Law Commission Working Paper No. 78 *op. cit.*, paras. 8.15–8.22.

116.   Rushdie, *Shame*, *op. cit.*, p. 28.

117.   Roberston, *op. cit.*, p. 240.

118.   J. Hick (ed.), *The Myth of the God Incarnate* SCM Press, 1977.

119.   This point was first put forward by Clifford Longley in *The Times*, 18 July 1977.

120.   Quoted in N. Walter, *Blasphemy Ancient and Modern* Rationalist Press Association, 1990, p. 72.

121.   See, for example, an advertisement placed in *The Times* by the Birmingham Central Mosque (*The Times*, 3 March 1989).

122.   J. Waldron, 'Too Important for Tact', *Times Literary Supplement*, 10 March 1989.

123.   Rushdie, 'Is Nothing Sacred?' in Rushdie, *Imaginary Homelands, op. cit.*, p. 420.

124.   G. Steiner, *Real Presences* Faber and Faber, 1989, p. 11.

125.   See, for example, Norman Mailer's statement extracted in L. Appignanesie and S. Maitland (eds), *The Rushdie File* Fourth Estate, 1989, p. 174.

126.   See pp. 21–25 above.

127.   See, for example, Lee, *op. cit.*, chp 13, *passim*. Professor Lee regards international law as a non-discriminatory foundation for arguments about the proper limits of expression. It seems unlikely that Muslims would agree. '[I]nternational legal materials must be discounted as too often these are the product of self-serving political factors aimed more at protecting the position of states than reflecting a reflexive moral consensus.' (I. Scobbie, 'Mercenary Morality: A Reply to Professor Coady' in A. Bradney (ed.), *International Law and Armed Conflict* Franz Steiner, 1992, p. 77.) Both Istvan Pogany and M. Reisman have expressed the view that the tenets of Islamic fundamentalism are in conflict with the principles of international law (see I. Pogany, 'Religion, the Palestinian–Israeli Conflict and International Law' in Bradney (ed.), 1992, *op. cit.*; M. Reisman, 'Islamic Fundamentalism and its Impact on International Law and Politics' in M. Janis (ed.), *The Influence of Religion on the Development of International Law* Martinus Nijhoff, 1991).

128.   S. Rushdie, 'One Thousand Days in a Balloon' in Rushdie, *Imaginary Homelands*, 1992, *op. cit.*, p. 439. This essay is to be found only in the paperback edition of this book.

129.   See, for example, D. Caute, 'Prophet Motive' in *New Statesman and Society*, 16 February 1990 and Akhtar, *op. cit.*, p. 23.

130.   Foote's arguments were quoted by Lord Coleridge CJ (*R. v. Ramsay and Foote* 48 *Law Times* 733 at p. 739.)

131.   A. Burgess, *You've Had Your Time* Heinemann, 1990 p. 308.

132.   The *Guardian*, 25 February 1989.

133.   F. Weldon, *Sacred Cows* Chatto and Windus, 1989, p. 6.

134.   See Akhtar, *op. cit.*, chp 3 and Webster, *op. cit.*, chp 2.

135.   *R. v. Chief Magistrate ex parte Choudhury op. cit.*, p. 318.

136.   [1991] 4 All ER 481, HL.

137. The line comes from MacNeice's poem 'Meeting Point'.
138. D. Moraes, *My Son's Father* Secker and Warburg, 1968, p. 167. The book itself contains a note saying that the publishers have not included one poem but giving no reason for the omission (G. Barker, *Collected Poems: 1930–1955* Faber and Faber, 1957, p. 13).
139. G. Barker, *The True Confessions of George Barker* Fore Publications, 1950; G. Barker, *The True Confessions of George Barker* McGibbon and Kee, 1965.
140. Thorensen, a Dane, was prevented from coming into Great Britain to make the film (*The Times*, 10 February 1977). The then Home Secretary, Merlyn Rees, had previously said, when the film had originally been proposed, that the law would be upheld. Which legal rules were in his mind at the time is unclear but the law of blasphemy was presumably one of them (*The Times*, 17 September 1976).
141. Sir Michael Havers (as he then was), the then Attorney General, refused to prosecute *The Wild Girl* having been asked to so by Sir Peter Mills MP (see *Hansard*, HC, Vol 78, col 185 and *The Times*, 6 July 1985). The then Director of Public Prosecutions, Allan Green, refused to prosecute *The Last Temptation of Christ* after a general outcry about the film's release (*The Times*, 2 September 1988). It is noticeable that, as with Kirkup's poem, both works, whilst not denying the divinity of Christ, concentrate on his human side more than is usually the case in the dominant Christian tradition in this country. (See D. Thompson and I. Christie (eds), *Scorsese on Scorsese* Faber and Faber, 1989, p. 124; and M. Roberts, *The Wild Girl* Methuen, 1985, p. 67.)
142. *The Times*, 15 December 1989. Although the relevant legislation, the Video Recordings Act 1984, makes no reference to the law of blasphemy, the Board seems to have felt that any issue of a classification certificate on their part implied that they were certifying the general legality of the video. A résumé of the content of the video is to be found in J. Herrick, 'Visions of Censorship' (January 1990) 104 *New Humanist* 5.
143. s 9 Video Recordings Act 1984.

6 Religion and work

Introduction

Family life and education are desires; free expression is a corollary of existence. Work, for most people, is a necessity. As with the law of education, the law effecting families and the law of blasphemy therefore, employment law offers a good opportunity to understand the reality of religious freedom in Great Britain.

Casual observation would suggest that the structures of employment in Great Britain are dominated by Christianity. In his first Reith Lecture, Rabbi Jonathan Sacks, in giving a negative answer to his own question, 'is Britain yet a post-religious society?', observed that anyone first visiting Britain, 'would be struck by the fact that a large number of businesses stopped on a Sunday and, asking why, would receive an explanation that could hardly fail to mention Christianity'.[1] From this cessation of trading it might appear that the dominant tradition in Christianity, which associates the fourth commandment, 'Remember the sabbath day, and keep it holy', with Sunday, receives legal recognition.[2] Sunday, the Christian sabbath, is a day of rest.[3] Public bank holidays, also days of rest which intersperse the working year, in the main owe their origins to Christian holy festivals.[4] Working life in Great Britain is punctuated by opportunities to attend Christian services. However, whilst to say this might be an accurate account of the actual structure of working life, it would be a misleading analysis of the structure and content of employment law.

Sunday

Legal prohibition of employment on Sunday in England and Wales owes its historical antecedents to the Sunday Observance Act 1677.[5] Present day prohibition, however, is by no means complete and, legally, is now restricted to relatively limited areas of employment and very specific classes of workers. The main limitation of the form of work to be done by those employed on Sundays is now to be found in the Shops Act 1950. The only specific limitation on employing people on Sunday is contained in the Factories Act 1961. There are also other, more minor, pieces of legislation, such as the Sunday Observance Act of 1780, which, by limiting the forms of entertainment or other matters which can legally be pursued on Sunday, limit legal forms of employment.

The Shops Act 1950 prohibits shops opening on a Sunday to sell various kinds of goods.[6] As the Auld Committee commented, when describing those goods which could and could not be sold on a Sunday, 'anomalies [in the 1950 Act] have been widely canvassed'.[7] Except in the case of parts of the country where exemptions from the provisions of the Act have been obtained, the Act allows the sale of gin but not cream, newspapers but not bibles, fried fish and chips except in a fried fish and chip shop (though fried fish and chip shops can sell other freshly cooked meals on a Sunday) and so on and so forth. There is no clear rationale to what can and what cannot be sold under the Act's provisions. Equally, the precise interpretation of what sales the Act permits is fraught with difficulty. In one case, where the court sought to define the exact limits of the 1950 legislation, Lord Goddard commented that, 'this Act really is unworkable to a very great extent'.[8] However, despite the difficulties of determining the precise ambit of the Act, and despite the restrictions that it does impose, it is clear that, whatever else the Act does, it does not protect, except in a very limited and tangential way, the sabbatarian beliefs of those Christians who think no work should be done on a Sunday.

The 1950 Act extends only to the retail trade. Thus, in large areas of employment workers will not be protected by the Act from being forced to engage in Sunday working.[9] Moreover, even in the case of shops, the 1950 Act prohibits not the employment of workers on a Sunday but the selling goods to customers.[10] Employees may, under the Act, be legally compelled to work on a Sunday filling shelves, stock-taking or on any other task which does not involve actual sales.[11] The only other significant piece of legislation in this area, the Factories Act 1961, adds little to the protection of those who do not wish to work on the Christian sabbath since, although the 1961 Act does prohibit Sunday working in factories, it does so only in the case of 'young persons'.[12]

For some, Sunday continues to retain its sabbatarian flavour. Such individuals, however, constitute only a part of what is, in any event, the small minority of the British population who continue to worship regularly in a Christian church.

> Increasingly Sunday has become a secular day, for most a day of leisure and recreation, an opportunity to engage in activities either individually or as a family for which there is no other time in the week...[13]

Many pieces of legislation continue to recognise that Sunday is not part of the normal business week by, for example, frequently excluding Sundays (along with Bank Holidays, and Christmas) from calculations of periods of time which are of statutory importance.[14] Nevertheless, legislation plainly plays only a small part in whatever special character Sunday may still have. Far more important are the social structures and conventions regarding Sunday first developed during the nineteenth century.[15]

Whilst the current legislation might play only a very small part in the compulsory celebration of Sunday, the part that it does play does have important implications for notions of religious freedom. The legislation that there is favours one religion's holy day. The legislation is not permissive,

allowing individuals to celebrate Sunday, but mandatory, making them
acknowledge it. The legislation is intended to close some businesses; to 'keep
Sunday special' in the words of one campaign. The legislation is not simply
intended to allow people to pursue their own inclinations on Sunday; rather it
allows some to enforce their sabbatarian beliefs on others. This mandatory
nature of the legislation is difficult to justify. One purpose of the Act is to
allow some individuals, sabbatarian Christians, to use other individuals, anyone
not being a sabbatarian Christian, in order that they may celebrate Sunday as
they wish. Because one set of individuals do not wish to work others may not
work. Such legislation clearly runs counter to the principle of the autonomy of
the individual, treating some people, as it does, as things for the use of others.
Moreover, at a lower level of analysis, from a religious perspective, the
legislation is especially difficult to justify in a society where active sabbatarian
Christians are a small minority of the total population.

Given the value now supposedly placed on religious tolerance, and the
recognition of the existence of a multi-faith society, it is not surprising to find
that arguments in favour of limiting trading on Sundays are increasingly
couched in secular rather than religious terms. The Auld Committee reported
that even for the Churches,

> [T]he main argument [against Sunday trading]...is not, and has not been for a long
> time, to protect and encourage Sunday worship...The Churches' argument has been
> rather to emphasize the human need to preserve one day a week as a day different
> from others...[16]

and also noted that, '[the Churches] acknowledge...that it would be wrong to
use the law, and the criminal law at that, as a tool to enforce or even encourage
Christian beliefs and practices'.[17] This is not to say that the Churches have
become any less concerned with the protection of Sundays. For example, in
February 1986 the General Synod of the Church of England voted by 427 to six
against, to oppose Sunday trading.[18] In analysing the defeat of the Shops Bill
1985, which would have abolished the prohibition on Sunday opening, Regan
writes that, '[t]he most important work in building up opposition at a local level
was done by religious bodies'. He instances as evidence for this proposition the
formation of the Pro-Sunday Coalition by the British Evangelical Council,
CARE Campaigns, the Evangelical Alliance, the Jubilee Centre and the Lord's
Day Observance Society, the publication by this group of a leaflet urging
people to write to their MPs protesting about the Bill and the result that, '[a]
very large number of MPs received hundreds of letters on the subject'.[19] What
has changed is the form of argument which is seen as being likely to be
persuasive, not the desired end result.[20]

Even with the increased emphasis in argument on the supposed need for one
day of rest in any week, the coincidence of the particular day chosen and the
Christian sabbath can hardly be dismissed as fortuitous. In the various pieces of
legislation which refer to Sunday other religions are simply treated less
favourably than Christianity. Although the arguments put forward by the
main Christian Churches have become paternalistic rather than theological,
arguing for Sundays to be kept free of employment for people's own good
(whether they want that good or not), the arguments continue to have a

theological consequence – the protection of the Christian sabbath. Moreover, notwithstanding the official attitude of the major Christian Churches in Great Britain, the protection of Christianity remains for some in itself a justification for this less favourable treatment for other religions.[21] The purpose of the legislation remains as being to, 'legislate for uniformity...to reflect the views of some members of the community as to how Sunday should be, whilst disregarding the wishes and needs of others.'[22]

The Shops Act 1950 attempts to ameliorate its otherwise discriminatory treatment of religions not celebrating Sunday as a holy day by making special provision for those who celebrate the Jewish sabbath. Under these provisions shopkeepers who conscientiously object to trading on a Saturday, the Jewish sabbath, can close their shops on a Saturday and open them until 2.00 pm on a Sunday.[23] This provision is in itself discriminatory since, as was pointed out in debate when the measure was first introduced in 1936, it allows for only half-day opening on Sunday in exchange for complete closure on Saturday.[24] Moreover, s 53 makes no allowance for Muslims who regard Friday as a holy day.[25]

The confusion of the Shops Act 1950, forbidding some sales whilst allowing others, is mirrored in the legislation relating to entertainment on Sundays. Whilst the Sunday Theatre Act 1972 and the Cinemas Act 1985 has largely freed these forms of entertainment from Sunday restrictions, failure to pass Sunday sport legislation means that the legality of much of professional Sunday sport is at best dubious.[26]

Consideration of the wider issues surrounding the merits or demerits of special legislative treatment for Sundays lies outside the legitimate limits of this volume. However, whatever the arguments surrounding the economic efficiency or even the legality of such treatment,[27] it is clear that both that special treatment and the exemptions from that special treatment contribute to religious discrimination by the legal system. To the extent that it is effective, the legislation attempts to impose one religion's holy day on the population at large. At the same time, because of its severe limitations, the legislation fails to protect many workers' sabbatarian wishes. Finally, the legislation does not acknowledge, or treats as less important than Christian holy days, the holy days of non-Christian workers.

Religious observance during working hours and unfair dismissal

For those committed to their faith religious observance can frequently conflict with the dictates of their working lives. British employment law sometimes provides partial protection for such workers but there is no general legislation whose specific purpose is to prevent discrimination in matters of employment on religious grounds.[28]

Three classes of legal rules may be relevant for those who find their religion and their work in conflict. First there is the general protection from unfair dismissal given to workers under the Employment Protection (Consolidation) Act 1978. Secondly, there is the protection given by the Race Relations Act 1976. Finally, there is a very limited number of special pieces of legislation which may protect workers in individual fields of employment.

Under s 54(1) of the 1978 Act every employee has a right not to be unfairly dismissed.[29] Once an employee has shown that he or she has been dismissed it is for the employer to establish that the reason for the dismissal falls within the permitted reasons for dismissal in s 57(2) of the 1978 Act.[30] The employer must also show that he or she has acted reasonably in dismissing the employee bearing in mind all the circumstances of the case, including the size and administrative resources of the employer's undertaking.[31]

In the unreported case of *Post Office* v. *Mayers* Mayers claimed he had been unfairly dismissed after he had refused to work after sunset on Friday.[32] Mayers had joined the World Wide Church of God which celebrated the sabbath from sunset on Friday to sunset on Saturday and forbade any form of work during those hours. The Employment Appeal Tribunal found that Mayers' dismissal had been fair. However, one of the reasons that Mayers was unsuccessful was that the Post Office had made efforts, albeit unsuccessful efforts, to accommodate Mayers' religious convictions. They had attempted to secure him alternative employment with more suitable hours and it was clear that he was unwilling to accept employment on a part-time four and a half day week basis. It was this attempt to accommodate Mayer which made the dismissal fair and not the mere fact that Mayers' religious convictions conflicted with his contractual duties. Similarly, in *Ali and others* v. *Capri* Muslim employees failed in an action for unfair dismissal when an employer refused to allow them to have lunch breaks at different times from other workers in order to allow them to attend a Mosque on Friday. Once again it was not just the fact that the workers religious convictions conflicted with their contractual duties which made the dismissal fair. The employer had made efforts to change lunch breaks in order to fit in with the Muslim workers' needs. The production process required that all employees be in the factory at the same time. The employer had provided a place to pray in the factory for Muslim workers.[33] It was this context that made the dismissal fair.[34]

Religious observance will sometimes be part of a reason why a dismissal which was otherwise fair has become unfair. In *George* v. *Plant Breeding International* an employee was required to work a 12-hour, seven-day week during the ten weeks of harvest. George claimed that this prevented him being with his family and attending church on a Sunday. In holding that George's dismissal was unfair the Industrial Tribunal noted the possible danger to George's health caused by the work load and its effect on his family life. No specific mention was made of his wish to attend church.[35]

It seems unlikely that George's desire to attend church would, on its own, have justified his refusal to work on Sundays in the eyes of the tribunal.[36] In *Esson* v. *London Transport Executive* Esson refused to work on a Saturday because he was a member of the Seventh Day Adventists who take Saturday as their sabbath. His subsequent dismissal was ruled to be fair because, if Esson had been allowed to take Saturdays of, it would have been necessary to make other employees work on Saturday instead of taking it as their rest day.[37] A different approach to *Esson* was taken in an unreported tribunal decision, *Lindhorst-Jones* v. *Aber Building Supplies*, in 1986 where the dismissal of a woman who refused to work on Sundays because she was a bellringer was found to be unfair.[38] The employee's bellringing was described as 'a commitment rather than a hobby'. Since such a description would be appropriate to any committed believer's attitude to their religion's holy days, *Lindhorst-Jones* might thus be taken to justify a finding of unfair dismissal if any believer were dismissed because of their refusal to work on such days. However, it seems that as important as the commitment to bellringing in the tribunal's eyes was the fact that the dismissal had been made 'in a fit of pique'. The failure to give any thought to the possibility of accommodating the employee's needs made the process of the dismissal unreasonable and thus unfair. Thus it seems unlikely that the law relating to unfair dismissal can be used as a simple mechanism for furthering the interests of those who do not wish to work on what they take to be holy days.[39]

In a limited sense religious discrimination will make a dismissal unfair but the limitations are very severe. There is some evidence that tribunals treat religious convictions as 'involuntary behaviour' and therefore, like ill-health, something that has to be treated sympathetically.[40] The religious convictions of an employee and ways of accommodating them must at least be considered by an employer if a dismissal is not to be unfair. But that consideration may, it seems, be fairly short and the needs of the believer must yield very quickly to the needs of the employer or other workers.

Religion and racial discrimination

Under the Race Relations Act 1976 a person has a right not to be discriminated against on grounds of race in relation to employment.[41] Race and religion are different things. The exclusion of religion from the 1976 Act was a matter of deliberate policy. In debate on an amendment which would have introduced religion into the Act, Brynmor John, then the relevant Minister of State, argued that, 'the Bill was trying to combat racial discrimination not religious discrimination as such'.[42] But the Minister went on to say that, 'the Bill is a considerable advance in protecting the religions of people in its concept of indirect discrimination'.[43]

Complaints of discrimination under the 1976 Act can be made in two different ways. First, the complaint might be one of direct discrimination, where the complainant alleges that he or she has been less favourably treated on racial grounds.[44] Secondly, the complaint might be one of indirect discrimination, where the complainant alleges that a requirement or condition which is applied equally to all is one which a considerably smaller proportion of one racial group can meet.[45]

In the instance of both types of complaint under the 1976 Act the question of what is meant by the concept of race is crucial to the final outcome of a case. Both 'racial grounds' and 'racial group' are defined in the Act as meaning, 'colour, race, nationality or ethnic or national origins'.[46] In *Mandela* v. *Dowell Lee* the House of Lords had to consider whether or not Sikhs constituted a racial group for the purposes of the Act.[47] In his judgement Lord Fraser held that the term 'ethnic' did not have a 'strictly racial or biological sense'.[48] Rather, Lord Fraser went on, the term ethnic referred to a community which shared certain characteristics. Two of these characteristics, a long shared history and a cultural tradition of its own, were necessary for the existence of an ethnic group. Other characteristics were relevant and if they existed, in addition to the two necessary characteristics, would indicate the existence of an ethnic group which was, in turn, a racial group. Amongst these relevant characteristics Lord Fraser listed a common religion, different from neighbouring groups or the general community surrounding the group in question.[49] On this basis Sikhs were held to constitute a racial group for the purposes of the Act.

Although the decision in *Mandela* is of assistance in allowing some members of religious groups to use Race Relations legislation to counter discrimination against them, it is important to note the limitations of the decision. If all that a group shares is its common religion it will not constitute a racial group for the purposes of the 1976 Act. In his judgement Lord Fraser specifically noted that the 1976 Act was 'not concerned at all with discrimination on religious grounds'.[50] The finding that Sikhs were a group which was, 'no longer purely religious in character' was a necessary precondition to the conclusion that they constituted a racial group.[51]

In *Seide v. Gillette Industries* the Employment Appeal Tribunal had to decide whether or not Jews constituted a racial group for the purposes of the 1976 Act.[52] The Employment Appeal Tribunal accepted that 'Jewish' could indicate either a racial group or a religious group.[53] If this distinction is accepted it raises the possibility that even if a religious group does constitute racial group for the purposes of the Race Relations legislation members of it may still fail to gain the benefit of the 1976 Act because a particular act of discrimination was aimed at the religious group not the racial group. However, although the distinction has a clear conceptual basis it is difficult to see how it will have any operative affect. The fact that, for example, a person has Jewish parents, and is therefore Jewish in racial terms, does not debar him or her from being an atheist. He or she could then be a member of the Jews as a racial group but not as a religious group. Nevertheless, any act of discrimination against Jews as a religious group, such as, for example, refusing to employ people who attend synagogues, would almost necessarily be indirect discrimination against Jews as a racial group because it would affect a greater proportion of Jews as a racial group than any other group.[54]

Sikhs and Jews represent cases where there is an obvious overlap between religious and racial groups. Other cases are more difficult. In *Crown Suppliers* v. *Dawkins* the group in question was the Rastafarians.[55] Although the Employment Appeal Tribunal was referred to expert evidence given at the previous Industrial Tribunal hearing to the effect that Rastafarians had a shared history going back 60 years and distinctive beliefs and practices, they nevertheless held that Rastafarians were not an ethnic, and therefore not a racial, group for the purposes of the 1976 Act. Mr Justice Tucker in his judgement on behalf of the tribunal said that, '[t]here is in our view insufficient [evidence] to distinguish them [Rastafarians] from the rest of the Afro-caribbean community...They are a religious sect and no more'.[56] Central to this conclusion was the Employment Appeal Tribunal's assertion that, '[i]t cannot reasonably be said that a movement which goes back 60 years, ie within the living memory of many people, can claim to be long in existence'.[57] On this basis the Employment Appeal Tribunal held that the first of Lord Fraser's necessary conditions for ethnic status, shared history, had not been met. Too much can be made of this decision. An Employment Appeal Tribunal has limited value as a precedent, binding only Industrial Tribunals. Moreover, the decision, overturning the previous Industrial Tribunal finding, was only reached by a majority verdict.[58] Nevertheless, *Dawkins* does suggest that comparatively new and small religious groups are unlikely to meet the test for ethnic status and, thus, protection under the Race Relations Act 1976.

The Muslim religion is almost the antithesis of the Rastafarian faith. Islam has a long history, dating back to 622 AD and Muhammad's *hijra* to what came to be called Medina. It is a religion of great size with adherents throughout the world. Precisely this long history and great size provide problems with according Muslims ethnic status under the 1976 Act. Although Islam may have a common heritage it now takes different forms depending, in part, on the cultural context in which it is found.

> Just as there were distinctive differences between the tribal shamans of central Asia and the village spiritual leaders in the East Indies and Africa, local Muslim Leadership also presents a picture of diversity.[59]

Present-day, predominantly Muslim Iran is radically different from present-day, predominantly Muslim Indonesia.[60] This cultural diversity make it difficult for Muslims to be accorded ethnic status. Neither of Lord Fraser's 'essential conditions' for ethnic status, a shared history and common culture, can clearly be established for Islam.[61] Many parts of the life of Muhammad are part of the common consciousness of Muslims but the Sunni and Shi'ite interpretations, the major traditions within Islam, differ in their view of the later development of Muslim history.[62] More importantly, the history of the establishment of Islam within various groups and countries, and the culture created within different groups, is a very individual matter.[63] Of Lord Fraser's five 'relevant conditions' when establishing ethnic status only a common religion is true for Islam.[64] No Employment Appeal Tribunal has yet ruled on the ethnic status of Muslims. Although one Industrial Tribunal has treated Muslims as an ethnic group it would seem more likely that the view that Muslims are not part of an ethnic group, previously adopted in other Industrial Tribunals, will prevail.[65] However, because, despite its number of adherents, Islam is unevenly spread through the world, many Muslims may be able to show that acts of discrimination against Muslims are, in turn, acts of indirect discrimination against the ethnic group to which they belong.[66]

Where a religious group has established their status as a racial group they are then entitled to have their religious practices taken into account by employers. Under the *Code of Practice for the Elimination of Racial Discrimination and the Promotion of Equality of Opportunity in Employment* issued by the Commission for Racial Equality, employers are enjoined to consider whether 'it is reasonably practicable to vary or adapt...[work] requirements' to fit in with the religious needs of their employees.[67] Specific examples of variations to consider include those necessary for the observance of prayer times or religious holidays or accommodations necessary to allow the wearing of particular forms of dress.[68] Failure to observe this Code of Practice is not in itself a breach of the law, but in proceedings under the Race Relations Act the Code is admissible in evidence. If any part of the Code is seen as being relevant to a case by an Industrial Tribunal then the provisions of the Code must be taken into account in determining the issue in the case.[69]

Even if a religious group can prove their ethnic status and thus establish that they are a racial group it does not then follow that they will be protected from acts of discrimination. Discriminatory actions may be justified under the 1976 Act. In *Kingston and Richmond Area Health Authority* v. *Kaur* it was argued that refusing to allow trainee nurses to wear trousers as part of their uniforms was an act of indirect discrimination against Sikhs.[70] In his judgement on behalf of the Employment Appeal Tribunal the then Mr Justice Browne-Wilkinson argued that it was justifiable for the Health Authority to insist on the wearing of a uniform and that, if it did so insist, the Authority was bound to adhere to the very strict terms of The Enrolled Nurses Rules Approval Instrument 1969.[71] This precluded the Authority from allowing the wearing of trousers and thus justified the act of discrimination.[72]

Religion and the employment of teachers

From the above it seems that employment law affords only very limited protection to the religious beliefs and needs of employees. One group of employees in Britain however, teachers in state-maintained schools in England and Wales, receive more positive legal protection from religious discrimination on the part of their employers.

According to section 30 of the Education Act 1944,

> ...no person shall be disqualified by reason of his religious opinions, or of his attending or omitting to attend religious worship, from being a teacher in a county school or in any voluntary school...

Paragraph 14 of Schedule 2 of the Education (Approval of Special Schools) Regulations 1983 provides similar protection for teachers employed in state-maintained special agreement schools. Section 30 was intended to implement the then government's view that, 'the religious opinions of a candidate for a teaching post will not disqualify him'.[73] However, the section, like the government's statement of commitment is hedged about with restrictions and caveats.

Section 30 only has limited application to teachers in voluntary-aided schools and reserved teachers in voluntary-controlled schools.[74] Such teachers are protected only from being paid less or deprived of promotion or other advantage because of their religious opinions or because they give religious education or because they attend religious worship.[75] Religion can be part of the qualification for employment in a voluntary-aided school or as a reserved teacher in a voluntary-controlled school.[76] This reflects the concordat inherent in the Education Act 1944 which allowed the Churches to retain religious control of their schools even though they became largely state funded.

A second serious limitation to section 30 can be demonstrated in the case of *Ahmad* v. *ILEA*.[77] Ahmad was a Muslim employed by the Inner London Education Authority as a teacher. In order to attend Friday prayers at the nearest mosque to his place of employment he had to take time off, missing about 45 minutes of teaching duty every Friday. Some schools at which Ahmad worked contended that this short absence could not be accommodated in the time-table. Ahmad was permitted to take all of Friday afternoon off in order to attend Friday prayers but told that he would then be treated as a part-time teacher working a four and a half day week. Ahmad was not willing to accept non-payment for the half day he was forced to take off and resigned. Later he sued for unfair dismissal citing section 30, '...no teacher...shall...receive any less emolument...by reason of his...attending...religious worship...', in argument.

In his judgement in the Court of Appeal Lord Denning held that section 30 should be read, 'subject to the qualification "if the school time-table so permits"'.[78] Orr LJ supported this view.[79] On this basis Ahmad failed in his claim. Lord Denning did suggest that head teachers would attempt to accommodate the needs of devout Muslims.[80] However, this requirement (if it is a requirement and not just a pious belief in the civilised attitudes of head teachers) does not even seem to go as far as the requirements of the law relating to unfair dismissal. Orr LJ held that Muslim teachers would not have a right to absent themselves from a school even if the inconvenience to the school was small. Any absence would be a breach of contract whatever the actual practical difficulties caused by the absence.[81] Thus schools faced by section 30 and the religious needs of their teachers, unlike employers faced by unfair dismissal law and the religious needs of their employees, can simply stand by the terms of the contract.[82]

Only one other recorded case has considered the implications of section 30. In *Lal v. Board of Governors, Sacred Heart Comprehensive School, Dagenham*, Lal sought to argue that religious discrimination was a reason for his dismissal. In a Court of Appeal hearing, he instanced an alleged insistance that he attend assemblies as a breach of section 30.[83] At an earlier Employment Appeal Tribunal hearing of his case Lal's contention that he had been subjected to religious discrimination was rejected. The tribunal judgement does not make clear whether section 30 was ever specifically raised in argument.[84] The Court of Appeal found that no point of law had been raised and it therefore did not have to consider the merits of Lal's arguments.[85] Had the matter come to full judgement, however, it seems unlikely, on the basis of *Ahmad*, that Lal would have succeeded. If Lal's contract of employment put him under a duty to attend assemblies then the fact that his conscience led him to act in breach of that duty would no more mean that section 30 would be of assistance to him than it had been to Ahmad.

The scope of section 30 is thus in practice very little more than the scope of normal employment law. It does, in the case of those teachers to whom it applies, prevent religious discrimination when the decision as to employment is made. However, it does little to protect the special religious needs of teachers once they have been employed.

Conclusion

Employment law provides evidence of contradictory attitudes towards religion. The provisions which seek to protect Sunday and to a lesser extent

Bank Holidays represent just as much an attempt to make people conform to religious notions as does the law relating to marriage. These laws penalise those whose religious attitudes depart from the presumed norm. They represent an attempt to coerce individuals which can only be justified by justifying treating individuals as creatures who may be bent to another's will merely because the other wishes it. Yet, insofar as these laws are given a religious justification, the protection of the Christian sabbath, this is done in the context of a system of employment law which largely ignores workers' religious needs, whether they be Christian or otherwise. The law seeks to protect the Christian sabbath but only sometimes and for some people. There is no structure to its protection and thus it is arbitrary. Employment law both offends against the basic principle of individual autonomy and, at the same time, fails to realise an apparent desire to protect a particular religion.

Whilst the above sections make it quite clear that the law gives very little protection for those whose religious beliefs conflict with the desires of their employers one might, from the standpoint outlined in chapter 2, legitimately query whether this gives rise to any grounds for concern. People choose to enter into employment. They are thus in a radically different position to those seen in the previous two chapters who find themselves in conflict with the law relating to families or education. In these cases the problems discussed arise not out of the individual's desire to enter into a family or to pursue education. Rather the difficulties come out of the fact that standards relating to family life and education have been set by others. These standards have conflicted with the religious convictions of some to whom the law applies. The question has then been, how far are those who have set the standards in the law justified in making others do what their conscience tells them not to do? In employment the matter is different. No employer tells a person what to do. Rather, the employer's command is always a contingent one: if you wish to remain employed, obey me. The relationship is a voluntary one. If a command by an employer offends against a worker's religious convictions the worker may always leave the employment avoiding the difficulty. The law does not bind the employee to the employer nor does it bind the employee to follow a particular course of action. The dictates of education law or family law cannot be avoided and it is that which can give them their particularly offensive character.

In times of high unemployment it might be considered unrealistic to ask a worker to leave his or her employment. In ordinary terms this might be so. Yet the defence of the principle of individual autonomy is founded on the high ground of the existential nature of the human being. It is not possible to base a concept of radical autonomy on an acknowledgement of the fact of individual freedom and then, at the same time, to deny that there is such freedom in an individual choosing to remain employed. To leave one's employment because of one's religious convictions might be a hard choice. Nevertheless it is a choice which can be made. In this context why should the law seek to limit an employer's contingent commands, at least in so far as the commands do not involve harm to others?

One answer to this might be seen by drawing an analogy between discrimination on grounds of religion and discrimination on grounds of race or sex. It might be argued that discrimination in employment on these latter grounds is not permitted. Nor, then, should discrimination be permitted on grounds of religion. This, after all, is the approach in Northern Ireland with the Fair Employment (Northern Ireland) Act 1989. But such a step, in the context of the argument of this book, would be a form of question-begging or avoidance. Discrimination on grounds of both sex and race is permitted within Great Britain. Both the Race Relations Act 1976 and the Sex Discrimination Act 1975 contain provisions allowing acts which would otherwise be ajudged to be discriminatory to be justified.[86] What, in legal terms, does and does not constitute race and sex discrimination, what is and what is not illegal, is a complex question. It is difficult to see how any easy movement can be made from the amorphous concepts of sex and race discrimination to the notion of religious discrimination. More importantly, the question at issue in this book in general, and this chapter in particular, is one of justification not rationalisation. The subject being pursued is what should the relationship be between religious convictions and legal rules. The fact that something already is illegal does not lead to the necessary conclusion that it should be illegal. Expository jurisprudence is therefore of little help in pursuing censorial jurisprudence. To follow this line of argument, comparing sex and race discrimination with religious discrimination, it would be necessary to ask first, should race and sex discrimination be made illegal and then, secondly, in what way, if at all, is religious discrimination analogous to discrimination on grounds of race or sex? To follow such a path would be to add to the scope of this enquiry without obviously making the task any easier.

To seek to provide protection against religious discrimination in the work environment is to go much further than the arguments in the previous chapters. Hitherto it has been argued that the principle of radical autonomy prevents any justification of treatment of individuals which seeks to deny the fact that as individuals they freely choose; which seeks to hold individuals to standards other than those principles which are themselves necessary corollaries of the principle of radical autonomy. For example, to insist on a right to absent oneself from work on holy days would be to reverse this argument. Others would be forced to take on one's work because of one's own religious beliefs. To make them work for you, whether they choose to or not, would be to seek to deny their autonomy. However, the matter does not rest there. At a lower level of argument where the law does make allowance for the needs of others then it must do so coherently and consistently. If one group's religious needs and beliefs are taken account of in, for example, the law relating to unfair dismissal then all other's religious needs and beliefs must equally be taken into account.

Notes

1. J. Sacks, 'The Environment of Faith'(15 November, 1990) 124 *The Listener* at pp. 4 and 5.
2. Not all Christians regard Sunday as the sabbath. Seventh Day Adventists, for example, celebrate Saturday as the sabbath. However, for stylistic reasons, this chapter will refer to Sunday as the Christian sabbath. For a history of the development of the Christian tradition of associating Sunday with the sabbath see

J. Wigley, *The Rise and Fall of the Victorian Sunday* Manchester University Press, 1980, chp 1.

3. '...Sunday should provide an opportunity first, for corporate worship and, second, for rest and recreation and for family pursuits.' Evidence of British Council of Churches and the Roman Catholic Body of England and Wales to the Crathorne Committee (*Report of the Departmental Committee on the Law of Sunday Observance* (the Crathorne Committee), Cmnd 2528 (1964) quoted at para. 40.

4. Such holidays find legislative expression in the Bank and Financial Dealings Act 1971 Schedule 1. The only such holidays not having an obvious Christian provenance is the August holiday taken in England and Wales and the May Day holiday taken in Scotland.

5. There had been previous legislation which limited recreation and put some limits on trading on a Sunday. For the full history of the early development of Sunday legislation, see Wigley, *op. cit.*

6. s 47. There is, however, a list of exempt transactions in Schedule 5 to the Act. Under s 48 a local authority may make a 'partial exemption order' for the sale of goods referred to in Schedule 6 of the Act. In holiday resorts, under s 51 of the Act, local authorities may allow shops to sell goods referred to in Schedule 7 of the Act. There are also special provisions regarding the retail sale of meat in ss 60 to 63 of the Act. The Act does not extend to Scotland (s 66).

7. *The Shops Act: Late-Night and Sunday Opening: Report of the Committee of Inquiry into Proposals to Amend the Shops Act* (Auld Committee), Cmnd 9376 (1984) para. 22.

8. *Newberry* v. *Cohen's Smoked Salmon Ltd* (1956) LGR 343, QBD, at p. 344.

9. Figures produced by the Department of Employment for June 1990 showed that 2,245,300 people were employed in retail distribution. The workforce numbered 22,231,800 in total (98 (1990) *Employment Gazette* Table 1.4). Not all the people engaged in retail distribution would be covered by the Shops Act 1950.

10. 'Every shop shall...be closed for the serving of customers...' (s 47 Shops Act 1950).

11. However, an employee cannot be compelled to work on a Sunday unless there is an express or implied term to that effect in their contract. As with the case of Sunday, legislation has only a small part in contributing to the general lack of business on Bank Holidays. There is no general legal prohibition of employment on Bank Holidays (Poulter, *op. cit.*, p. 253).

12. s 93 Factories Act 1961. This Act applies to both England and Wales and to Scotland (s 185).

13. Auld Committee Report, *op. cit.*, para. 64. Alan Sillitoe's 'Saturday night...a violent preamble to a prostrate Sabbath' in the case of the single man and 'fishing on a Sunday morning' in the case of the married man offers a more prosaic, but essentially similar, account of the same phenomena (A. Sillitoe, *Saturday Night and Sunday Morning* W.H. Allen, 1958).

14. For example, in the last three years see s 5(8) Local Government and Housing Act 1989, s 53(5) Food Safety Act 1990 and s 98(2) New Roads and Street Works Act 1991. LEXIS lists 237 statutory references to 'Sunday' many of which are references in this kind of context.

15. See Wigley, *op. cit.*, passim.

16. Auld Committee Report, *op. cit.*, para. 11.

17. Auld Committee Report, *op. cit.*, para. 130.

18. P. Regan, 'The 1986 Shops Bill' (1988) 41 *Parliamentary Affairs* 218 at p. 227.

19. Regan, *op. cit.*, pp. 226–227.

20. It would, however seem that the Churches have not always been fully aware of the full ambit of the legislation they support. In 1986 the Consumers' Association found that many cathedral shops were selling goods on Sunday in contravention of the 1950 Act (the *Guardian*, 20 February 1986; *The Times*, 20 February 1986). One

result of the Churches opposition to the amend the Shops Act 1950 seems to have been a heightened awareness amongst their own shop workers of the legislation and a consequent unwillingness to work on Sunday (the *Guardian*, 19 March 1987).

21. Thus, for example, several MPs used religious arguments when speaking against the last major attempt to abolish the restrictions on Sunday trading, the Shops Bill 1985 (see *Hansard*, HC, Vol 86, cols 165–166, 176–178 and 186, November 7, 1985).

22. This being the Auld Committee's reason why the Shop Act provisions on Sunday trading should be abolished (Auld Committee Report *op. cit.*, para. 143).

23. s 53 Shops Act 1950. The shop may be open on a Sunday after 2.00 pm for the sale of such items whose Sunday sale is not otherwise prohibited by the Act (s 53(1)(c)).

24. *Hansard*, HC, Vol 308, col 2179, February 21, 1936

25. The Muslim attitude to Friday is not entirely analogous to the Christian and Jewish attitude to their respective sabbaths. Whilst there is a duty to attend midday prayers on Fridays there is no general duty to abstain from work for the whole day (Mustafa Yousuf McDermott and Muhammad Manazir Ahsan, *The Muslim Guide* The Islamic Foundation, 1986, pp. 39–40; A. Welch, 'Islam' in J. Hinnells (ed.), *A Handbook of Living Religions* Penguin Books, 1985, pp. 139–143). The Crathorne Report recommended that Muslim traders receive special treatment (The Crathorne Report *op. cit.*, para. 201). However, despite four attempts to provide special dispensation for Muslims, there are still only exemptions with respect to the Jewish sabbath.

26. Andrew Mackay's Sunday Sport Bill in 1989 was the third such Bill to fail to secure a passage through Parliament in three years (*The Times*, 18 February 1989). On course betting on a race-course also remains illegal on a Sunday (s 5 Betting, Gaming and Lotteries Act 1963).

27. On the former see D. de Meza, 'The Fourth Commandment: Is it Pareto Efficient?' (1984) 94 *The Economic Journal* 379. On the latter see A. Arnull, 'What Shall We Do on Sunday?' (1991) 16 *European Law Review* 112.

28. Such legislation does exist in Northern Ireland in the form of the Fair Employment (Northern Ireland) Act 1989.

29. Providing that that worker has been employed by the employer for a period of at least two years continuous service prior to the dismissal (s 64(1) Employment Protection Consolidation Act 1978 as amended by the Unfair Dismissal (Variation of Qualifying Period) Order 1985 SI 1985/782). Dismissal includes constructive dismissal (ss 55(2), 83(2) EPCA 1978).

30. s 57(1) EPCA 1978.

31. s 57(3) EPCA 1978 as amended by s 6 Employment Act 1980.

32. A full transcript of this case is to be found on LEXIS.

33. The case is unreported but is discussed in 'Religious Observance at Work' (1991) 439 *Industrial Relations Legal Information Bulletin* pp. 5–6. The over-riding dictates of a production process also seem to have been the important factor in deciding that the dismissal of a Muslim factory worker who took time off to pray was fair. Again this Industrial Tribunal case is unreported but is discussed in D. Pearl, 'Legal Decisions Affecting Immigrants and Sex Discrimination – No. 5' (1976/77) 5 *New Community* 259 at p. 261.

34. For another similar finding see *Hussain* v. *London Country Bus Services Ltd* where it was held that it was unreasonable to expect the company to allow a Muslim 'bus cleaner to clock off so as to pray'. (This case is unreported but a full transcript is available on LEXIS.)

35. This case is unreported but is discussed in 'Religious Observance at Work' *op. cit.*, p. 4. There is also a news report of the case in *The Times*, 7 October 1991.

36. In both *Mayers* and *Ali* the religious objections by the employees were accepted by all sides as being genuine. In *George* the employers challenged the sincerity of

George's claims to strong Christian beliefs (the *Guardian*, 5 September 1991). It will be for the employee to show that they do have religious objections.

37.   Esson had been allowed to seek private arrangements with other employees to swop Saturday work with them (*Esson* v. *London Transport Executive* [1875] IRLR 48, IT).

38.   There is a news report of this case in *The Times*, 19 November 1986.

39.   In *Storey* v. *Allied Breweries* a chambermaid was judged to have been fairly dismissed when she refused to work on Sundays because she wished to attend church (St John Robilliard, 'Discrimination and Indirect Discrimination: the Religious Dimension' (1980) 8 *New Community* 261 at p. 263). It is important to remember that unfair dismissal is an area of statute law. Industrial Tribunal decisions have no value as binding precedents. 'The modern approach of both the Court of Appeal and the EAT is to treat the accumulation of case law in these areas circumspectly and to deprecate over-reliance on previous authorities...' (I. Smith and J. Wood, *Industrial Law* Butterworths, 1989, p. 302).

40.   The description and comparison is taken from Wood's judgement in *Post Office* v. *Mayers op. cit.*

41.   ss 1(1), 4(1) Race Relations Act 1976.

42.   Standing Committee A, Standing Committee Reports 1975–76, col 101.

43.   Standing Committee A, *loc. cit.*

44.   s 1(1)(a) Race Relations Act 1976.

45.   s 1(1)(b)(i) Race Relations Act 1976. Such a requirement or condition will not constitute indirect discrimination if the person applying it can show that it is justifiable or that it is not to the detriment of the racial group in question (ss 1(1)(b)(ii), 1(1)(b)(iii) Race Relations Act 1976).

46.   s 3(1) Race Relations Act 1976.

47.   *Mandela* v. *Dowell Lee* [1983] 2 AC 548, HL.

48.   *Mandela* v. *Dowell Lee op. cit.*, at p. 561.

49.   *Mandela* v. *Dowell Lee op. cit.*, at p. 562. Lord Fraser also noted the necessary cultural tradition which an ethnic group had to possess was 'often but not necessarily associated with religious observance'.

50.   *Mandela* v. *Dowell Lee op. cit.*, at p. 562.

51.   *Mandela* v. *Dowell Lee op. cit.*, at p. 565. Lord Templeman in his judgement said that Sikhs were 'more than a religious sect' (*Mandela* v. *Dowell Lee op. cit.*, at p. 569).

52.   *Seide* v. *Gillette Industries* [1980] IRLR 427, EAT.

53.   *Seide* v. *Gillette Industries op. cit.*, at p. 432.

54.   The distinction raised in *Seide* does not seem to have been raised in any subsequent case law. In *Simon* v. *Brimham Associates* the Court of Appeal accepted that a candidate who had been asked whether he was of the Jewish faith might have a good cause of action under the Race Relations Act 1976. (*Simon* v. *Brimham Associates* [1987] IRLR 307, CA.)

55.   *Crown Suppliers* v. *Dawkins* [1991] IRLR 327, EAT.

56.   *Crown Suppliers* v. *Dawkins op. cit.*, at p. 331.

57.   *Crown Suppliers* v. *Dawkins loc. cit.*

58.   Although this is also true of the Industrial Tribunal decision.

59.   J. Voll, *Islam: Continuity and Change in the Modern World* Westview, 1982 p. 28.

60.   Cf. N. Keddie (ed.), *Religion and Politics in Iran* Yale University Press, 1983 and K. Jackson, *Traditional Authority, Islam and Rebellion: A Study of Indonesian Political Behavior* University of California Press, 1980. This diversity within Islam is captured in V.S. Naipaul's book *Among the Believers* Andre Deutsch, 1981 (though from Naipaul's own very individual perspective).

61.   *Mandela* v. *Dowell Lee op. cit.*, at p. 562.

62.   There are also many smaller groups within Islam whose version of Islamic history differs from both those of the dominant Sunni and Shi'ite groups and from each other (see, for example, A. Guillaume, *Islam* Penguin Books, 1956, chp 6).

63. See, for example, Akbar Ahmed, *Discovering Islam* Routledge and Kegan Paul, 1988, chps 4, 6 and 8.
64. *Mandela* v. *Dowell Lee loc. cit.*
65. In *Malik* v. *Bertram Personnel Group Ltd* it was decided that Muslims would be treated as an ethnic group. In *Tariq* v. *Young and others* and *Commission for Racial Equality* v. *Precision Manufacturing Services Ltd* Industrial Tribunals reached the converse conclusion. None of these decisions are reported. They are, however, discussed in 'Religious Observance at Work', *op. cit.*, p. 3.
66. In turn, this produces the problem that some Muslims, but only some Muslims, are protected against discrimination (see St John Robilliard, 1980, *op. cit.*, p. 262).
67. *Code of Practice for the Elimination of Racial Discrimination and the Promotion of Equality of Opportunity in Employment* SI 1983/1081 para. 1.24.
68. *loc. cit.*
69. *Code of Practice for the Elimination of Racial Discrimination and the Promotion of Equality of Opportunity in Employment op. cit.*, para. 1.2.
70. *Kingston and Richmond Area Health Authority* v. *Kaur* [1981] IRLR 337, EAT.
71. SI 1969/1674. *Kingston and Richmond Area Health Authority* v. *Kaur op. cit.*, pp. 338–339. The Commission for Racial Equality's *Code of Practice for the Elimination of Racial Discrimination and the Promotion of Equality of Opportunity in Employment* specifically mentions that employers should consider whether or not a refusal to allow a Sikh to wear a turban is justified. (*Code of Practice for the Elimination of Racial Discrimination and the Promotion of Equality of Opportunity in Employment op. cit.*, para. 1.24.)
72. Whether employers can justify an act of discrimination is a question of fact to be decided on the individual circumstances of the case. Thus, whilst an Industrial Tribunal accepted that Walls Meat Co Ltd's refusal to allow an employee to wear a turban and beard was justified, another Industrial Tribunal refused to accept that a chocolate factory's refusal to allow an employee to wear a turban was justified (*Gill* v. *The Walls Meat Co Ltd, Bhakherd* v. *Famous Names Ltd.* Both these cases are unreported but are discussed in 'Religious Observance at Work', *op. cit.*, p. 7.) Similarly in *Chowdhury* v. *FW Woolworth* an Industrial Tribunal accepted that a refusal to allow an employee to wear trousers was indirect racial discrimination. (Again this case is unreported but is noted in the (1984) Vol VI No 1 CRE *Employment Report* p. 8.)
73. *Educational Reconstruction*, Cmd 6458 (1943) para. 41.
74. Reserved teachers are those who are appointed by the religious denomination concerned.
75. s 30 Education Act 1944.
76. Religion can also be a qualification for employment in denominational schools in Scotland (s 21(2)(i) Education (Scotland) Act 1980).
77. *Ahmad* v. *ILEA* [1978] 1 All ER 574, CA.
78. *Ahmad* v. *ILEA op. cit.*, at p. 577d.
79. *Ahmad* v. *ILEA op. cit.*, at p. 581b.
80. *Ahmad* v. *ILEA op. cit.*, at p. 577e.
81. *Ahmad* v. *ILEA op. cit.*, at p. 581d–e.
82. For example see the process of attempted accommodation required by the Industrial Tribunal in *Ali and others* v. *Capri supra.*
83. *Lal* v. *Board of Governors, Sacred Heart Comprehensive School, Dagenham*, 7 November 1990. This case is unreported but a full transcript is to be found on LEXIS.
84. *Lal* v. *Board of Governors, Sacred Heart Comprehensive School, Dagenham*, 5 March 1990. This case is unreported but a full transcript is to be found on LEXIS.
85. *Lal* v. *Board of Governors, Sacred Heart Comprehensive School, Dagenham*, 17 January 1991. This case is unreported but a full transcript is to be found on LEXIS.
86. Race Relations Act 1976 s 5, Sex Discrimination Act 1975 s 7.

7 Charity

Introduction

Paul, in his first letter to the Corinthians, commended charity to the Corinthians, saying that it was more important than either faith or hope.[1] Paul's insistence on the virtue of charity is one example of a stress that is placed on altruism in many religions. For Muslims almsgiving, *zakat* and *sadaqat*, is one of the religious duties imposed by Islam.[2] Sewa, service to the community, is an integral part of Sikh life.[3] Hindus regard charity as more important than either religious ceremonies or sacrifices.[4] Many other similiar examples could be given.[5] Thus the attitude of the law towards charity is of considerable importance to many believers.

English law has long given a special status to charity, alloting charities privileges denied to other institutions.[6] Broadly, these privileges can be divided into two kinds: trusts law privileges and fiscal privileges. Charitable gifts do not, as is normally necessary, have to have a specific human beneficiary. Equally, and again contrary to the usual practice, charitable gifts may be made in perpetuity. Charities are also exempt from certain taxes.[7] By these and other similar means the law encourages charity. Those entities which are charities are advantaged. Those entities which are not charities are disadvantaged. Through this policy, the law can be said to aid and even foster religious observance, encouraging that practice which many religions demand of their adherents.

Charity in English law, unsurprisingly, receives a legal definition. What the law considers to be charity, and thus what the law accords special privileges to, depends not simply upon the subjective 'charitable' intentions of the donor of a gift but objective criteria of charitable status developed through a series of legal decisions made over many centuries.[8] The origins of English charity law lie in judicial consideration of the preamble to the Charitable Uses Act 1601 which listed various matters as charitable. Judicial statements about this preamble eventually resulted in Lord MacNaghten's attempt to classify charity under four different heads in *IRC* v. *Pemsel*.[9] One of Lord MacNaghten's four heads of charity was, 'the advancement of religion'.[10] Thus the law of charity favours religion not simply by advantaging that virtue, charity, which most religions think desirable, but also by treating as charitable the very pursuit of religion itself. This is fortunate since many religions derive a significant proportion of their income from voluntary donations by their adherents.[11] However, in doing this, the law inevitable raises the question: what will count as the advancement of religion for the purposes of the law of charity? The question is of crucial importance for, in defining what constitutes the advancement of religion, the law of charity selects those religions which are to be advantaged and those which are not.

In 1954, in his introduction to Crowther's book, *Religious Trusts*, H.G. Hanbury wrote,

> Fifty years have passed since Maitland told us that 'Religious liberty and religious equality are complete'. But this was true then, and is still true, only of the criminal law. As a statement of the law relating to charitable trusts, his remark can rank merely as an optimistic anticipation.[12]

Notwithstanding this statement, '[t]he leading commentaries on the law of charitable trusts in England maintain that the present state of the law is now one of virtually unqualified toleration of every religion or sect, irrespective of the truth or falsity of its doctrines'.[13] This divergence of academic opinion accurately reflects the muddled conceptual content of an area of law where, on the one hand, a judge can state that, '[a]s between different religions the law [of charity] stands neutral...' and yet, on the other hand, a gift to a Dominican Convent can be declared not to be charitable because, *inter alia*, the value of the example offered by the nuns in their prayers was judged 'too vague and intangible'.[14]

Neutrality towards religion

A defence of the proposition that the law of charities is neutral on matters of religion might well begin with *Thornton v. Howe*.[15] This involved a bequest for the propagation of the works of Joanna Southcott. Southcott had taught that she was pregnant by the Holy Ghost and had said that, at the age of 65, she would give birth to a second Messiah.[16] The then Master of the Rolls, Sir John Romilly, said of Southcott, '[s]he was, in my opinion, a foolish, ignorant woman' and that he found in her writings, 'much that, in my opinion, is very foolish'.[17] Nevertheless, holding that, 'the Court of Chancery makes no distinction between one religion and another', Sir John Romilly went on to decide that the bequest was valid.[18]

In *Re Watson* the testatrix left money to set up a charitable trust for the publication of various pious works which an expert witness described as having no intrinsic worth. Their only possible value, in the eyes of the expert witness, was to the few members of a group who agreed with the author of the works, in that they might, by reading them, be confirmed in their faith.[19] Plowman J noted the case of *Re Pinion* in which Harman LJ, having referred to *Thornton v. Howe*, had said that in the case of religious trusts the courts would 'assume without enquiry that the teaching [of a sect or religious group] will do some good if it is not shown to be subversive of morality'.[20] On this basis, and on the basis of *Thornton v. Howe* itself, Plowman J decided that, since the courts were neutral as regards the content of different religions, the charitable bequest in *Re Watson* had to be considered to be valid.

Religion and morality

It has been said that *Thornton v. Howe* constitutes 'the high-water mark of tolerance' towards religions in the law of charity.[21] However, the judgement in this case is also indicative of one of the ways in which the law of charities distinguishes between those religions which it finds acceptable and those which it does not. English courts have long held that charities which are established for purposes which are contrary to public policy will be declared invalid.[22] In the course of his investigation of Joanna Southcott's works, Sir John Romilly enquired into whether there was anything in those works which would tend to make 'persons who read them either immoral or irreligious'.[23] Had the works failed to meet this test the charity would then have been invalid on grounds of public policy. It was only because he felt able to answer this question in the negative that he was able to declare the gift to be a valid charitable bequest.

Examples of religions which might fail to meet the morality test are rare. However, one possible instance is Scientology. Academic commentators are all agreed in thinking that Scientology could not attain charitable status.[24] Given previous judicial descriptions of the 'harmful' nature of Scientology it seems likely that such commentators are correct and that the courts would regard Scientology as being immoral and, for that reason, amongst others, incapable of achieving charitable status.[25] More dubiously, it may be that the Exclusive Brethren is also an example of a religion which fails to meet Sir John Romilly's criteria. Although the Exclusive Brethren have had trusts accepted for registration by the Charity Commissioners, following a court decision accepting their charitable status, there is still room to argue that a future court might find their practices contrary to the public interest.[26] In *Holmes* v. *Attorney-General* Walton J found that the disciplinary practices of the Exclusive Brethren, 'Shutting-up' and 'Withdrawal', both of which involved ostracism of an individual, were not something to which exception could be taken. However, in finding in this way, he noted that the evidence about these disciplinary practices came solely from the Exclusive Brethren themselves. He went on to add that evidence from other sources 'may very well put the matter in a much more charitable light than it wears in reality'.[27] More detailed evidence on the disciplinary methods of the Exclusive Brethren might persuade the courts that they fail to meet the test of morality in *Thornton* v. *Howe*.

In the case of private, non-charitable trusts those which have included a condition separating parent and child have been declared void on grounds of public policy.[28] On analogy with such cases, Picarda has argued that any religious trust, where the religion concerned is adjudged to break up families, might similarly be declared to be void on grounds of public policy.[29] Equally, Picarda has argued that, 'a religion whose basic tenets and practices include psychological pressures on initiates could be accounted contrary to public policy as being inimical to public health in the mental sphere'.[30]

The difficulty in operating the morality test in *Thornton* v. *Howe* in a legal context is self-evident. What the courts are required to decide is not whether or not the religions in question have breached any civil or criminal legal rule (although evidence about such matters might be relevant to their operation of the morality test). If the religions are in breach of such rules legal action will follow in the normal way. Rather, the courts have to ask whether, despite the legality of the religion's actions, the religion is in some sense so detrimental to the functioning of society that it should not be accorded charitable status. Courts are not the obvious institution within which to debate what is and what is not a matter of fundamental morality; nor do they have manifest authority to decide on matters of social policy. Judges do not have any training in dealing with matters of purely ethical significance. Operation of the test makes the courts a vehicle for social policy-making alongside, and in addition to, the legislative role of Parliament.

One instance is sufficient to demonstrate the potential dangers involved in the operation of the morality test. If Picarda's suggestion about the potential invalidity of religious trusts where the religions are ajudged to break up families is taken seriously and literally, any charity connected with Christianity is put at risk. In Mark, Christ is reported as having said,

> For I have come to set a man against his father, a daughter against her mother, and a daughter-in-law against her mother-in-law.[31]

Nothing can be more calculated to split up families. Nor is this point one of purely academic theological conjecture. Any proselytising religion which holds itself out as having a unique truth will tend to split families in at least some instances. There are those who suggest that new religious movements, such as the Unification Church ('the Moonies'), are uniquely likely to sunder established families.[32] However, this is to misunderstand the relationship between such new religions and more traditional religions. The only difference between the Church of England and the Unification Church, with respect to their attitude towards the comparative merits of an adherent's loyalty to their church or their family, is the social context within which they operate. The Unification Church, being new and small, will, by the preaching of its truths, tend to draw its adherents further and further away from the social life they previously had. It 'offers the potential recruit the chance to be part of a family of like-minded people...'. '[P]arents will be unable to understand how their offspring could give up a promising future when everything seemed to be going exactly the way they wanted it to go for him.'[33] The Church of England, being older, larger and more deeply ingrained in the social fabric of English society, will, by the teaching of its truths, tend to confirm its adherents in the broad pattern of the social life that they and those around them have always enjoyed. Both churches offer truths and, in the end, believe those truths to be more important than familial contact. Does the mere fact that the Unification Church's truths are new mean they are contrary to public policy?[34]

Notwithstanding the objections to the morality test in *Thornton* v. *Howe* some have argued for its extension. The Goodman Committee stated that,

> however liberal or tolerant a society may be it has the duty to determine what is and what is not beneficial to it; accordingly between good and evil it cannot be neutral. It must exclude from charitable status what it regards as evil just as it can and does outlaw what it regards as detrimental to its moral welfare.[35]

On this basis the Committee concluded that the law should be extended so that those religions wishing to achieve charitable status should be required to 'satisfy the Charity Commissioners or the courts that their advancement is for the benefit of the community according to certain basic concepts which should be established.'[36]

As the government noted, in their most recent White Paper on charities, the Goodman Committee gave no guidance as to what the 'basic concepts' by which religions should be judged might be.[37] The Goodman Committee appear to be advocating a further departure from the principle of neutrality towards religions (in itself already brought into question by the morality test in *Thornton* v. *Howe*) in favour of an imposed standard of social morality which goes beyond the normal civil or criminal legal rules. Such a standard would not mean that some religions were made illegal. However, the operations of those religions which failed to meet the standard would be considerably disadvantaged in financial and other terms. Given the language of the Goodman Committee Report, the 'basic concepts' which the Committee had in mind seem to be ones which would be fundamentally illiberal, judging the religion not on the basis of whether or not it enables its adherents to follow what they determine are their own best ends but on the basis of what benefit the actions of those adherents bring to an undefined and vague concept of 'society' or 'community'. Personal autonomy would be sacrificed to an ill-conceived idea of the interests of society as a whole.

Those religions most at risk of falling foul of the Goodman test are clearly those whose status is suspect under the present *Thornton* v. *Howe* test. In Australia, Scientology, one example of such a religion, has been the beneficiary of a completely different approach to the question of its moral status and social effects to that used in *Thornton* v. *Howe* and expanded upon by the Goodman Committee. In *Church of the New Faith* v. *Pay Roll Tax Commissioners* the Australian High Court held that, '[r]egardless of whether...the practices of Scientology are harmful or objectionable...Scientology must, for all relevant purposes, be accepted as a religion in Victoria'.[38] In the course of his judgement in the case Murphy J stated that, '[a]dministrators and judges must resist the temptation to hold that groups or institutions are not religious because claimed religious beliefs or practices seem absurd, fraudulent, evil or novel.'[39] Mason ACJ and Brennan J, in their judgement, observed that, 'charlatanism is a necessary price of religious freedom'.[40] Since such an approach does not involve the courts making contingent and highly debatable judgements on the effects of particular religions it seems more likely to facilitate each individual's pursuit of their own autonomy in choosing their religion and is thus a preferable approach.

The definition of religion

English courts have rarely attempted to define religion either in the law of charities or in any other context. In 1917 Lord Parker gave what he believed to be the first judicial description of what constituted a religion for the purposes of the law of charities.[41] However, this description was little more than a history of the changing legal rules which had either penalised or tolerated various religions within Great Britain. Unsurprisingly, given the general history of Great Britain, Lord Parker's account of religion referred only to monotheistic religions. This led some commentators to infer that only monotheistic religions were recognised for the purposes of the law of charities.[42]

In *R. v. Registrar General ex parte Segerdal*, in defining the phrase 'religious worship', Lord Denning said,

> It connotes to my mind a place of which the principal use is as a place where people come together as a congregation or assembly to do reverence to God. It need not be the God which the Christians worship. It may be another God, or an unknown God, but it must be reverence to a deity. There may be exceptions. For instance, Buddhist temples are properly described as places of meeting for religious worship.[43]

This definition of religious worship is not of itself of direct relevance when deciding what meaning is to be given to the word 'religion' in the law of charities unless it is argued that 'religion' necessarily implies 'worship'.[44] Nevertheless, the decision has been one reason for a change in the attitude towards what constitutes a religion in the law of charities, leading commentators and judges to accept that monotheism is not always necessary.[45] In *Re South Place Ethical Society* Dillon J accepted, partly on the basis of the judgements in *R. v. Registrar General ex parte Segerdal*, that, in order for there to be a religion, there had to be a theistic element or some belief in a supreme being or supernatural element but he made no specific reference to any need for the religion to be monotheistic.[46] The government, in their most recent White Paper on charities, noted that Hinduism, a religion which is usually polytheistic, was one of the religions which had charities registered by the Charity Commissioners.[47] However, because they have no theistic content to their beliefs, groups such as the Secular Society and the South Place Ethical Society still cannot be registered as charitable religious trusts.

The increasing liberalisation of charity law, with the movement from requiring a monotheistic faith before a trust is accepted as charitable to the acceptance of polytheistic faiths, must be seen as being likely to enhance religious tolerance and, thus, increase religious freedom. More religions will gain the fiscal and other advantages of charitable status and thus religious pluralism is encouraged. Nevertheless, despite this advance, the judgements in cases like *R. v. Registrar General ex parte Segerdal* and *Re South Place Ethical Society* create as many problems as they solve.

In his judgement in *R. v. Registrar General ex parte Segerdal* Lord Denning noted that there might be exceptions to the test of religious worship that he had propounded.[48] He instanced Buddhism. Similarly in his judgement in *Re South Place Ethical Society* Dillon J observed that Buddhism might have to be treated as an exception to the rule that a religion was necessarily theistic.[49] A definition which contains an exception raises several questions. If the exception does not meet the terms of the definition why should it be encompassed in the definition? Does the need to accept the exception suggest a defect in the definition? If the exception is to be accepted are there further exceptions? According to what criteria should such putative exceptions be tested? If there are such criteria do they not then constitute a further and more sophisticated definition? If such criteria do not exist, how can one ever know what legitimately constitutes an exception to the normal definition?

Theravandic Buddhism is not the only belief, commonly described as a religion, which fails to exhibit any theistic elements. Jains, for example, do not recognise any supreme deity or creator and do not worship any gods.[50] If such religions are to be accepted as suitable objects for charitable religious trusts the question will then be how to justify the distinction drawn between them and organisations such the South Place Ethical Society. To say, as was said in *Re South Place Ethical Society*, that it does not meet the test in *R. v. Registrar General ex parte Segerdal* is not enough for the question must remain, why, like Buddhism and presumably Jainism, is the South Place Ethical Society not another exception to criteria used in the test?

In *Church of the New Faith v. Pay Roll Tax Commissioners* the Australian High Court described the British definition of religion as 'too narrow' and went on to produce rather more sophisticated tests to be used in determining whether or not something is a religion.[51] All three of the different tests in the Australian High Court accepted that a theistic element was not necessary for something to be characterised as a religion. Mason ACJ and Brennan J suggested that there was a need for a 'belief in a supernatural Being, Thing or Principle' plus an acceptance of canons of conduct which gave effect to that belief.[52] Murphy J looked for one out of a number of different constellations of beliefs of which the widest was, '[a]ny body which claims to be religious, and offers a way to finding meaning and purpose in life'.[53] Wilson and Deane JJ enumerated a number of different 'indicia', any of which might help to suggest that a body was religious. Although these indicia referred in the main to the supernatural they made no reference to deities or even, directly, to worship.

The advantage of the Australian tests lies not only in the fact that they are more liberal than the approach in *R. v. Registrar General ex parte Segerdal* and *Re South Place Ethical Society*. Indeed the degree to which the approaches really are broader and more liberal can be over-emphasised. Although the Australian approach did result in Scientology being characterised as a religion it is difficult to think of any other religion which it is clear that Australian courts would accept as a religion but British courts would reject. Plainly, the Australian courts would accept religions such as the Exclusive Brethren. However, the difficulty for British courts in such cases rests not in whether the body is a religion but whether, because of the morality test, the body is a religion which should be recognised for charitable status. It seems unlikely that the Australian courts would recognise the Secular Society as a religion. The Secular Society fails to pass even the most liberal test on offer in *Church of the New Faith v. Pay Roll Tax Commissioners*, whether the body offers a way to find meaning and purpose in life and holds itself out as being religious, since, although the Society arguably passes the first limb of the test, it clearly does not pass the second limb.[54] The position of the South Place Ethical Society in relation to the Australian tests is more difficult. Since one of the Society's objects is the 'cultivation of a rational religious sentiment' it arguably would fall within at least some of the *Church of the New Faith v. Pay Roll Tax Commissioners* tests.[55] The great strength of the Australian tests, however, lies in their individual intellectual coherence. It seems inconceivable that the British courts, anymore than the Australian courts, would fail to accept that the Jain faith is a religion. British courts, as noted above, have already accepted that all forms of Buddhism are religious sects. However, the Australian tests have the merit of providing a justification for the courts reasoning whilst the British courts are forced to rely on the creation of *ad hoc* exceptions to the general rule; these exceptions being *ex cathedra* statements made by people manifestly ill-equipped to assess the matters at issue.

Benefiting the public

The issue which has attracted the greatest criticism in analysis of the relationship between religion and the law of charities has been the court's treatment of the linked issues of what constitutes the advancement of religion and public benefit.

It has long been generally accepted that, in order for a religious trust to be charitable, the purposes of the trust must encompass some element of public benefit. Even Newark, in his article arguing against this proposition, begins by noting that the idea is commonly held amongst and has been applied by, the judiciary.[56] This proposition follows naturally from the broader suggestion that,

> the law recognizes no purpose as charitable unless it is of a public character. That is to say, a purpose must, in order to be charitable, be directed to the benefit of the community or a section of the community.[57]

In the case of putative religious charities either or both of two questions may arise. First, does the trust benefit a sufficient number of people to constitute 'a section of the public'? Secondly, what, in the context of religious trusts, may be said to be 'benefit'?

Crowther, in his book on religious trusts, summarises the rules relating to what can constitute a section of the community thus:

> Firstly, the beneficiaries who may benefit must not be numerically negligible, and, secondly, the quality which distinguishes the persons forming the class from other members of the community must not be dependant on their relationship to a particular person.[58]

In *Baddeley* v. *IRC* the Court of Appeal approved Harman J's first instance suggestion that a charitable trust might be properly constituted for the members of a particular church. In the instant case the trust was intended for such of the members of Stratford Newtown Methodist Mission, or such people who were likely to become members of the church, as who were of 'insufficient means' to otherwise enjoy the advantages provided by the trust.[59] In the Court of Appeal, as in the High Court, the decisive factor in the argument about whether members of a particular church were a sufficient section of the community for the purposes of the law of charities was that which united the members, their religious beliefs, was not something which was a 'relationship by the fact of blood, employment, or otherwise to some specified person or persons'.[60] Thus they could be said to constitute a section of the public.

In the House of Lords decision in the same case two judges held that membership of a particular church could not constitute a sufficient group of people so as to be a 'section of the public'. Viscount Simmonds argued that, although those who might be helped by the particular trust in the case might be a large section of the community, to accept the suggestion that religious groups could in themselves be a section of the community was to begin on 'a slippery slope' which might involve accepting very small numbers of people as being a section of the public; 'suppose the area [from which the church draws its membership] is a single street and the beneficaries to those whose creed commands few adherents'.[61] However, this rejection of the notion that membership of a particular church can constitute something which is for the benefit of a sufficient section of the community has to be seen in the light of the particular kind of charitable trust at issue in the case. The trust in *Baddeley* was argued to be one falling under the fourth head of charity in Lord MacNaghten's classification, trust for general purposes beneficial to the community.[62] Viscount Simmonds' arguments were explicitly put in this context and Lord Somerville, the other Law Lord who took the same view as Viscount Simmonds, said that, 'there might well be a valid trust for the promotion of religion benefiting a very small class', implicitly accepting that church membership might be sufficient to constitute a section of the community for the purposes of charitable religious trusts.[63] Neither Lord Tucker nor Lord Porter expressed any opinion on this point. Lord Reid in upholding the Court of Appeal did note that, '[t]here may be small sects which are not sufficiently numerous to form an appreciably important class of the community but no one would suggest that that is true of the Methodist Church'. However, once again one should note that Lord Reid's caveat was entered in the context of a charitable trust which was not held out as being a religious charitable trust.[64]

The view taken by the minority of the House of Lords may have some merit in the context of charities which do not fall under the first three specific heads of charity but which are, rather, supposed to be generally beneficial to the community. In such circumstances the notion of community becomes central to the essence of the charity and is therefore put under greater scrutiny. However, the minority House of Lords view seems to be of little merit in the context of religious trusts where the public benefit test is there simply to ensure that the fiscal and other advantages of charitable status do not accrue to private ends. As a purely empirical matter it is quite clear that religious trusts for the benefit of members of particular churches, chapels and synagogues have existed for several centuries and have long been regarded as charitable.[65] The Court of Appeal view does no more than recognise this fact. Yet it is arguably difficult to reconcile the Court of Appeal view in *Baddeley* with both earlier and later cases.

One earlier case which may seem to run counter to the Court of Appeal's view in *Baddeley* is the House of Lords decision in *Gilmour* v. *Coats*. In this case a trust for an enclosed order of Carmelite nuns was denied charitable status because, it was held, the trust failed the public benefit test.[66] Surely, it might be argued, an enclosed order of nuns is a religious community par excellence. If this group fails the public benefit test so must any church or sect. Picarada has suggested that such an argument would confuse the necessity for *benefit* and the necessity for *public* benefit. In *Gilmour* v. *Coats* the matter at issue was not, directly, whether there was a sufficient class of the community involved but whether there was any benefit at all.[67] The House of Lords held that the value of intercessory prayer and edification by example were matters which were either incapable of legal proof or were too vague and intangible to be capable of being a benefit for the purposes of the law of charities.[68]

Two later cases, *Neville Estates Ltd* v. *Madden* and *Holmes* v. *Attorney-General*, offer greater difficulties for those who wish to advance the proposition that an individual church can constitute a section of the community. In *Neville Estates Ltd* v. *Madden* the court held that a religious trust for the benefit of the members of Catford Synagogue was a valid charitable religious trust. However, in doing so Cross J said that, 'the members for the time being of the Catford Synagogue are no more a section of the public than the members for the time being of a Carmelite Priory'.[69] Cross J held that the trust was only valid because the members of the synagogue, unlike the Carmelite nuns, mixed with their fellow citizens and the court was, 'entitled to assume that some benefit accrues to the public from the attendance at places of worship of persons who live in this world and mix with their fellow citizens'.[70] The practical significance of this different analysis is small. Following Cross J's approach, since all religious groups (with the exception of enclosed contemplative orders) mix with outsiders to at least some limited extent religious trusts for the benefit of all such groups are valid charitable trusts. However, as will be seen below, Cross J's approach causes difficulties when looking at the court's general approach to what can constitute benefit.

In *Holmes* v. *Attorney-General* Walton J held that, 'it is not for the benefit of the adherents of the religion themselves that the law confers charitable status, it is in the interests of the public'.[71] Were this literally true the Court of Appeal's analysis in *Baddeley* would be wrong. However, it seems unlikely that Walton J's stark statement was meant to fully explain his analysis of public benefit. Holding that the trust whose status was at issue, which was for the benefit of the Exclusive Brethren, was a valid charitable religious trust, Walton J referred to the fact that the sect were willing to accept the participation of outsiders in some of their services and the existence of attempts by some of the Brethren to proselytise. For him these things provided sufficient contact with the wider community for there to be an element of public benefit. As with Cross J's approach above, the practical significance of the difference in Walton J's approach is small. Religious trusts for most, and probably all, Christian sects would be charitable under Walton J's test. However, Walton J's approach causes more problems for non-Christian groups. Whilst proselytising is not a feature unique to the Christian religion it is something more central to that faith than it is to many others. For religions such as Judaism, Islam and Hinduism Walton J's test would create more difficulties. Individual mosques, synagogues and temples might find it difficult to show that they engage in either of the activities that Walton J thought necessary to show public benefit. For this reason alone Walton J's approach seems to be a less expedient analysis of the law than that in *Baddeley* if the courts wish to maintain the stance that they make no distinction between different faiths.[72]

The definition of benefit

Determining what counts as benefit for the purposes of charity law has been a difficult conceptual task for the courts. In the leading case of *Gilmour* v. *Coats* the House of Lords decided that neither intercessory prayer nor edification by example constituted benefit.[73] In the view of the Law Lords it was necessary for the value of something to be capable of proof before it could be said to be a benefit. However, none of the Law Lords addressed the question of what criteria might be appropriate for determining proof of benefit.

As the Irish courts have observed, the House of Lords' failure in *Gilmour* v. *Coats* to specify the nature of the objective test to be applied for public benefit leaves the difficulty of deciding 'on what basis or criterion, unless a purely arbitrary one, the line [between that which is and that which is not benefit] can be drawn at any particular point?'.[74] For the Irish courts the activities of Carmelite nuns are 'a strong force in the advancement of religion' and are of 'spiritual benefit to a large section of the public'.[75] For the British courts, where the Protestant Church of England is the established church in much of the land, that which the Roman Catholic church accounts to be a benefit is of no account. The conclusion that, '[t]here could be no clearer statement of the Protestant insistence upon the utility of religious activity and the rejection of the pre-Reformation notion of spiritual improvement' is difficult to rebut.[76]

If the British court's vagueness about what constitutes benefit is one major difficulty in the law of charities the inconsistency in their application of the idea is another. In *Neville Estates* v. *Madden* the court found the element of benefit to be the fact that members of the Catford Synagogue, having worshipped in the synagogue, then mixed in ordinary society. 'As between different religions the law stands neutral, but it assumes that any religion is at least likely to be better than none.'[77] Thus, presumably, the proposition that those who have a faith, no matter what faith or how weak their faith, are thereby better citizens is deemed by the courts to be capable of proof and, indeed, to have been proven.[78] It is not clear from the cases where this proof is to be found.[79] Moreover, even this flawed notion of benefit has been inconsistently applied. In the earlier case of *Re Warre's Will Trusts* Harman J held that a gift to create a retreat house where members of the Church of England could stay for a short space of time 'for religious contemplation and the cleansing of the soul', was not for an activity which affected the public and therefore could not create a valid charitable trust.[80] If the judgement in *Neville Estates* v. *Madden* is correct Harman J should have held that the trust was charitable since people visiting the retreat were confirmed in their faith and such confirmation is of benefit to those people with whom they mix in the outside world. In a later case, *Re Banfield*, a gift to the Pilsdon Community was held to create a valid charitable religious trust because the community took in those who needed help for various reasons, 'such as drug addiction, or drink, or having been in prison, or even loneliness or mere failure to stand up to the strains of life'.[81] Goff J, in his judgement in *Re Banfield*, distinguished *Re Warre's Will Trusts* by saying the Pilsdon Community 'opens out to reach the community'. Earlier in his judgement he had commented that the Pilsdon Community existed, *inter alia*, 'to do the will of God in practical Christianity'.[82] Once again there is a clear contrast between the unacceptable face of pre-Reformation Christianity and the acceptable face of the Protestant reforms.

Further difficulties in applying the benefit test occur when different attitudes to what constitutes the advancement of religion are considered. In *Re Hummeltenberg* the court decided that a trust for the training of mediums was not a valid charitable trust since there was 'nothing but vague expressions of opinions and belief, directed in the main to alleged powers of diagnosis and healing attributed to some mediums' to show any element of public benefit.[83] However, the Charity Commissioners have held that a trust to further the work of Church of England clergymen as exorcists is a valid charitable religious trust.[84] What difference is there between the work of medium and that of exorcists except those differences consequent upon different religious beliefs? Gifts for a memorial stain glass window for a church are charitable.[85] In such cases, as Newark has observed, it is difficult to see where the element of benefit is to be found. There is a clear aesthetic advantage in such gifts but in what sense do they advance religion?[86] Gifts for a memorial tombstone are not charitable.[87] If memorial windows advance religion and benefit the public why is it not the same true for memorial tombstones? Trusts for the saying of masses are charitable but only so long as the masses are said in public.[88] If there is a public benefit in a public mass it is presumably in the fact that those worshipping will be strengthened in their faith. But, under Catholic doctrine, adherents are strengthened in their faith by their knowledge of the existence of private masses. Why should the absence or presence of a congregation make a difference to the law?

Newark, in an article which sought to show that public benefit was not an element necessary for a charitable religious trust, commented,

> If we are content to say that the advancement of religion...is charitable, and to abandon the search for public benefit, we are relieved from investigation into many matters with which the Courts are manifestly incompetent to deal. Divine Bounty and Edification are matters incapable of accurate analysis and evaluation by lawyers who are not trained as theologians, and the attempts of judges to make such analysis and evaluation merely distress the faithful and amuse the cynical.[89]

Whilst subsequent case law has shown Newark's expository account to be incorrect the passages in this book above suggest that, as censorial jurisprudence, his remarks remain true.

Conclusion

A supreme effort of synthesis might find a reconciliation for all the apparent contradictions in the law of charities' attitude towards religions. Such an effort, however, would miss the point. Lord Simmonds said of the law relating to charities, '[a] great body of law has...grown up. Often it may appear illogical and even capricious'.[90] So it does. So it is.

Commentators on the law through the years have been consistent in their criticism of the bias and incoherence of the law. Newark, writing in 1946, wrote that, 'legal historians of the future will trace the effect of Protestant thought on the development of trusts in post-reformation times'.[91] Hanbury's remarks in 1954 about the elements of bias in this area of law have already been noted at the beginning of this chapter.[92] Brady, in 1968, observed that, '[t]he very phrase "advancement of religion" has the ring of puritan evangelism about it...'.[93] Blakeney's comments about Protestant bias in his 1981 article have already been referred to above.[94] Other examples could be given. The need for reform is clear. At present the law is unjust because it distinguishes between different religious adherents in a manner which is arbitrary and incapable of rational defence. To clarify the law in a manner which would promote religious freedom would be a difficult task involving, as it necessarily would, the need to address the question of the definition of religion. It is perhaps a combination of the difficulty of the task and the small number of people actively mistreated by the present law which has resulted in the failure of successive governments to address the issues involved. However, neither matter justifies such failure and the present law of charity provides yet another illustration of the mixture of bias and muddle which characterises British law's attitude towards religions.

Notes

1. I Corinthians 13:13. This is to be found in the Authorised Version of the Bible. Some other translations substitute 'love' for 'charity'.
2. A. Guillaume, *Islam* Penguin Books (2nd ed., 1956) p. 69. *Zakat* are compulsory alms; *sadaqat*, voluntary alms.
3. W. Owen Cole and P. Singh Sambhi, *The Sikhs* Routledge and Kegan Paul, 1985 p. 178.
4. N. Chandrasekharan Aiyar (ed.), *Mayne's Treatise on Hindu Laws and Usage* Higginbothams Ltd., (11th ed., 1953) p. 911.
5. 'Though frequently neglected in practice...tenets [such as "good neighbourliness and the obligation to meet human need"] lay at the heart of the more ethical religions of the past, as well as the great living religions of today' (*Report of the Committee on the Law and Practice Relating to Charitable Trusts*, Cmd 8710 (1952) para. 34).
6. Scots law has traditionally not recognised a special category of charitable trusts. (K. Norrie and E. Scobbie *Trusts* W. Green, 1991, pp. 30–31; H. Picarda, *The Law and Practice Relating to Charities* Butterworths, 1977, pp. 12–14.)
7. For a fuller examination of the legal privileges accorded to charities see S. Bright, 'Charity and Trusts for the Public Benefit – Time for a Rethink?' (1989) 53 *Conveyancer and Property Lawyer* 28 at pp. 29–31. For an analysis of the fiscal benefits that charities have, see N. True, *Giving: How to Encourage Charity More* Centre for Policy Studies, 1990, p. 13.
8. *Hoare* v. *Osborne* (1866) LR 1 Eq 585 at p. 588.
9. *IRC* v. *Pemsel* [1891] AC 531 at p. 583, HL. Although this classification of the different heads of charity has generally been accepted it is not determinant of what, at law, constitutes a charity. In *Scottish Burial Reform and Cremation Society Ltd* v. *Glasgow Corporation* [1968] AC 138, HL Lord Wilberforce observed (at p. 154) that there might be charities which did not neatly fall under any of the four heads in Lord MacNaghten's classification.
10. *Ibid.*
11. Thus, for example, Brady notes that, '[t]he Catholic Church derives much of its revenue from mass honoraria and the bequest for masses is a ubiquitous feature of Catholic wills'. J. Brady, 'Some Problems Touching the Nature of Bequests for Masses in Northern Ireland' (1968) 19 *Northern Ireland Legal Quarterly* 357 at p. 357.
12. C. Crowther, *Religious Trusts* George Ronald, 1954.
13. M. Blakeney, 'Sequestered Piety and Charity – A Comparative Analysis' (1981) 2 *Journal of Legal History* 207 at p. 211.
14. See respectively Cross J in *Neville Estates Ltd* v. *Madden* [1962] 1 Ch 832, ChD at p. 853 and Lord Simmonds in *Gilmour* v. *Coats* [1949] AC 426, HL at p. 446.
15. *Thornton* v. *Howe* (1862) 31 Beav 14.

16. An account of Southcott's life is to be found at 24 *Edinburgh Review* 453.
17. *Thornton* v. *Howe op. cit.*, at p. 18 and p. 19 respectively.
18. *Thornton* v. *Howe op. cit.*, at p. 19.
19. *Re Watson* [1973] 1 WLR 1472, ChD, at p. 1477.
20. *Re Pinion* [1965] Ch 85, CA, at p. 105. These remarks are *obiter* since *Re Pinion* concerned a putative educational charitable trust.
21. Picarda, *op. cit.*, p. 55.
22. *Thrupp* v. *Collett* (1858) 26 Beav 125.
23. *Thornton* v. *Howe op. cit.*, at p. 19.
24. See, for example, Picarda, *op. cit.*, p. 56 and D. Hayton (ed.), *Hayton and Marshall: Cases and Commentary on the Law of Trusts* Sweet and Maxwell (9th ed., 1991) at p. 329.
25. For critical judicial comment about Scientology see *Hubbard* v. *Vosper* [1972] 2 QB 84, CA, *Church of Scientology* v. *Kaufman* [1973] RPC 635, CA and *Re B and G* [1985] 1 FLR 134, FD. Scientology might also fail to meet some of the other tests which trust for the advancement of religion have to pass in order to acquire charitable status.
26. The Commissioners noted their willingness to register such trusts in *Report of the Charity Commissioners for England and Wales for the Year 1981* (1982) HC 363 paras 22–30.
27. *Holmes* v. *Attorney-General The Times*, 12 February 1981. A full report of this case is to be found on LEXIS.
28. See, for example, Parker J in *Re Sandbrook* [1912] 2 Ch 471, ChD at p. 478.
29. H. Picarda, 'New Religions as Charities' (1983) 131 *New Law Journal* 436 at p. 437.
30. Picarda (1983) *loc. cit.*
31. Mark 10:35. See also Matthew 19: 28–30, Mark 10: 29–30 and Luke 12: 51–53 for other similar pronouncements.
32. See, for example, remarks in a debate in the House of Commons on the Unification Church at (1981–82) *Hansard*, HC, Vol 24, cols 1165–116, May 28, 1982.
33. E. Barker, *The Making of a Moonie* Basil Blackwell, 1984, pp. 244, 252.
34. In their 1982 report the Charity Commissioners reported that they had decided that there was no good reason why trusts operated by the Unification Church should be denied charitable status (*Report of the Charity Commissioners for England and Wales for the Year 1982* (1983) HC 370 paras 36–38 and Appendix C).
35. *Charity Law and Voluntary Organisations* (The Goodman Report) Bedford Square Press, 1976, p. 24.
36. Goodman Committee, *loc. cit.*
37. *Charities: A Framework for the Future*, Cm 694 (1989) para. 2.27.
38. *per* Wilson and Deane JJ in *Church of the New Faith* v. *Pay Roll Tax Commissioners* (1983) 57 AJLR 785 at p. 808.
39. *Church of the New Faith* v. *Pay Roll Tax Commissioners op. cit.*, at p. 795.
40. *Church of the New Faith* v. *Pay Roll Tax Commissioners op. cit.*, at p. 791. This particular statement should be contrasted with the failure by British courts to recognise the Church of the Agapemonites (see Picarda (1977) *op. cit.*, at p. 56).
41. In *Bowman* v. *Secular Society Limited* [1917] AC 406 at pp. 448–450.
42. See, for example, *Tudor on Charities* Sweet and Maxwell (6th ed., 1967) p. 59.
43. *R.* v. *Registrar General ex parte Segerdal* [1970] 2 QB 697, CA at p. 707.
44. Something that would be difficult to maintain in the light of those beliefs, apparently religious, which include both evil and good gods (see, for example, the figure of Angra Mainyu in the Zoroastrian faith) and those which suggest that God should be ignored in the search for enlightenment (see, for example, the Gnostic teachings described in E. Pagels, *The Gnostic Gospels* Penguin Books, 1982 p. 18).

45. See, for example, S. Maurice (ed.), *Tudor on Charities* Sweet and Maxwell (7th ed) (1984) p. 55.

46. *Re South Place Ethical Society* [1980] 1 WLR 1567 at pp. 1572–1573.

47. *Charities: A Framework for the Future, op. cit.*, para. 2.19. For discussion of monotheistic forms of Hinduism see P. Bowes, *The Hindu Religious Tradition: A Philosophical Approach* Routledge and Kegan Paul, 1977, pp. 33–34.

48. *R. v. Registrar General ex parte Segerdal op. cit.*, at p. 707.

49. *Re South Place Ethical Society op. cit.*, at p. 1573.

50. See K. Folkert, 'Jainism' in J. Hinnells (ed.), *A Handbook of Living Religions* Penguin Books, 1985, p. 262.

51. *Church of the New Faith* v. *Pay Roll Tax Commissioners op. cit.*, pp. 790 and 791.

52. *Church of the New Faith* v. *Pay Roll Tax Commissioners op. cit.*, p. 789.

53. *Church of the New Faith* v. *Pay Roll Tax Commissioners op. cit.*, p. 796.

54. *Church of the New Faith* v. *Pay Roll Tax Commissioners loc. cit.* and *Bowman* v. *Secular Society* [1917] AC 406 at pp. 418–419.

55. *Re South Place Ethical Society op. cit.*, p. 1569.

56. F. Newark, 'Public Benefit and Religious Trusts' (1946) 62 *Law Quarterly Review* 234 at p. 234.

57. This passage, which comes from the fifth edition of *Tudor on Charities*, was cited with approval by Lord Greene MR in *Re Compton* [1945] Ch 123, CA at p. 128.

58. Crowther, *op. cit.*, p. 21.

59. *Baddeley* v. *IRC* [1953] 3 WLR 135, CA approving *Baddeley* v. *IRC* 1 WLR 84, ChD.

60. *per* Evershed MR *Baddeley* v. *IRC* [1953] 3 WLR 135 at p. 145 (see also Jenkins LJ at pp. 161–162).

61. *Inland Revenue Commissioners* v. *Baddeley* [1955] 2 WLR 552 at p. 561.

62. *IRC* v. *Pemsel op. cit.*, p. 583.

63. *Inland Revenue Commissioners* v. *Baddeley op. cit.*, p. 582.

64. *Inland Revenue Commissioners* v. *Baddeley op. cit.*, p. 575. Given the conditions in the trust, Lord Reid presumably meant that no one could suggest that members of a particular Methodist Church were not sufficiently numerous to constitute a section of the public, not that no one could contend that the Methodist Church as a national body was not sufficiently numerous to be a section of the public. However, if this is so, Lord Reid is surely incorrect. If a sect can be too small to constitute a section of the public it is by no means implausible, given the level of church membership noted in chapter 1, to suggest that some groups of Methodists are too small to constitute a section of the public.

65. See, for example, those referred to by Cross J in *Neville Estates Ltd* v. *Madden* [1962] 1 Ch 832, ChD, at p. 854.

66. *Gilmour* v. *Coats* [1949] AC 426, HL.

67. Picarada, *op. cit.*, p. 17.

68. See Lord Simmonds in *Gilmour* v. *Coats op. cit.*, at p. 446, Lord du Parcq at p. 453 and Lord Reid at p. 459.

69. *Neville Estates Ltd* v. *Madden op. cit.*, at p. 853.

70. *Neville Estates Ltd* v. *Madden loc. cit.*

71. *Holmes* v. *Attorney-General The Times*, 12 February 1981. All quotations in this book are taken from the full report of the case available on LEXIS.

72. In any event both Walton J's analysis and that of Cross J are merely High Court dicta.

73. *Gilmour* v. *Coats op. cit.*, at pp. 446, 453 and 459.

74. *per* Dixon J in *Re Sheridan* [1957] IR 257 at p. 275.

75. *Re Sheridan op. cit.*, at p. 279.

76. Blakeney, *op. cit.*, at p. 215.

77. *per* Cross J in *Neville Estates Ltd* v. *Madden op. cit.*, at p. 583.

78. There is a similar statement by Walton J in *Holmes* v. *Attorney-General op cit.* and other equivalent propositions can be found in earlier cases (see, for example, Lord Reid in *Gilmour* v. *Coats* at p. 459).

79. It might well be argued that this proposition is simply one that the courts take from the accretion of case-law without having to hear argument on the matter. Whilst this argument might explain the position that the law has reached it will not clarify the conceptual muddle that has resulted.

80. *Re Warre's Will Trusts* [1953] 1 WLR 725, ChD, at pp. 728–729.

81. *per* Goff J *Re Banfield* [1968] 1 WLR 846, ChD at p. 850. Some members of the community also went out into the outside world to provide help where required. Whilst it is clear that this could also be regarded as a form of public benefit, Goff J's judgement does not seem to regard this extra element as being necessary to show public benefit overall.

82. *per* Goff J in *Re Banfield op. cit.*, at p. 850 and p. 852.

83. *per* Russell J in *Re Hummeltenberg* [1923] 1 Ch 237 at p. 241. The case concerned an attempt to establish that the trust was a valid charitable trust under the fourth head of charity, purposes generally beneficial to the community.

84. *Report of the Charity Commissioners for England and Wales for the Year 1976* (1977) HC 389 paras 65–68.

85. *Hoare* v. *Osborne* (1866) 1 Eq 585.

86. Newark, *op. cit.*, pp. 236–237.

87. *Mellick* v. *Asylum President and Guardians* (1821) Jac 180.

88. *Re Hethrington* [1990] 1 Ch 1, ChD.

89. Newark, *op. cit.*, at p. 245.

90. *Gilmour* v. *Coats op. cit.*, p. 443.

91. Newark, *op. cit.*, at p. 235.

92. See n. 9 and the text thereto.

93. Brady, *op. cit.*, at p. 375.

94. See n. 13 and the text thereto.

Part 3:

Solutions

8 Protecting the religious conscience

Introduction

The various chapters in Part 2 of this book have illustrated some of the different points at which religions and legal rules interconnect and often conflict with each other in Great Britain. Most of these illustrations have shown how individual legal rules affect social practices which result from the religious beliefs of different individuals or groups of individuals. The contact and conflict has not been the direct result of a legal rule seeking to forbid a particular religious practice; still less have the illustrations shown cases where there has been any attempt to question the legal status of any religion taken as a whole. However, the illustrations have usually been of a negative character, showing the problems that legal rules cause for believers. This is a fair reflection of the relationship between legal rules and religions in Great Britain. The general picture is one where legal rules, if they impact upon faith at all, are usually detrimental to the lives of believers.

Notwithstanding this general picture, there are occasions when legal rules attempt to take account of the particular difficulties inherent in an attempt to live a life of faithful adherence to the dictates of a religion. Reference was made to some such rules in Part 2 where they took the form of particular exemptions from a general legal pattern for those of specific individual faiths. Thus, for example, in chapter 3 there was discussion of the legal rules that exist for those who wish to marry using Jewish or Quaker procedures. This is one way in which the law seeks to accommodate the needs of believers. Another way in which the law seeks to take account of the special position of those who have a strong religious belief is to provide overall exemptions to particular legal regimes on general grounds of religious faith. It is on examples of these kinds of rules that this chapter concentrates.

Religion and trade union membership

In 1971, with the passing of the Industrial Relations Act, the closed shop first received statutory recognition. Under the 1971 Act, where there was either 'an agency shop agreement' or 'an approved closed shop agreement', a worker, who refused to join the appropriate union, could be dismissed by the employer, because of that refusal, without the employer being liable for unfair dismissal.[1]

However, the 1971 Act did not permit a fully 'closed' shop. Where there was an agency shop agreement a worker was given the right, under s 6(1), to make payments to the union in lieu of membership. Under s 9(1), any worker who objected 'on grounds of conscience' both to being a member of a trade union and to making payments in lieu, could, instead, make equivalent payments to a charity. Where there was an approved closed shop, Part IV of Schedule 1 to the Act enabled a worker, who objected on grounds of conscience to being a member of a trade union, to make appropriate contributions to charity.

The implementation of the 1971 Act, with its general conscientious objection formulae, had relatively little actual effect on the position of conscience objectors *qua* objectors. The Act gave protection only to agreements concluded by unions registered under the Act.[2] The TUC decided that it would expel any union which continued its registration.[3] Only two unions of any size, the National Union of Bank Employees and the Bakers' Union, failed to deregister.[4] Consequently, very few agency shop agreements were drawn up. Similarly there were very few approved closed shops.[5] This is not to say that there were a similarly small number of *de facto* closed shops. Surveys indicated that the majority of employers attempted to maintain existing closed shops outside the framework of the law even though this caused them, 'difficulties and expense'.[6] In such cases, conscientious objectors could, if dismissed because of their refusal to join a union, sue for unfair dismissal. However, this was by virtue of their rights under sections 22 and 24 of the 1971 Act, as workers, rather than under section 6 or Schedule 1, as conscientious objectors. In law there was no closed shop for them to object to.

There were very few reported cases in which the tribunals and courts were asked to determine the precise ambit of the conscientious objection formulae under the 1971 Act. Two cases, *Drury* v. *The Bakers Union (Southern District)* and *Hynds* v. *Spillers-French Baking Ltd*, concerned agency shop agreements.[7] In *Drury*, decided before an Industrial Tribunal, the Tribunal noted that the 1971 Act gave no guidance on what constituted 'grounds of conscience'. The Tribunal held that religious grounds could 'justifiably be put forward as grounds of conscience.[8] In *Hynds* v. *Spillers-French Baking Ltd*, heard before the National Industrial Relations Court, the Court went much further, holding that '"grounds of conscience" necessarily pointed to and involved a belief or conviction based on religion in the broadest sense contrasted with personal feeling, however strongly held, or intellectual creed'.[9] Thus, following *Hynds*, 'conscientious objection' under the 1971 Act became 'religious objection'.

In support of its assertion in *Hynds* that conscientious objection necessarily involved objection on grounds of religion the National Industrial Relations Court simply cited two previous cases, *Drury*, which had merely said that a religious objection was a conscientious objection without averring to the possibility of reversing the proposition, and *Newell* v. *Gillingham Corporation*.

Newell was a case decided during the Second World War. Newell, who was registered as a conscientious objector under s 5 of the National Service (Armed Forces) Act 1939, was dismissed by his employers, Gillingham Corporation because of his registration. In his judgement in *Newell*, Mr Justice Atkinson said that Newell

was not a conscientious objector in the true sense. He was a political conscientious objector. A true conscientious objector, which is what Parliament had in mind [when passing the 1939 Act], is one who on religious grounds thinks it is wrong to kill and to resist force by force. He thinks that that is the teaching of Christ.[10]

Mr Justice Atkinson went on to quote the example of Quakers as 'true conscientious objectors'. These pronouncements by Mr Justice Atkinson seem to owe more to the emotions of the times than to any sustained attempt to analyse the meaning of the relevant parts of the National Service (Armed Forces) Act 1939. Later on in his judgement Mr Justice Atkinson called Newell, 'defeatist', 'pro-German' and a 'humbug'.[11] There is nothing in either Mr Justice Atkinson's judgement, nor the 1939 Act with which his judgement was ostensibly concerned, to justify the proposition that 'conscientious objection' should be treated as a synonym for 'religious objection'. Moreover, the actual bodies charged with interpreting and applying the conscientious objection clause in the 1939 Act, local tribunals and appellate tribunals set up particularly for that purpose under Schedule 1 of the Act, acknowledged four categories of legitimate conscientious objectors under the Act. One of these categories was indeed religious objection. However, the other three categories were those objecting on ethical grounds, those objecting on aesthetic grounds and those objecting on political grounds.[12]

Hynds illustrates the difficulty that the courts feel they have in dealing with concepts such as 'conscientious objection'. Faced with a seemingly indeterminate phrase the court sought to give it a concrete and limited meaning. That that meaning owed nothing to anything that could be found in the 1971 Act and rested on a single negligible High Court judgement mattered less than the apparent clarity of the definition that resulted.

Notwithstanding its manifest intellectual limitations, the decision in *Hynds* was used to support the Labour administration's reforms which overturned the 1971 Act, limiting the right to object to joining a closed shop to religious objection only. Under Schedule 1, para 6(5), of the Trade Union and Labour Relations Act (1974), an employee could object to joining a properly constituted union membership agreement (the 1974 Act's new formula for a statutorily recognised closed shop) only if the employee had an objection 'on grounds of religious belief to being a member of any trade union whatsoever or on any reasonable grounds to being a member of a particular trade union'. Section 1 of the Trade Union and Labour Relations Act 1976 further restricted the right of objection by deleting everything after 'whatsoever'.

Citing *Hynds* and the unreported case of *Woolam* v. *National Union of Insurance Workers* in debate in the House of Lords, Lord Jacques argued that the 1974 changes only reflected the way in which the courts and tribunals had already interpreted the seemingly broader conscience clause in the 1971 Act.[13] Further, it was argued by others, religious objections represented a more objective phenomena than the vague and inherently subjective notion of conscience.[14] In debate on the 1971 Act, Lord Pearson, then a Law Lord, had assured the House of Lords that 'religious conscience' would be an 'easy formulation' for the courts to interpret.[15] Pragmatically, the 1974 and 1976 changes seemed to produce a formulation which was much more mangeable for the courts. Subsequent case-law was to suggest a very different story.

In successively reported cases concerning the 1976 Act the courts and tribunals began by rejecting the notion that the Act imported any suggestion that objectors must show a written rule in the Church to which they claimed adherence forbidding trade union membership, went on to say that objectors need not show that other adherents shared their conception of their Church's beliefs and finished by saying that an objector came within the terms of the Act even though his belief about non-membership of a trade union was an individual conviction about Christian principles which was at odds with the teaching of his Church and the beliefs of his fellow adherents.[16] The objective phenomenon of religious belief had come to be determined using the purely subjective phenomenon of personal conviction.

Whilst the court's interpretation of the 1976 Act was clearly at odds with the intentions of at least some of those who had supported the Act as it passed through Parliament it is not clear how else the courts could have approached the religious objection clause without depriving it of most of its operative effect. The proponents of the religious objection clause in the 1974 and 1976 Acts simply failed to understand the full measure of the complexity of religious behaviour.

Church membership is often objectively ascertainable. Many religious groups will have a core membership whose identity is beyond question. For some groups a clear statement of membership of the group will be an inalienable part of the beliefs that distinguish the group from other faiths. Thus, for example, Beckford writes that, '[b]y contrast with some other modes of religious sociation…it is theoretically impossible to be a Jehovah's witness without joining a local congregation and without remaining firmly in association with it'.[17] Even here however, where membership of a particular church or sect is concerned, groups may be amorphous, fluid bodies whose precise membership is difficult to settle. Thus, to take as an example a religious group which is well-established in Great Britain, who is correctly to be considered a member of the Quakers? Is it someone who attends Meeting (the Quaker service of worship) on an occasional basis, someone who is classified by the Society officially as an 'attender' or only someone who has become a full, official member of the Society?[18] And if the criteria of membership is taken to be the latter, why is someone who is a full, official member of the Society to be counted, despite the fact that they may be both irregular and occasional in their attendance at Meeting, whilst a person who regularly but occasionally attends is not counted?

The question of determining what is and what is not a religious belief is even more difficult than determining church membership. Plainly it is not possible to limit the definition of a religious belief to something that is an accepted belief reduced to a written form by a particular religious group. It does not usually lie in the nature of religious groups to produce detailed official rule-books prescribing all social behaviour for adherents.[19] Religious belief, even in one group, is rarely uniform and there is usually room for a degree of individual interpretation. Even if belief were uniform, the process of schism would neccesitate allowance for the believer who is moving away from the main body of the group. Luther is constantly in the process of nailing his Ninety-five Theses to the church door and his beliefs are religious long before a new Church has formed behind him. Religious belief is as subjective as any other form of intellectual or emotional belief.[20] It was almost inevitable that the courts would recognise this.

When the principle of objection to trade union membership based only on religious conviction had been introduced the then Labour administration had recognised the weakness of their ethical position in privileging religion over conscience, arguing that they were doing so because of a matter of legislative expediency rather than principle.[21] Subsequent case-law showed this expediency to be chimerical thus casting a stronger light on the law's unequal treatment of the secular and the religious.

The only attempt to separate religious objection off from general conscientious objection as a discrete conceptual category had been founded on the argument that religion, but not conscience, was a matter of faith.[22] Conscience, it was argued, was, by definition, a matter of reasoning. Conscience could objectively be questioned. Faith could only be accepted or ignored. And, it was said, 'in a civilised society' religious consciences should be recognised.[23] Not everyone had accepted this distinction. Lord Houghton of Sowerby had asserted that, 'most grounds of conscience are unreasonable, which means that they are not open to reason'.[24] Christopher Tugenhadt had argued that, '[c]onscience can take many different forms. A sign of the civilised society is that it respects the form that conscience takes.'[25]

In 1980 the statutory formula allowing someone to object to being made to join a closed shop, changed once again. Under s 7 of the Employment Act 1980 the right of objection was widened to include anyone who 'genuinely objects on grounds of conscience or other deeply held personal conviction to being a member of any trade union whatsoever or of a particular trade union'.[26]

Any proposal for a general right of conscientious objection to any individual law risks the objection that the proposal usurps the very purpose of law. After all, if any individual may be excused obedience to the law simply because of the dictates of their conscience, what imperative message does law have? And, if law looses its imperative content, what does it have left? An examination of the judgements interpreting the conscientious objection formula in the 1980 Act suggests that there is some strength in such remarks.

In *Home Delivery Services* v. *Shackcloth* the Employment Appeal Tribunal held that the phrase, 'deeply held personal conviction' in the 1980 Act did not impute any moral consideration on the part of the objector.[27] Moreover, the Employment Appeal Tribunal held specifically that a belief that the union had failed to look after the interests of the objector could amount to a deeply held personal conviction.[28] Shackcloth, who sought to leave the trade union USDAW, had been a member of the union for the four years between his joining Home Delivery Services and deciding to leave the union. He had also been a member of the union during his one year's previous employment with the firm. He had no objection in principle to joining trade unions. The examples of his complaints given by the Employment Appeal Tribunal either related to the union's relationship with its members or to its dealings with Home Delivery Services Ltd.[29] Shackcloth simply did not think USDAW was a good union for him to belong to.

The decision in Shackcloth considerably widened the scope of possible legitimate reasons for objection to trade union membership which had been developed under previous legislation. In *Westhead* v. *National Union of Seamen*, Westhead had been denied the status of a conscientious objector under the 1971

Act by an Industrial Tribunal.[30] Westhead had history of union membership both before his employment as a seaman and for some time whilst he was a seaman. His objections to the NUS were based on his assessment of the way in which the union treated its members and his opinion of it negotiating competence. The case is thus almost precisely analogous with *Shackcloth*. Like Shackcloth, Westhead would have been willing to join a trade union if he considered that it was acting in his best interests. The tribunal characterised these objections as 'grounds of expediency' rather than grounds of conscience.[31] In *Shackcloth* it was held that a matter of expediency could amount to a deeply held personal conviction.

Taken alone, the decision in *Shackcloth* might suggest that any reason for not wanting to join a trade union would be sufficient for the purposes of the 1980 Act. Moreover, other decisions would seem to add weight to this contention. In *Thorpe* v. *General Motors* an Industrial Tribunal held that the reason an employee had for not wanting to join a trade union did not even have to be 'reasonable, correct, justifiable or anything of the sort'; it simply had to be 'a deeply held personal conviction'.[32] In *Wellstead* v. *Foilwraps Ltd* an employee who, like Shackcloth, left a union because of his disagreement with its policies, again like Shackcloth, succeeded in convincing an Industrial Tribunal that he had a deeply held personal conviction which prevented him continuing his union membership.[33] Such cases appear to confirm the thesis that the formula in the 1980 Act allows any dissenter to avoid the normal affect of the law. However, the case-law is not all one way.

In *McGhee* v. *British Road Services Ltd* an Employment Appeal Tribunal refused to overturn an Industrial Tribunal's finding that McGhee did not have a 'deeply held personal conviction' to being a member of a trade union.[34] Like Shackcloth and Wellstead, McGhee had a history of trade union membership but had come to object to the way the union treated him and, to some extent, his fellow employees. Noting that they could only overturn the Industrial Tribunal's decision if it contained an error of principle, the Employment Appeal Tribunal held that they could detect no such error in the Tribunal's handling of McGhee's case. The Employment Appeal Tribunal held that, in assessing matters 'as personal and subjective as an individual's conscience and the depth of his conviction', the tribunal which actually hears the person claiming the conviction giving evidence is almost uniquely qualified to make the decision. However, the Employment Appeal Tribunal did say that a majority of its members, had they been members of the original Industrial Tribunal, would have been minded to find for McGhee.[35] In the similar case of *McKenzie* v. *Nairn Floors Ltd* a Scottish Employment Appeal Tribunal refused to overturn an Industrial Tribunal's decision that an employee whose 'views on trade union membership were shallow and superficial and had not been formed after considering the matter in detail' did not have a genuine deeply held personal conviction preventing them joining a trade union.[36] As in *McGhee*, the Employment Appeal Tribunal held that, providing the Industrial Tribunal addressed itself to the correct question, decisions about whether or not someone actually had a genuine deeply held person conviction were primarily matters for the Industrial Tribunal. The Industrial Tribunal had accepted that a genuine conviction might be ill-founded or absurd. The shallowness and superficiality of McKenzie's beliefs simply led them to refuse to accept that they were genuinely 'deeply held'. Finally, there is the case of *Chauhan* v. *Ford Motor Company*.[37] Chauhan's membership of his union lapsed. Three years later this lapse in membership came to the attention of the relevant union. At this point Chauhan refused to rejoin the union although he did offer to pay a sum to charity equivalent to the amount of union dues. Chauhan explained that his membership of the Radhaswami sect, a Hindu body, prevented him joining a union and he quoted from the Hindu scripture, *The Laws of Manu*, in support of his position.[38] Having explained his position, Chauhan refused to take part in a company appeals procedure designed to test whether or not he had sufficient conscientious or other objection to trade union membership. Given this refusal, and in the light of Chauhan's three-year silence about his objection to union membership, the Employment Appeal Tribunal accepted that an Industrial Tribunal could legitimately conclude that Chauhan had not got a genuine deeply held personal conviction preventing him joining a union.[39]

The then government did not intend the formula introduced by the 1980 Act, 'to cover those with trivial, superficial or transitory objections to union membership'.[40] The history of attempts by tribunals to interpret and apply the formula in the 1980 Act illustrates how difficult it is to both give full weight to the scope of genuine deeply held personal convictions, allowing for the almost infinite variety of what idiosyncratic individuals can regard as matters of great moment, whilst all the time keeping sight of the fact that the convictions have to be deeply held. In making determinations on such matters the actual composition of the tribunal can be the most important factor dictating the outcome of the case.[41] However, the full history of the interpretation of the 1980 Act indicates that the tribunals have sought to avoid holding that every objection to trade union membership is a deeply held personal conviction whilst remembering that every objection to trade union membership can be a deeply held personal conviction.[42] This liberality gives the fullest possible weight to objections to union membership based on religious conviction.[43]

Religion and conscientious objection to abortion

The history of the legislative reaction to conscientious objection to the closed shop shows the courts trying to grapple with the problem of giving a definite meaning to broadly constructed legal formulae. Section 4 of the Abortion Act 1967 illustrates two very different problems with a similar provision.

The Abortion Act 1967 laid down certain conditions under which a pregnancy might lawfully be terminated. Section 4(1) of the 1967 Act says, *inter alia*, that,

> [N]o person is under any duty, whether by contract or by any statutory or other legal requirement, to participate in any treatment authorised by this Act to which he has a conscientious objection.

Anybody claiming the benefit of section 4 must, themselves, prove that they have a conscientious objection.[44] Furthermore, section 4(1) does not apply if there is any duty to participate in treatment which is necessary to save the life or prevent grave permanent injury to the physical or mental health of a pregnant woman.[45]

Although the conscience clause in the Abortion Act is a secular provision, protecting all consciences whether they have a religious basis or not, a desire to protect religious and specifically Roman Catholic consciences was part of the motivation which led some people to press for the provision. Simon Mahon, in Standing Committee debate, asserted that the National Health Service depended upon foreign nurses, mentioning in particular Irish nurses. He argued that a conscience clause had to be inserted into the Act to satisfy these people or they would take their skills elsewhere.[46] Whilst Mahon did not base his argument solely on the proposition that these foreign nurses were Roman Catholics, elsewhere in debate it was the position of those of the Roman Catholic faith that was constantly adverted to. Thus, for example, Bernard Braine argued that Roman Catholics would no longer be recruited into the Health Service if there was no conscience clause.[47] Norman St John Stevas, as he then was, argued that, in the absence of a conscience clause, Catholics already in the Health Service would have to leave.[48] However, although for some people the major importance of the conscience clause lay in its ability to protect religious conscience, they often grounded their argument for the necessity of protecting such consciences on a more universal ethical base. Thus, Bernard Braine argued that, 'it is...one of the best features of our way of life in Britain that we recognise the right of conscientious objection on moral grounds'.[49] Norman St John Stevas rested his arguments for a conscience clause on the need for a pluralistic reciprocity in recognising one group's belief in the need for more liberal abortion laws and other people's abhorrence of the idea.[50]

The effectiveness of the conscience clause in the Abortion Act has to be judged by taking into account a number of factors. One of those factors is the interpretation given to the clause by the courts. To date the only reported instance where the interpretation of the conscience clause has been a central issue in court is in a case which concerned the dismissal from her employment of a Mrs Janaway, a medical secretary and receptionist.[51] Janaway had declined to type a letter of referral arranging for a patient to see a consultant with a view to an abortion. After a series of meetings with her, the Area Health Authority, her employers, dismissed her. A subsequent Appeal Tribunal, at the Authority, upheld Janaway's dismissal. She then made an application for judicial review, seeking an order of *certiorari* quashing the Authority's decision and a declaration that, by reason of the combined effect of her conscientious objection and s 4(1) of the 1967 Act, she was under no duty to type letters of the kind in issue.

Nine judges heard the Janaway case; one at first instance, three in the Court of Appeal and five in the House of Lords. Although all nine judges concurred in concluding that Mrs Janaway could not claim the benefit of s 4(1), they did not agree in the reasons they gave for reaching this conclusion.

All the reasoned judgements in the case were based on the premise that the interpretation of the conscience clause is central to the outcome of the case.[52] However, the precise question(s) that judges thought had to be addressed varied greatly from judgement to judgement. Stocker LJ found that the one central question was 'whether the conscience clause is available to all those exempted from criminal liability by section 1(1) [of the Abortion Act 1967] or whether it is confined to those concerned with "treatment" at a prescribed hospital'.[53] Slade LJ, on the other hand, saw three questions as arising: who could claim exemption from criminal liability for taking part in an abortion under s 1, to whom did s 4(1) apply and could Janaway invoke s 4(1)?[54] Balcombe LJ adopted Slade LJ's classification of the issues but, in his judgement, addressed himself only to Slade LJ's second question.[55] Neither Nolan J nor Lord Keith amplified the statement that the case turned upon the interpretation of section 4(1).[56]

Differences in the formulation of the issues in the case may, in part, be due to mere stylistic preferences. Plainly Stocker LJ's question is not the only one that he will have to answer. At some stage he too will have to face Slade LJ's third question. Balcombe LJ looked at matters pertaining to Slade LJ's first question in answer to his own second. Equally Slade LJ's first two questions are subsumed under one heading by Stocker LJ. Lord Keith and Nolan J implicitly expanded on their opening statements by the manner of their subsequent arguments. However, the different questions are also suggestive of different approaches to the interpretation of the conscience clause. For Stocker LJ and Slade LJ the conscience clause and s 1(1) were closely linked together. Balcombe LJ, by referring only to Slade LJ's second question, broadens the range of possible answers to it. He left open, at least at the beginning of his judgement, the possibility of a more distant connection between the conscience clause and s 1(1).

For both Slade LJ and Stocker LJ Janaway's case was essentially one concerned with criminal law. When discussing whether or not Janaway 'participated' in treatment under the 1967 Act so as to be able to take advantage of the conscience clause it is to the criminal law that they turned for assistance in defining 'participate'.[57] Lord Keith and Balcombe LJ, however, explicitly held that 'participate' in the Abortion Act did not have to mean the same thing that it meant in the criminal law.[58] They preferred to adopt the type of reasoning used by Nolan J at first instance which determined the interpretation of 'participate' by reference to 'plain English'. Thus the very different routes that individual judges took to reach the conclusion that Janaway could not benefit from the conscience clause in the Abortion Act can be grouped into two categories; those who held that she did not 'participate' in the abortion treatment within the meaning of the term in the criminal law and those that held that she did not 'participate' in the treatment in the word's ordinary and natural usage.

Faced with these two different approaches by judges seeking to interpret 'participate', to ask, simply, what section 4(1) means is unnecessarily naive. Words are inherently open-textured. Until given a context by those using them, words can mean, if not anything, certainly a wide range of different things. For lawyers, and thence often legal academics, the context influencing meaning is usually supplied by the courts. Traditionally it has been said that lawyers seek a stipulative meaning for words and phrases, where the 'right' answer is determined not by the quality of the argument that is advanced for a certain interpretation but by the position that the judge putting forward a definition has within the hierarchy of the courts. However, even for the decreasing number who fully accept traditional doctrinal presuppositions relating to precedent and statutory interpretation, to suppose that that stipulative meaning has been supplied by one judgement in the House of Lords, given the strength of the opposing argument put forward in the Court of Appeal, seems excessively optimistic.[59] *Janaway* is important, not because the House of Lords decision necessarily determines how the courts will interpret the conscience clause in the future, but because either of the two broad paths chosen by the judiciary involved in the decision suggest a major conflict between judicial thinking and a possible approach of those who might consider themselves conscientious objectors.

For those judges who took the criminal law approach to *Janaway* the final question in the case became what could have been said of Janaway's state of mind had she typed the letter of referral? In Slade LJ's view,

> [w]hatever might be said of the doctor whose letter she was being asked to type, she herself, in typing the letter, would have been intending merely to carry out the obligations of her employment, and not endeavouring to produce the result consisting of an abortion.[60]

Slade LJ's decision was based solely upon a consideration of whether, if Janaway had typed the letter, she would have had sufficient *mens rea* to be guilty of the crime of procuring an abortion were it not for the effects of s 1 of the 1967 Act. This is a completely different matter from whether Janaway felt that, by typing the letter, she was promoting abortion. Her refusal to type the letter and her subsequent attempts to take advantage of the conscience clause demonstrate that she did indeed feel that her typing of the letter would have been participation in any subsequent abortion.[61] Her affidavit, quoted by Nolan J in his judgement at first instance, specifically said, 'I would have strenuous objections to participating in any activity which would assist in or would be a necessary step in bringing about the termination of a pregnancy'.[62] The same problem arises when the judgements of those who favoured the 'plain English' approach to the conscience clause are analysed. Balcombe LJ held that participation involved physical proximity.[63] In the first instance decision Nolan J had held that 'participate' referred only to those who were engaged in the 'team effort' of the treatment of the patient in hospital. In the House of Lords Lord Keith concluded that 'participate' referred to those 'actually taking part in treatment authorised in hospital'.[64] Whilst these slightly different formulations might have varying consequences for some hospital staff, they all excluded Janaway for the simple reason that her job was too remote from the actual site of treatment. Yet, as with the criminal law approach to participate, the ordinary language approach results in the courts accepting the genuiness of Janaway's objections but rejecting the notion that she is participating in that which she says she is participating in.

There is nothing inherently paradoxical in accepting that someone is genuine in their beliefs and yet contending that they are wrong. Yet, in the case of a piece of legislation which, upon its face, is designed to protect individual subjective consciences, drawing a distinction between genuiness and correctness creates particular difficulties. To deny that Janaway 'participates' in the abortion treatment is tantamount to saying that, although one accepts that she genuinely thinks she has a conscientious objection, objectively (according to the tests of the criminal law or plain language) she does not. It thus comes close to arguing that her objections, inspired by her Roman Catholic faith, are merely frivolous, personal whims.

The effect of the two approaches adopted by the courts is especially problematic given the very wide approach taken to matters of participation and responsibility by many of those who have concerned themselves with ethical issues. Paul, in his first epistle to the Corinthians, writes of the organic nature of the Christian community; all are members of one body.[65] 'And where one member suffereth, all members suffer with it; or one member is honoured, all the members rejoice with it.'[66] Ethical questions are, for Paul, determined in the context of a framework where each Christian can neither disavow another Christian's connection with their actions nor their own connection with another Christian's actions. Each participates fully and wholly in the lives of others.[67] John Donne's seventeenth Meditation is a development of this same theme in Christian theology. 'Any Man's death diminishes me because I am involved in Mankinde.'[68] This extended notion of participation is not a specifically Christian idea. Gabriel García Márquez, in his novel *Chronicle of a Death Foretold*, contrasts a town's attendance at a marriage feast and its contribution to later murder. Each member of the town attends the feast. Many know about the intended murder but do little or nothing to prevent it. In Gregory Rabassa's English translation of the novel all the people are said to have 'participated' in the feast.[69] One woman's 'participation' in the later murder 'was having seen two bloody knives that weren't bloody yet' although she was not present at the murder itself.[70] In an ethical context, participation and the responsibility it connotes, for Márquez, loses the implication of physical proximity; we are responsible for more than our immediate surroundings and circumstances. The inhabitants of his town were responsible for, and participated in, the murder, even if they were not present when it occurred.

It is not necessary for the purposes of this chapter to argue that the approaches to the definition of participate put forward immediately above are superior to those advanced in the courts. It is enough to say that they suggest that Janaway's approach to her own feelings about abortion, which reflects a much wider understanding of ethical responsibility than that which can be encompassed by using any of the judges' reasoning in *Janaway*, is one which is not uncommon. The gap between the the approaches of the courts and commonly existing ethical beliefs means that the conscience clause is much less effective, protecting far fewer people, than might at first be supposed.

Whilst the interpretation of the conscience clause is an important factor to take account of in determining the effectiveness of the provision it is not the only matter which is relevant. Equally important is the attitude to the clause of those people who might be protected by it; this includes both their knowledge of the contents of the clause and their perception of the possible result of their seeking to use the clause. If those who might potentially benefit from the clause are unaware of it or fear using it because of potential adverse consequences the clause is therefore less effective.

Knowledge of legal rules is obtained either through a direct reading of cases and statutes or is mediated through the commentaries of others. For those without a legal training, who might doubt their ability to interpret primary material, commentaries will take on a greater significance than the primary material. For them the law is largely what others say it is. Sources of information about the conscience clause vary depending upon the occupational groups concerned. The then DHSS drew the attention of all hospital authorities to the conscience clause in a memorandum of guidance issued in April 1968. However, 'it is a matter of local management how it [the conscience clause] is brought to the attention of all concerned'.[71] Information is, thus, as likely to come from manual, journals and guides as it is from official sources. Such information can be contradictory. Thus, for example, a nurse consulting one manual on nursing and the law will find that, '[t]he nurse has no right to opt out of caring for any patient admitted for an abortion either before or after the event, only from the actual abortion'.[72] However, on consulting the Royal College of Nursing, the same nurse will be told that,

> It is the view of the RCN that nursing care is a continuous process and that therefore nurses who object to participation in abortion treatment should be facilitated by nurse management to non-participation in that continuous process.[73]

Given the contradictory advice available, contradictory beliefs about the law are to be expected. However, the range of beliefs about the conscience clause may be even wider than that which might legitimately be derived from commentaries on the law. For example, Kemp, in her 1984 survey of nurses, observed that 75 per cent of her sample thought the conscience clause exempted them from participating in all instances of abortion if they had a conscientious objection to them and not simply from participation in those abortions to which the Abortion Act applied.[74]

Perceptions about what might happen if one implements the conscience clause are as important in influencing the effectiveness of the clause as knowledge of its contents. Since very soon after the 1967 Act was first introduced, allegations have been made that those who have attempted to take advantage of the conscience clause have found that their careers have thereby been hindered. The Lane Committee, reporting in 1974, noted such complaints.[75] A later report by a Select Committee on Abortion recommended that the conscience clause be liberalised. They suggested that it should be made clear that objection could be on religious, ethical or other grounds. It also suggested that the burden of proof be removed from the objector.[76] Neither of these two committees had been centrally concerned with assessing the working of the conscience clause. In 1989, the Social Services Committee of the House of Commons addressed itself to just this task.

The Social Services Committee concluded that whilst evidence about discrimination in employment was, by its very nature, difficult to obtain '[g]iven the number of those doctors who claim that they have been discriminated against because of their anti-abortion views it has to be accepted that such discrimination does take place'.[77] However, the Committee went on to observe that, given the need to appoint doctors who would take part in abortions so as to service the needs of pregnant women, there was no easy way to reconcile the interests of objecting doctors and pregnant women.[78]

The conscience clause in the 1967 Act is concerned with negating a legal duty that a person might otherwise have to take part in a abortion. It does not, however, prevent an employer discriminating against a person who makes use of the clause. In particular it does not prevent an employer from refusing to employ or promote someone who reveals that they intend to make use of the clause. The omission of employment protection from the conscience clause was not mere inadvertence on the part of the legislature. In the House of Lords, during the passage of the Abortion Bill, Lord Craigmyle proposed an amendment to the conscience clause outlawing discriminatory employment practices.[79] This amendment was rejected after a debate during which Baroness Stocks had argued that

> hospitals...ought to be allowed to exercise a certain amount of discretion against getting too many members of their staff who are not prepared to carry out what is part of the medical policy of the hospital.[80]

Thus, whilst the conscience clause may protect medical staff from dismissal, it does not protect them from disadvantage.

Conclusion

The general protection clauses discussed in this chapter clearly provide a measure of protection for those with strong religious convictions. However, several problems seem to recur.

General conscience clauses cause great problems for the judiciary. In part these difficulties may be due to the judicial unfamilarity with such provisions. In *Janaway* the conscience clause was described as 'unique'.[81] Even then, given the very similar clauses in legislation relating to trade union membership and national service, this was an exaggeration. Now the 1967 Act conscience clause is replicated in almost precisely the same terms by s 38 of the Human Embryo Act 1990. However, there are still very few such clauses. More importantly, the issues they relate to are ones which are seldom discussed in the courts. Judges rarely discuss conscience in ethical terms in court.[82] The infrequency with which they are faced with such matters does not encourage sophistication when dealing with them.

Limiting the ambit of general clauses is difficult both technically and philosophically. Objective definitions of 'religion' or 'conscience' seem frivolous when examined in the light of the variety of subjective human experience. Limits set by tests of frequency or rationality of the objection are difficult to justify when most religions rest their claims on faith not evidence. Once one religious conscience is given weight it is difficult to deny the merits of another conscience whether religious or not. Where technical arguments do produce an area of demarcation, policy considerations generally seem to suggest that the boundaries of the legal rule be moved further outwards. Thus the rejection of religion as a sole criterion for entitlement to refusal to join a closed shop and thus the Social Services Committee's recommendation that, in the light of *Janaway*, 'the Department of Health considers extending the provision of section 4 of the 1967 Act to cover some ancillary staff'.[83]

Conscience clauses, however excellent their form, do not live up to their promise in application. The Abortion Act clause does not protect medical staff from feeling that their conscientious objections set them apart from other staff. Nor can they be expected to do more than they do. Those who have a conscientious objection are by definition 'peculiar people' set against the world to the extent of their objection. A conscience clause can ameliorate their position but it cannot put them in the same place as their non-objecting fellows.

Finally, a conscience clause in any particular area of law, to the extent that it is successful, always breeds the question, if this area why not others?

Notes

1. The concepts of the agency shop agreement and the approved closed shop agreement are outlined in sections 11 and 17 of the Industrial Relations Act 1971. The employee's right not to be unfairly dismissed was then contained in sections 22 and 24 of the same Act.
2. s 63(1) Industrial Relations Act 1971.
3. Under s 78 of the 1971 Act a provisional register of trade unions was drawn up using as a base those unions which had registered under the voluntary scheme originally started by the Trade Union Act 1871. (See R. Rideout, *Principles of Labour Law* Sweet and Maxwell (1st ed, 1972) pp. 299–301, 308–311.)
4. The 1972 Annual Congress of the TUC suspended these unions and 30 others who had failed to deregister under the Act. (1972) 41 *Industrial Relations Review and Report* p. 16.
5. Both the NUS and Equity were suspended from the TUC when they applied to the Commission on Industrial Relations to complete approved closed shop agreements. (1972) 39 *Industrial Relations Review and Report* p. 10.
6. C. Hanson, S. Jackson and D. Miller, *The Closed Shop* Gower, 1982, p. 5.
7. *Drury* v. *The Bakers Union (Southern District)* [1973] IRLR 171, IT, *Hynds* v. *Spillers-French Baking Ltd* [1974] IRLR 281, NIRC.
8. *Drury* v. *The Bakers Union (Southern District) op. cit.*, at p. 172.
9. *Hynds* v. *Spillers-French Baking Ltd op. cit.*, at p. 283.
10. *Newell* v. *Gillingham Corporation* [1941] 1 All ER 552, KBD, at p. 554.
11. *Newell* v. *Gillingham Corporation loc. cit.*
12. G. Field, *Pacificism and Conscientious Objection* Cambridge University Press, 1945 p. 3. The 1939 Act explicitly deprived the ordinary courts of any jurisdiction to determine who was and who was not a conscientious objector (s 5(12) National Service (Armed Forces) Act 1939).
13. *Hansard*, HL, Vol 357, col 802, February 25, 1975.
14. See, for example, Maurice Edelman, *Hansard*, HC, Vol 876, col 1707, July 11, 1974.
15. *Hansard*, HL, Vol 318, col 661, May 10, 1971.
16. *Cave and Cave* v. *British Railways Board* [1976] IRLR 400, IT, *Goodbody* v. *British Railways Board* [1977] IRLR 84, IT, *Saggers* v. *British Railways Board (No 2)* [1978] IRLR 435, EAT.
17. J. Beckford, *The Trumpet of Prophecy* Basil Blackwell, 1975, p. 70.
18. Quakers classify a person as a member if their name is recorded as such in a minute of a Monthly Meeting (*Church Government* London Yearly Meeting of the Religious Society of Friends, 1980, para. 832). However, there is also an official list of 'attenders' (*Church Government op. cit.*, para. 849). There are no 'clear-cut tests of doctrine or outward observance' which define membership (*Church Government op. cit.*, para. 831).
19. Specific rules on behaviour during worship, generalised commentaries on social duties consequent upon membership of the particular group and unofficial tracts written by group members do not meet the point.
20. Although, like any other form of intellectual or emotional belief, religious belief may also be constantly striving to be objectively, or at least absolutely, true.

21. Lord Shepherd, *Hansard*, HL, Vol 357, col 685, February 25, 1975.
22. Tom King, *Hansard*, HC, Vol 876, col 1703, July 11, 1974.
23. Albert Booth, *Hansard*, HC, Vol 876, col 1701, July 11, 1974.
24. *Hansard*, HL, Vol 358, col 118, March 10, 1975.
25. *Hansard*, HC, Vol 886, col 548, February 12, 1975.
26. This section amended s 58(3) Employment Protection (Consolidation) Act 1978.
27. *Home Delivery Services* v. *Shackcloth* [1984] IRLR 470, EAT, at p. 473.
28. *Home Delivery Services* v. *Shackcloth loc. cit.*
29. *Home Delivery Services* v. *Shackcloth loc. cit.*
30. *Westhead* v. *National Union of Seamen* [1973] IRLR 275, IT.
31. *Westhead* v. *National Union of Seamen op. cit.*, at p. 276.
32. This decision is unreported. The quotation is taken from a transcript of the case.
33. The case is recorded in a news report in *The Times*, 12 June 1984.
34. *McGhee* v. *British Road Services Ltd* [1985] IRLR 198, EAT.
35. *McGhee* v. *British Road Services Ltd op. cit.*, at p. 203.
36. *McKenzie* v. *Nairn Floors Ltd* (1984) 271 *Industrial Relations Legal Information Bulletin*, p. 6.
37. *Chauhan* v. *Ford Motor Company* (1985) 280 *Industrial Relations Legal Information Bulletin*, p. 11. There is a full report of the case on LEXIS.
38. The report of the case cites only the chapter in *The Laws of Manu* that Chauhan referred to; this being chapter VI entitled 'The Hermit in the Forest; the Ascetic'. As the title indicates, the chapter relates to the stage of life where there is a withdrawal from the world. Section 42 of the chapter reads, 'Let him wander alone, without any companion, in order to attain (final liberation), fully understanding that the solitary (man, who) neither forsakes nor is forsaken, gains his end' (G. Buhler (trans.), *Laws of Manu* Motilal Banarsidwass, 1964). There is an obvious parallel between this passage and the Pauline injunction, '[b]e not unequally yoked with unbelievers' (2 Corinthians 6:14), which led some Christian groups to reject trade union membership (see, for example, *Goodbody* v. *British Railways Board op. cit.*). The Industrial Tribunal seem to have regarded Chauhan's beliefs as unusual. However, Raja Rao writes "[a]ll indians know of the forest." (Raja Rao, *The Chessmaster and His Moves* Vision Books, 1988, p. 44.)
39. It is, of course, possible that Chauhan would have felt that raising his objection and taking a full part in the company appeals procedure would have been in contradiction of the spirit of withdrawal from the material world recommended in the sixth chapter of *The Laws of Manu*. However, his continued employment might also be regarded as being in contradiction of this spirit. Equally, it is relevant that Chauhan had at one stage raised non-religious reasons, such as possible bias on the part of those assessing his case, as justifications for his withdrawal from the appeals procedure.
40. *Hansard*, HL, Vol 411, col 913, July 7, 1980.
41. As in *McGhee* (see n. 35).
42. One decision, *Sakals* v. *United Counties Omnibus Co Ltd* [1984] IRLR 474, EAT, runs counter to this general trend. In *Sakals* the Employment Appeal Tribunal held that Sakals objections 'were not objections to being a members of the union or any union as such…they were only objections to being compelled into union membership by the threat of loss of his job' (p. 476). As such the objection was not an objection to trade union membership in itself. Such reasoning is plainly defective. Following the argument of the Employment Appeal Tribunal in *Sakals* any person who objected to trade union membership for a reason would thereby exclude themselves from the protection of the formula precisely because they had a reason for their objection. The only legitimate objector would be the person who objected to belonging to a trade union and was unable to articulate any justification

for their stance. On this basis all of the cases relating to the 1980 Act, discussed above, whether they find for the putative objector or not are decided on the wrong basis. However, it seems unlikely that *Sakals* was rightly decided. Presumably the 1980 Act was not only intended to protect the bovine.

43. Following on from the Employment Act 1980 subsequent legislation reduced the legal protection for the closed shop. Sections 10 and 11 of the Employment Act 1988 finally removed all forms of legal protection rendering the conscientious objection provisions otiose. (See I. Smith and J. Wood, *Industrial Law* Butterworths (4th ed., 1989) pp. 457–458.)

44. s 4(1) Abortion Act 1967. In Scotland a statement on oath by a person to the effect that she or he has a conscientious objection will suffice (s4(3)).

45. s 4(2) Abortion Act 1967.

46. H of C Standing Committee Reports 1966/67, Vol X, col 576, March 22, 1967.

47. H of C Standing Committee Reports *op. cit.*, col 551.

48. H of C Standing Committee Reports *op. cit.*, col 561.

49. H of C Standing Committee Reports *op. cit.*, col 552.

50. H of C Standing Committee Reports *op. cit.*, col 555.

51. *Janaway* v. *Salford Area Health Authority* [1988] 3 All ER 1079., HL. The Court of Appeal decision in the case is reported as *R.* v. *Salford Area Health Authority* [1988] 2 WLR 442, CA. The first instance hearing is briefly reported in *The Times*, 13 February 1987. A full report of the first instance decision is available on LEXIS.

52. Not all the judgements in the case are reasoned. In the House of Lords only one judge, Lord Keith, gave a full judgement. Three other judges in the House of Lords, Lord Brandon, Lord Griffiths and Lord Goff, concurred with Lord Keith. One judge, Lord Lowry, supplemented his concurrence with four extra lines of judgement.

53. *R.* v. *Salford Area Health Authority op. cit.*, at p. 455.

54. *R.* v. *Salford Area Health Authority op. cit.*, at p. 447.

55. *R.* v. *Salford Area Health Authority op. cit.*, at p. 453.

56. *Janaway* v. *Salford Area Health Authority op. cit.*, at p. 1081.

57. See particularly Slade LJ, *R.* v. *Salford Area Health Authority op. cit.*, pp. 449–451, and Stocker LJ at p. 455.

58. Lord Keith in *Janaway* v. *Salford Area Health Authority op. cit.*, at p. 1082, Balcombe LJ in *R.* v. *Salford Area Health Authority op. cit.*, at p. 453.

59. For the the traditional arguments regarding precedent and statutory interpretation, see R. Cross and J. Harris, *Precedent in English Law* Clarendon Press (4th ed., 1991) and J. Bell and G. Engle (eds), *Cross on Statutory Interpretation* Butterworths (2nd ed., 1987). For an opposing view see the increasingly voluminous literature from the Critical Legal Studies movement. The possibility of future courts diverging from the House of Lord's decision in *Janaway* is still greater given the (possibly inevitable) internal inconsistencies in the judgement's favouring the approach taken in the House of Lords. However, the alternative 'criminal law' approach also has its own logical failings and inconsistencies (see A. Bradney, 'Making Cowards' [1990] *Juridical Review* 129 at pp. 136–141).

60. *R.* v. *Salford Area Health Authority op. cit.*, at p. 452. Stocker LJ adopted Slade LJ's reasoning, see *R.* v. *Salford Area Health Authority op. cit.*, at p. 459.

61. It was common ground in all judgements that Janaway was completely genuine in her protestations of objection (see, for example, Slade LJ in *R.* v. *Salford Area Health Authority op. cit.*, at p. 447).

62. This passage is included in the LEXIS report of the first instance decision.

63. *per* Balcombe LJ in *R.* v. *Salford Area Health Authority op. cit.*, at p. 453.

64. *per* Lord Keith in *Janaway* v. *Salford Area Health Authority op. cit.*, at p. 1082.

65. I Corinthians 12: 12–27.

66. I Corinthians 12: 26.
67. For a full discussion of this passage from Corinthians, see C. Dodd, *Gospel and Law* Cambridge University Press, 1951, pp. 32–39.
68. John Donne, *Selected Prose* Clarendon Press, 1987, p. 124.
69. Gabriel García Márquez (trans. G. Rabassa), *Chronicle of a Death Foretold* Jonathan Cape, 1982, at p. 17.
70. Márquez, *op. cit.*, p. 98.
71. Sir K Joseph, *Hansard*, HC, Vol 813, col 171, March 11, 1971.
72. A. Young, *Legal Problems in Nursing Practice* Harper and Row, 1981 p. 148.
73. Internal briefing paper supplied to the author by the Royal College.
74. J. Kemp, 'Attitudes to Abortion' (1984) 158, 17 *Nursing Mirror* 34 at p. 35.
75. *Report of the Committee on the Working of the Abortion Act* (Lane Committee), Cm 5579 (1974) para. 340.
76. *First Report from the Select Committee on Abortion* (1975–76) HC 573–I para. 98.
77. *Tenth Report of the Social Services Committee* (1989–90) HC 123 para. 43.
78. *Tenth Report of the Social Services Committee loc. cit.*
79. *Hansard*, HL, Vol 285, col 1094, July 26, 1967.
80. *Hansard*, HL, Vol 285, col 1095, July 26, 1967.
81. *R. v. Salford Area Health Authority op. cit.*, at p. 458.
82. None of the judges in *Janaway* had been involved in more than two previous cases where conscience in its ethical sense had been discussed (for precise figures on this point see Bradney, *op. cit.*, pp. 142–143).
83. *Tenth Report of the Social Services Committee op. cit.*, para. 47.

9 Conclusion

Whilst I am writing this final chapter the courts are deciding whether or not to honour the wishes of a woman who, before she lost consciousness in hospital, said that her religious beliefs prevented her from having a blood transfusion.[1] At the same time an attempt is being made to circumvent the laws which prevent commercial horse-racing and its normal accompanying activities on a Sunday.[2] Whatever ensues in either case it is unlikely that the imperatives of religious belief will receive much attention in the courts or the legislature; the fora in which these issues will finally be settled. The existence of these two disputes at the date of writing this conclusion is not simply fortuitiously adventious. The foregoing chapters of this book have demonstrated that conflict between religions and legal rules is an everyday occurence in Great Britain. Moreover, they have shown that the conflict is one where the religious adherent is usually the loser. The idea that Great Britain is a country where freedom of religion can, unproblematically, be taken to have been achieved has been shown to be a myth. The notion that the courts are neutral, whatever that might mean, in matters of religion has been seen, despite the protestations of the judges themselves, to be false.

Gladstone argued that,

> [Religious toleration requires] that civil penalty or prohibition be not employed to punish or to preclude a man's acting on his own religious opinions...it requires that no privilege or benefit which a person is capable of receiving rightly and of using beneficially be withheld from him on account of his religious opinions as such.[3]

Understood in this fashion, religious tolerance has still to be achieved in Great Britain. People are materially disadvantaged because of their religious beliefs. They may lose their jobs or control of their children because of their religion. If they have the wrong faith they will not be able to create a charitable trust. If they have the right faith, they will see the state take that faith to its heart, promoting it by making its celebration a compulsory part of the educational system, its service of divine worship part of the core of the marriage laws, its tenets the subject of the protection of the law of blasphemy and its mores a standard of behaviour for judgements in the courts. In these and numerous other ways legal rules select out some religions for favour and some for disapproval. Sardurski has commented that, '[t]he relationship between the state and religion in modern secular states is regulated by two principles: the separation of the state and religion, and the freedom of religion'.[4] Great Britain does not have the former. Can it be said to have the latter?

Classically it has been argued that, '...the real test of religious freedom and tolerance [is]...the extent to which the general law accomodate[s] different practices. But there must be limits to this. The society's own basic values must be respected and must not be undermined.'[5] Derogations from a general stance of religious freedom can thus be justified on the grounds that they represent instances where particular religions conflict with the fundamental mores of the society at large. In this tradition, individual examples of discrimination on grounds of religion within the system of legal rules are acknowledged but held not to be sufficient to invalidate the thesis that religious freedom exists within Great Britain.

In part the popularity of the traditional view of the relationship between law and religions in Great Britain may result from an empirical misunderstanding of the degree of conflict between legal rules and religions in the country. The comparative lack of research and scholarship in the area of the relationship between religions and legal rules in Great Britain was noted in the opening chapter of this book. The traditional understanding of the place of religious freedom in the British legal systems relies, in part, on an assumption of a comparative fit between the religious beliefs of those living in Great Britain and legal rules of the country rather than on any demonstration of that fit. The usual practice in legal education, whereby legal rules are studied in different categories which owe their origins to the presumed purpose of the rules, serves further to exacerbate an intuitive under-estimate of the degree of conflict between religions and laws. Within 'criminal law' or within 'family law', taken as a whole, there are very few instances of discrimination in the laws because of religious belief. Thus the conclusion that the law does not customarily discriminate on grounds of religion naturally follows. If, however, the law is divided in another manner, by, for example, asking how does the law treat Hindus, then the examples of differential treatment take on a greater proportionate significance and the result might be a different conclusion.[6]

The strength of the traditional view of religious freedom and the law does not just lie in any under-estimate of the number of examples of difficulties caused to adherents by legal rules. Its strength also lies in the conceptual cheat that is involved in the basic proposition at its heart. Religious freedom in law is usually said to exist if religious adherents are allowed to follow their beliefs providing those beliefs do not strike at the fundamental mores of the society. But it is difficult to gainsay any proposition that a particular religious belief strikes at the fundamental mores of the society in a society which still treats one religion, Christianity, as characterising those mores. This is especially the case if the religion being judged is one which is new to the country. And any number of such religions, whose tenets are discounted because it is said that their beliefs strike at the society's mores, will not then count as instances showing an absence of religious freedom. Thus, the proposition that there is religious freedom in Great Britain becomes unfalsifiable and, because it is unfalsifiable, becomes mere rhetoric.

This rhetoric of religious freedom is not without function. The concept of religious freedom in Great Britain might be a myth but, if it is, it is part of a myth in the technical sense.[7] The importance of the idea of religious freedom in Great Britain lies not in its narrative truth but in the values it reflects. The notion hymns a homogenous nation. It speaks of a country where all are essentially the same, where there are 'our traditions' which unify 'us' and divide 'us' from other nations. 'We' know there is religious freedom because 'we' can follow our religion (which 'we' take lightly) and if others are different they are different in no significant way. If the religious beliefs of others vary in any important manner, altering the way in which they view the family or children or education or whatever, then this indicates that their beliefs take them outside the magic circle of acceptable standards; this, in itself, justifying their different treatment.

This traditional view of religious freedom is both condescending and complacent. It is also dangerous because it refuses to acknowledge the very dimension on which some wish to protest their experience. Nobody can be heard to testify to their mistreatment as a believer because there is religous freedom in Great Britain. Thus their experience as a believer, as a Muslim, as a Sikh, is denied. It is not as a Hindu or a Jain that they are treated differently. It is not because they are a Jehovah's witness or a member of the Exclusive Brethren. It is because they have an unacceptable attitude to women or the place of computers in education or whatever else it is that, for the moment, counts as being part of the fundamental mores of Great Britain. On the one hand their beliefs result in them being less favourably treated than others with different beliefs. On the other hand they are denied the dignity of having those beliefs described as religious beliefs because they are assured that, despite their differential treatment, there is no denial of religious freedom in Great Britain. Moreover, such judgements are not infrequently made on the basis of casual ignorance and studied indifference. A society which claims religious freedom as a victory which it has won regards education about just one faith as being a *sine qua non* for its children. Even then, it is only the tenets of the sect of that faith which is numerically dominant which must be explored in the educational system. The everyday lives and beliefs of a whole range of Christian and non-Christian believers remain an apparent mystery to most British citizens including their judges and legislators. This is the context within which the myth of religious freedom is maintained. There is a need for a more serious basis on which to assess whether there is, and whether there should be, religious freedom within the British legal systems.

Chapter 2 of this book demonstrated that, philosophically, each person is alone. The chapters in Part 2 illustrated some of the variety of ways in which people within Great Britain choose to arrange a number of different aspects of their lives. Either approach is sufficient to dispel any idea that legal rules can serve to promote any common identity. There is, in the end, nothing 'British' to protect. That which is numerically most common in the behaviour of people in Britain owes its origins to accidents of history and whims of fashion. That which is most common is never that which is universal. Whatever it is that the most people in Britain have been or have been doing is also that which some people in Britain have long been opposing. To identify something as being 'British', to categorise it as constituting part of the basic values of Great Britain, is only possible using an arithmetic rule with a simple majority being the deciding factor. That which the majority of Britains do is a basic British value. Anything selected as a value in this fashion has all the intellectual attraction of choosing moral views by means of an popularity poll conducted on the population at large. There is, thus, no way in which people, acting in good faith, can authentically become 'British'. There are, and can only be, individuals trying to discover their own best ends. All legal rules can and should do is to try to facilitate this.

Religion is one way in which people try to discover themselves. True believers are people who are likely to be amongst those citzens who are most obdurate in their views.[8] True believers are not necessarily fundamentalists though genuine fundamentalists will be true believers. True believers need not believe in the inerrancy of the texts which form their sacred books (if they have any). Still less do they need to believe in their own personal infallibility in interpreting their religion's dictates. Finally, they need not hold the view that their religion demands that they impose their views on others. Bahai, Quakers and members of the Church of England can be true believers as much as Shi'ite Muslims or Southern Baptists. However, true believers share with the popular conception of the fundamentalist a peculiar dedication to their truths. It is this which separates them out from the majority of their fellow citizens.[9] It is this which makes their way of discovering themselves a special problem for legal rules.

Obdurancy does not give true believers a claim for different treatment by a legal system. It certainly does not give them a claim for better treatment. It does, however, guarantee the legal system's necessity to be able to justify its treatment of religious belief. True believers, because they are true believers, are far less likely than their average fellow citizens to simply accept, unchalleneged, a legal rule that makes something which they regard as part of the focus of their lives impermissible. Luther's declaration before the Diet of Worms, '[h]ere I stand, I can do no other', is characteristic of the true believer's greatest strength. All adherents to any religion aspire to the status of perfection in their faith. That which the believer has fully understood about the tenets of their faith they must comply with or account themselves blameworthy. They cannot bend with the wind. For them the injunction, 'obey the law', will be hollow rhetoric. They will always be a challenge to the coherence and justice of the legal system's rules.

The aim cannot be to create legal systems where the wishes of each believer are accommodated. Religious beliefs can be mutually incompatible with each other. Religious beliefs can treat other people, non–believers, as objects in the service of the religion. Religious beliefs can be, by whatever standards are chosen, as unreasonable and as undesirable as any other form of belief. Religious beliefs may fail to recognise the priority of radical autonomy. At the same time these beliefs remain genuine religious beliefs. The need is for those who frame and administer legal systems to decide how to accommodate religions and, where there is no accommodation for religions, to have a justification for that stance. Discrimination on grounds of religious belief within a legal system will be justifiable in some cases. What is never justifiable is inadvertent discrimination on grounds of religion within a legal system or discrimination which is based on an inaccurate view of the religion in question.

A Religious Discrimination Act, modelled on the lines of the Race Discrimination legislation and the Sex Discimination statutes, would, whilst it might well improve the lot of those presently hampered in the prosecution of their faith, be difficult to justify. Like its precursors, it would inevitably be based upon conceptual confusion. Neither the Race Discrimination legislation nor the Sex Discrimination statutes in fact seek to outlaw race or sex discrimination *per se*. Categories of justifiable differential treatment remain within the law. So it would be with any Religious Discrimination Act. In the case of the Race and Sex Discrimination legislation the conceptual confusion can be justified by the pragmatic arguments that the existence of the legislation has furthered the debate about what constitutes permissible discrimination and has reduced the harm caused by impermissible discrimination. It is difficult to see how this could be so in the case of a Religious Discrimination Act. Debate about what constitutes permissible and even desirable discrimination on grounds of religion has been forestalled by the proposition that there is religious freedom in Great Britain. In creating and applying such legislation Parliament and the courts would be working in an intellectual vacuum on problems they have not been noticeably good at addressing in the past.

One solution to problems of religious discrimination in the British legal systems is to treat all religions equally unfavourably; to apply normal legal rules in an entirely even way taking no account of religious belief at any point. Sadurski has argued that, 'the concept of the neutrality of law towards competing moral conceptions provides the best account of widely felt liberal intuitions about legally protected liberties, and...forms a comprehensive framework for a liberal model of law'.[10] With this as a foundation he has gone on to argue that, 'it is impossible to preserve neutrality between religious and non-religious beliefs while accommodating religions' claims for special protection and recognition'.[11] The attraction of this approach lies in the suggestion that no religion can ever claim any disadvantage if all religions are treated in the same way. Thus not only intentional but also inadvertent discrimination becomes impossible. However, this attractive idea rests on the unspoken premise that draining the legal system of specific references to particular religions will also remove all religious values from the legal rules. This is clearly not the case in Great Britain. Whilst it is the case that the special exemptions allowing Jews to trade on Sundays are an example of religious discrimination, since Muslims are not similarly advantaged, removing the exemptions would not make that particular law neutral towards all religions. The Sunday trading law would still be based on Christian concepts of the sabbath and its application to other religions thus an example of religious discrimination.

Identifying problems will always be simpler than suggesting solutions. The problems in the treatment of religions within the legal systems in Great Britain are clear. Legal rules are often created and applied without thought of the difficulties they will cause for some faiths. This in turn happens because neither judges nor legislators are acquainted with much of the variety of religious experience. In some cases faith is devalued because its form runs counter to those religious traditions which have historically dominated Great Britain. People are treated as citizens and not as individuals. Patterns of legal thought, in any event, rest uneasily in religious pastures. Judgements in some cases involving conflict between religions and laws suggest mutual incomprehension on both sides. Neither legal system in Great Britain is characterised by consistency in its attitude either to religion in general or to individual religions in particular.

The rise of non-Christian religious groups in Great Britain makes the need to develop a new and more ordered legal response to religions a pressing political problem. The number of references in this book to the problems that British legal rules cause for Muslims is indicative not only of the seriousness of those problems but also the degree of political and scholarly activity which has generated a literature analysing the issue. However, Muslims are not especially disadvantaged. Other religions, including non-mainstream Christian denominations, facing similar problems, will follow Islam in pressing their case for the myth of religious freedom in Great Britain to be reconsidered. Greater attention to the issue will in itself be a kind of solution. Political pressure will create more specific exemptions in individual legal rules and a greater general awareness of the need to take account of the dictates of faith. The danger is that reforms will be *ad hoc* and that their content may reflect the political power of interest groups rather than the genuine merits of different cases.

In the end for true believers the problem of the relationship between the British legal systems and religions can almost be seen as an irrelevance since they will benefit from the existentialist truth traced out in chapter 2. Faced with an individual conscience, resolved to act for itself alone, a mere legal system can do nothing. Penalties will not alter the true believer's mind. The only question for a legal system that is held out as being liberal is, in punishing or stigmatising a believer for their faith, what damage will the legal system do to the conception of itself?

Notes

1. At the date of writing, the Court of Appeal had ruled that the woman could be treated against her wishes. Reasons for its decision had not yet been given. The Official Solicitor, acting on behalf of the unconscious woman, was contemplating an appeal to the House of Lords. (*The Times*, 25 July 1992.)
2. Lord Hartingdon, the Jockey Club's senior steward, writing in *The Times* argued that Sunday racing should be permitted on the grounds of 'fair competition for racing, and freedom of opportunity for the public. (*The Times*, 25 July 1992.)
3. Quoted in St John Robilliard, *Religion and the Law* Manchester University Press, 1984, p. ix.
4. W. Sadurski, *Moral Pluralism and Legal Neutrality* Kluwer Academic Publishers, 1990, p. 167.
5. G. Zellick, *The Law, Religion and the Jewish Community* Jews' College, 1987, p. 13.
6. This argument mirrors that which has been developed in feminist critiques of the legal system's attitude towards women where traditional categories within legal education have been held accountable in part for the comparatively slow realisation of the ways in which legal rules can hinder women's lives (see, for example, S. Atkins and B. Hoggett, *Women and the Law* Basil Blackwell, 1984, Preface). An equally apposite argument in the context of religions and legal rules which can be

taken from feminist jurisprudence concerns the way in which traditional legal education concentrates on the exposition of legal rules, marginalising any questions which pertain to the operation of those rules. (See, for example, N. Naffine, *Law and the Sexes: Explorations in Feminist Jurisprudence* Allen and Unwin, 1990, pp. 29–34.)

7.   C. Levi-Straus, *Structural Anthropology* Penguin Books, 1972, chp XI.

8.   I use the term 'true believers' as a way of distinguishing those who hold to their faith in a serious fashion from those whose adherence is less secure.

9.   True believers are not unique in the way they hold to their consciences. Those with a secular stance may be equally firm in the way they hold to their views (see, for example, W. Schwarz, *The New Dissenters* Bedford Square Press, 1989). I would, however, contend that in modern Great Britain true believers remain numerically greater than those with a similarly strong secular conscience.

10.   Sadurski, *op. cit.*, p. 197.

11.   Sadurski, *op. cit.*, p. 193.

Select bibliography

M. Ahsan and A. Kidwai (eds), *Sacrilege versus Civility* The Islamic Foundation, 1991.

S. Akhtar, *Be Careful with Muhammed!* Bellew Publishing, 1989.

S. Akhtar, 'Is Freedom Holy to Liberals?' in *Free Speech* Commission for Racial Equality, 1990.

C. Alves, 'Just a Matter of Words? The Religious Education Debate in the House of Lords' (1991) 13 *British Journal of Religious Education* 168.

L. Appignanesie and S. Maitland (eds), *The Rushdie File* Fourth Estate, 1989.

J. Arthur, 'Catholic Responses to the 1988 Education Reform Act: Problems of Authority and Ethos' (1991) 13 *British Journal of Religious Education* 181.

The Shops Act: Late-Night and Sunday Opening: Report of the Committee of Inquiry into Proposals to Amend the Shops Act (Auld Committee), Cmnd 9376 (1984).

Z. Badawi, *Islam in Britain*, Ta Ha, 1981.

E. Barker, *The Making of a Moonie* Basil Blackwell, 1984.

S. Barton, *The Bengali Muslims of Bradford* Community Religions Project, University of Leeds, 1986.

J. Beckford, *The Trumpet of Prophecy* Basil Blackwell, 1975.

M. Blakeney, 'Sequestered Piety and Charity – a Comparative Analysis' (1981) 2 *Journal of Legal History* 207.

D. Bowen, *The Sathya Sai Baba Community in Bradford* Community Religions Project, University of Leeds, 1988.

A. Bradney, 'Arranged Marriages and Duress', [1984] *Journal of Social Welfare Law* 278, [1985] *Journal of Social Welfare Law* 2.

A. Bradney, 'Separate Schools, Ethnic Minorities and the Law' (1987) 13 *New Community* 412.

A. Bradney, 'Making Cowards' [1990] *Juridical Review* 129.

A. Bradney, 'And that man dying' in F. Patfield and R. White (eds), *The Changing Law* Leicester University Press, 1990.

J. Brady, 'Some Problems Touching the Nature of Bequests for Masses in Northern Ireland' (1968) 19 *Northern Ireland Legal Quarterly* 357.

S. Bright, 'Charity and Trusts for the Public Benefit – Time for a Rethink?' (1989) 53 *Conveyancer and Property Lawyer* 28.

P. Bromley and N. Lowe, *Bromley's Family Law* Butterworths (7th ed, 1987).

E. Cashmore, *Rastaman* Allen and Unwin, 1979.

Charities: A Framework for the Future, Cm 694 (1989).

Choice and Diversity: A New Framework for the Future, Cm 2002 (1992).

Church, School , Education and Islam Manchester Diocesan Council for Education (no date).

W. Cole and P. Sambhi, *The Sikhs* Routledge and Kegan Paul, 1978.

M. Couto, 'The Search for Identity' in M. Butcher (ed.), *The Eye of the Beholder* Commonwealth Institute, 1983.

E. Cox and J. Cairns, *Reforming Religious Education: The Religious Clauses of the 1988 Education Reform Act 1988* Kogan Page in association with the Institute of Education, University of London, 1989.

The Crathorne Committee, *Report of the Departmental Committee on the Law of Sunday Observance* Cmnd 2528 (1964).

S. Cretney and J. Masson, *Principles of Family Law* Sweet and Maxwell, (5th ed., 1990).

C. Crowther, *Religious Trusts* George Ronald, 1954.

M. Cruickshank, *Church and State in English Education* Macmillan, 1963.

R. Deakin, *The New Christian Schools* Regius Press on behalf of the Christian Schools Trust, 1989.

A. Denning, *Freedom Under Law* Stevens, 1949 p. 46.

R. Descartes, *Discourse on Method* Penguin Books, 1968.

M. Detmold, *Courts and Administrators* Weidenfeld and Nicholson, 1989.

Abdur Rahman I Doi, *Shariah: The Islamic Law* Ta Ha Publishers, 1984.

Education for All: Report of the Committee of Inquiry into the Education of Children from Ethnic Minority Groups (Swann Committee) Cmnd 9453 (1985).

P. Dooley, 'Muslim Private Schools' in G. Walford (ed.), *Private Schooling* Paul Chapman Publishing Ltd, 1991.

G. Duncan, *The Church School* National Society for the Propagation of Religious Education, 1991.

G. Field, *Pacificism and Conscientious Objection* Cambridge University Press, 1945.

J. Gay et al, *A Role for the Future* Culham Educational Foundation, 1991.

(The Goodman Report) *Charity Law and Voluntary Organisations* Bedford Square Press, 1976.

Guidelines and Syllabus on Islamic Education Union of Muslim Organizations for the United Kingdom and Ireland, 1976.

A. Guillaume, *Islam* Penguin Books (2nd ed., 1956).

J. Halstead, *The Case for Muslim Voluntary-Aided Schools* Islamic Academy, 1986.

J. Halstead and A. Khan–Cheema, 'Muslims and Worship in the Maintained School' in L. Francis and A. Thatcher *Christian Perspectives for Education* Gracewing, 1990.

J. Hinnells (ed.), *A Handbook of Living Religions* Penguin Books, 1985.

M. Hiskett, *Schooling for British Muslims* The Social Affairs Unit (no date).

W. S. Holdsworth, 'The State and Religious Nonconformity: An Historical Retrospect' (1920) *Law Quarterly Review* 339.

R. Homan, 'Teaching the Children of Jehovah's Witnesses' (1988) 10 *British Journal of Religious Education* 154.

J. Hull, 'Introduction: New Directions in Religious Education' in J. Hull (ed.), *New Directions in Religious Education* Falmer Press, 1982.

J. Hull, *Studies in Religion and Education* Falmer Press, 1984.

J. Hull, 'School Worship and the 1988 Education Reform Act' (1989) 11 *British Journal of Religious Education* 119.

J. Hull, *The Act Unpacked* University of Birmingham, School of Education, 1989.

E. Husserl, *Cartesian Meditations* Martinus Nijhoff, 1960.

M. Janis (ed.), *The Influence of Religion on the Development of International Law* Martinus Nijhoff, 1991.

W. Jordan, *The Development of Religious Toleration in England* George Allen and Unwin, 1932.

R. Kabbani, *Letter to Christendom* Virago Press, 1989.

C. Kenny, 'The Evolution of the Law of Blasphemy' (1922) 1 *Cambridge Law Journal* 127.

K. Knott, *Hinduisim in Leeds* Community Religions Project, University of Leeds, 1986.

G. Kumar, *Censorship in India* Har-Anand Publications, 1990.

Private International Law: Polygamous Marriages: Capacity to Contract a Polygamous Marriage and Related Issues Law Commission No. 42 and Scottish Law Commission No. 96, (1971).

Law Commission Report on Solemnisation of Marriage Law Commission No. 65, (1973).

Offences Against Religion and Public Worship Law Commission Working Paper No. 79, (1981).

S. Lee, *The Cost of Free Speech* Faber and Faber, 1990.

J. Lyotard, *The Postmodern Condition: A Report on Knowledge* Manchester University Press, 1984.

Mustafa Yousuf McDermott and Muhammad Manazir Ahsan, *The Muslim Guide* The Islamic Foundation, 1986.

Shaikh Abdul Mabud, 'A Muslim Response to the Education Reform Act 1988' (1992) 14 *British Journal of Religious Education* 88.

G. Maher 'Blasphemy in Scots Law' (1977) *Scots Law Times* 257.

S. Mason, 'Islamic Separatism?' (1986) 8 *British Journal of Religious Education* 109.

S. Maurice (ed.), *Tudor on Charities* Sweet and Maxwell (7th ed., 1984).

A A'la Mawdudi, *Human Rights in Islam* The Islamic Foundation (2nd ed., 1980).

Meeting the Needs of Muslim Pupils IQRA Trust, 1991.

W. Menski, 'Legal pluralism in the Hindu Marriage' in R. Burghart (ed.), *Hinduism in Great Britain* Tavistock Publications, 1987.

N. Middleton and S. Weitzman, *A Place for Everyone: A History of State Education from the Eighteenth Century to the 1970s* Gollancz, 1976.

K. Murad, *Muslim Youth in the West* Islamic Foundation, 1986.

J. Murphy, *Church, State and Schools in Britain* Routledge and Kegan Paul, 1971.

F. Newark, 'Public Benefit and Religious Trusts' (1946) 62 *Law Quarterly Review* 234.

J. Nielsen (ed.), *Islamic Family Law in the UK: Report of a seminar held at Woodbrooke College* Centre for the Study of Islam and Christian-Muslim Relations, Selly Oak Colleges, 1985.

B. O'Keefe, *Faith, Culture and the Dual System* Falmer Press, 1986.

E. Pagels, *The Gnostic Gospels* Penguin Books, 1982.

B. Parekh, 'Britain and the Logic of Social Pluralism' in Commission for Racial Equality, *Britain: A Plural Society*, 1990.

U. Parameswaran, *The Perforated Sheet: Essays on Salman Rushdie* Affiliated East–West Press, 1988.

D. Pearl, 'Immigrant Marriages: Some Legal Problems' (1972/73) 2 *New Community* 67.

D. Pearl, 'Legal Decisions Affecting Immigrants and Sex Discrimination – No. 5' (1976/77) 5 *New Community* 259.

D. Pearl, *Family Law and the Immigrant Communities* Family Law Publications, 1986.

D. Pearl, *A Textbook on Muslim Personal Law* Croom Helm (2nd ed., 1987).

L. Pfeffer, *Religious Freedom* National Textbook Company, 1977.

H. Picarda, *The Law and Practice Relating to Charities* Butterworths, 1977.

H. Picarda, 'New Religions as Charities' (1983) 131 *New Law Journal* 436.

D. Pipes, *The Rushdie Affair* Carol Publishing Group, 1990.

S. Poulter, 'Hyde v. Hyde – A Reappraisal' (1976) 25 *International and Comparative Law Quarterly* 475.

S. Poulter, *English Law and Ethnic Minority Customs* Butterworths, 1986.

S. Poulter, *Asian Traditions and English Law: A Handbook* Runnymede Trust with Trentham, 1990.

S. Qureshi and J. Khan *The Politics of the Satanic Verses* Muslim Community Studies Institute, 1989.

M. Raza, *Islam in Britain* Volcano Press, 1991.

P. Regan, 'The 1986 Shops Bill' (1988) 41 *Parliamentary Affairs* 218.

Registration: Proposals for Change Cm 939 (1990).

Report of the Commission on Religious Education in Schools (The Durham Report) National Society and the SPCK, 1970.

T. Robbins and D. Anthony, 'Deprogramming, Brainwashing and the Medicalisation of Deviant Religious Groups' (1982) 29 *Social Problems* 283.

G. Robertson, *Obscenity* Weidenfeld and Nicholson, 1979.

St John Robilliard, 'Discrimination and Indirect Discrimination: the Religious Dimension' (1980) 8 *New Community* 261.

St John Robilliard, *Religion and the Law: Religious Liberty in Modern English Law* Manchester University Press, 1984.

A. Rogerson, *Millions Now Living Will Never Die* Constable, 1969.

M. Ruthven, *A Satanic Affair* Chatto and Windus, 1990.

S. Rushdie, *Grimus* Grafton Books, 1979.

S. Rushdie, *Midnight's Children* Jonathan Cape, 1981.

S. Rushdie, 'The Empire writes back with a vengeance', *The Times*, 3 July 1982.

S. Rushdie, *Shame* Jonathan Cape, 1983.

S. Rushdie, 'The Indian Writer in England' in M. Butcher (ed.), *The Eye of the Beholder* Commonwealth Institute, 1983.

S. Rushdie, '"Errata" Unreliable Narration in Midnight's Children' in B. Olinder (ed.), *A Sense of Place* Goteborg, 1984.

S. Rushdie , *The Satanic Verses* Viking, 1988.

S. Rushdie, *Haroun and the Sea of Stories* Granta Books, 1990.

S. Rushdie, 'Is Nothing Sacred?' in S. Rushdie *Imaginary Homelands* Granta Books, 1991, Granta Books, 1992.

S. Rushdie, 'In Good Faith' in S. Rushdie *Imaginary Homelands* Granta Books, 1991, Granta Books, 1992.

S. Rushdie, *The Wizard of Oz* BFI Publishing, 1992.

W. Sadurski, *Moral Pluralism and Legal Neutrality* Kluwer Academic Publishers, 1990.

E. Said, *Orientalism* Penguin Books, 1978.

Y. Samad, 'Book Burning and Race Relations: Political Mobilisation of Bradford Muslims' (1992) 18 *New Community* 507.

A. Samuels, 'Custody and Access: Law, Principles and Practice' (1974) 4 *Family Law* 141.

Z. Sardar and M. Wyn Davies, *Distorted Imaginations* Grey Seal, 1990.

J.P. Sartre, *Being and Nothingness* Philosophical Library, (no date).

J. Scotland, *The History of Scottish Education: Volume 2* University of London Press, 1969.

K. Siddiqui (ed.), *The Muslim Manifesto* The Muslim Institute, 1990.

N. Slee, 'Conflict and Reconciliation Between Competing Models of Religious Education: Some Reflections on the British Scene' (1989) 11 *British Journal of Religious Education* 128.

I. Smith and J. Wood, *Industrial Law* Butterworths (4th ed., 1989).

P. Souper and W. Kay, *The School Assembly in Hampshire* University of Southampton, Department of Education, 1982.

D. Srivastava, 'Personal Laws and Religious Freedom', (1976) 18 *Journal of the Indian Law Institute* 551.

A. Stillman, 'Legislating for Choice' in M. Flude and M. Hammer (eds), *The Education Reform Act 1988* Falmer Press, 1990.

Tenth Report of the Social Services Committee (1989–90).

J. Thompson, *Family Law in Scotland* Butterworths, (2nd ed., 1991).

S. Tomlinson and S. Hutchinson, *Bangladeshi Parents and Education in Tower Hamlets* ACE, 1991.

J. Waldron, 'Too Important for Tact', *Times Literary Supplement*, 10 March 1989.

R. Wallis, *The Road to Total Freedom* Heinemann Educational, 1976.

B. Walsh, 'Religious Considerations in Custody Disputes' (1988) 18 *Family Law* 198.

N. Walter, *Blasphemy Ancient and Modern* Rationalist Press Association, 1990.

W. Weatherby, *Salman Rushdie: Sentenced to Death* Carrol and Graf, 1990.

R. Webster, *A Brief History of Blasphemy* The Orwell Press, 1990.

White Paper on Education The Muslim Parliament of Great Britain, 1992.

J. Wigley, *The Rise and Fall of the Victorian Sunday* Manchester University Press, 1980.

L. Wittgenstein, *On Certainty* Basil Blackwell , 1974.

Y. Zaki, 'The Teaching of Islam in Schools: A Muslim Viewpoint' (1982) 5 *British Journal of Religious Education* 33.

G. Zellick, *The Law, Religion and the Jewish Community* Jews College, 1987.

Table of Cases

Table of Statutes

Index

UNIVERSITY OF WOLVERHAMPTON
LEARNING RESOURCES